IMAGES
of America

TAMARAC

ON THE COVER: ADULTS AT PLAY. An iconic photograph of the first mayor, William Morse, Ken Behring's friend and attorney, shows life in early Tamarac. "Adults at Play" was the newly incorporated City of Tamarac's pledge and motto. (Courtesy of the Fort Lauderdale Historical Society. *Gene Hyde Collection*. H 43560.2.)

IMAGES
of America

TAMARAC

Tamarac Historical Society

ARCADIA
PUBLISHING

ISBN 978-0-7385-9981-6

Published by Arcadia Publishing
Charleston, South Carolina

Printed in the United States of America

Library of Congress Control Number: 2012954555

For all general information, please contact Arcadia Publishing:
Telephone 843-853-2070
Fax 843-853-0044
E-mail sales@arcadiapublishing.com
For customer service and orders:
Toll-Free 1-888-313-2665

Visit us on the Internet at www.arcadiapublishing.com

Dedicated to the residents of Tamarac, past, present, and future

Contents

Acknowledgments

The Tamarac Historical Society would like to thank its members for their contributions to this book with special recognition to Barbara Tarnove, Amy Redman, Rea Mills, and Marian Daly for compiling and editing the contents.

We would also like to thank the following for providing historical photographs, images, and information:

City developer Kenneth E. Behring;

From the city of Tamarac: mayor, city commissioners, city manager's office, city clerk's office, public information and media office, parks and recreation department, community development department, and Tamarac city employees;

Organizations: Broward County Historical Commission, Broward County Public Schools, Broward County Public Art and Design Program, Broward County Library (Tamarac Branch), Fort Lauderdale Historical Society, curator at the Boca Raton Historical Society, and South Florida Wildlife Center;

Local publications: *Tamarac Topics*, *Tam-A-Gram*, *Broward Times/South Florida Times*, *Fort Lauderdale News*, *Sun Sentinel*, and *Miami Herald*;

And individuals: Ilan Averbuch, Jane DeDecker, George Gadson, Leonardo Nierman, Raymond Olivero, and Beth Ravitz.

Finally, thank you to Chad Quinn, founder of the Tamarac Historical Society, for his inspiration, guidance and support in helping us preserve our history.

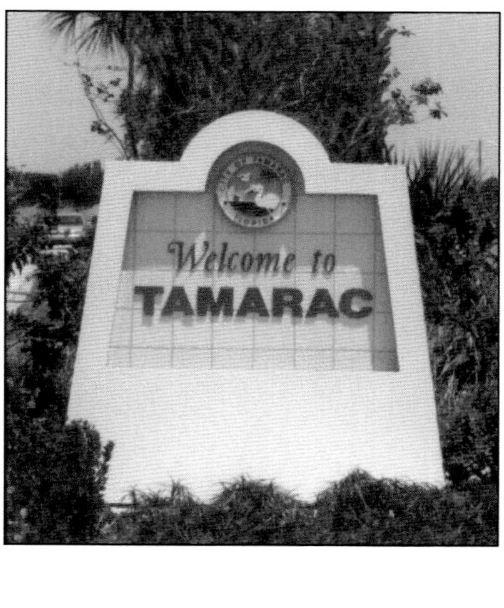

Welcome. An early welcome sign is found at the city limits. (Courtesy of the City of Tamarac.)

Introduction

From a cow pasture to a vibrant city, from wanting to do more to creating a great legacy, from zero population to 60,000-plus residents, from the average age of over 60 to the diverse population of 40-somethings, the city of Tamarac has seen many changes. These images will show the growth of Tamarac as it developed into a "City for Your Life."

The Tamarac Historical Society has uncovered many interesting stories and images, dispelled myths, and reawakened memories. This story begins with city developer and founder Kenneth E. Behring.

Kenneth E. Behring was born in 1928 and came to Florida in 1956. Initially involved in the construction of Fort Lauderdale apartments, he later began constructing single-family homes with condominium amenities. The first parcel of land he purchased was practically uninhabitable. In addition, building codes in Broward County restricted lot size. In order to get around these restrictions, Behring decided to create his own city.

Land had to be cleared and moved, canals and lakes had to be dug, and developments had to be laid out—all this to create the city that would become Tamarac. To help complete this work, Behring called upon friends from back home to contribute their expertise.

Along with 250 homes and a clubhouse with recreational amenities, the residents of Tamarac were better able to enjoy life because others handled the maintenance on their homes for a small monthly fee of $23. As this new way of life gained popularity, the population exploded and Behring ran out of land.

Additional land acquisitions took Behring to the Sunshine State Parkway, today the Florida Turnpike, but there was no means to cross the road to continue westward expansion. The only access was a stock tunnel that permitted cows only (and the occasional car while the cows were held back).

Behring petitioned the state to build an overpass at Commercial Boulevard. The state denied the request since there currently was no reason to travel to a place where nothing existed. Behring was undeterred and petitioned again, but this time, he included a donation of 29 acres of land to the state in exchange for the overpass. The overpass, which was dubbed "Behring Overpass," allowed for westward expansion.

In keeping with his original model, Vista Villas was erected on the R Bar Ranch on the west side of the Sunshine State Parkway. Behring employed the best architects and interior designers to build this unique country club community. Robert Von Hagge, a world-famous golf course architect, built the two championship courses. Now known as The Woodlands, this was the most ambitious of all Behring properties and included a magnificent home for his family. Business continued to grow and more land was again needed. Needless to say, the project was a huge success.

Coral Springs, Florida, was being developed at the same time by Coral Ridge Properties; its boundary to the south was the C-14 Canal on Southgate Boulevard. The Coral Springs land was once owned by Bud Lyons, a beanpole farmer. Looking for additional land, Behring's people negotiated with Lena Lyons (Bud Lyons's wife) to acquire 5,000 acres adjacent to Coral Springs. Legend has it that if Coral Springs had bought this parcel to extend its city, many of today's Tamarac residents would be living in Coral Springs. Tamarac won out, however, this final large acquisition completed the city, and one more golf course community called Colony West was added.

Behring then became interested in modular homes that could be erected on a lot in one week using prefabricated parts. Such an idea was practically unheard of at the time, but Behring built Modiflex to do just that. A manufacturing plant that gained national prominence as well as FHA approval (which was no small feat) led to an additional housing development called Heathgate, the first family-oriented development. Families with children flocked to Tamarac, which then needed better roads, schools, an expanded hospital, more houses of worship, restaurants and businesses. Although the "way of life" was changing, the city continued to thrive.

Behring soon decided to leave our city for yet another venture. Behring Properties merged with Leadership Housing, which would continue to build the city while keeping the original Behring model in mind. Leadership Housing erected Sunflower, Lime Bay, Westwood, and Woodmont Country Club.

Over time, Tamarac has become a full-service city with fully equipped parks, wider roadways, additional clean canals, manicured green areas, a fully expanded hospital, many more businesses, including an industrial park, and restaurants. The city has been reworked and refined many times over. Meanwhile, city officials keep residents informed.

A quarterly, *Tam-A-Gram* contains articles on the city improvements, ongoing city initiatives, upcoming events, and activities for all ages. Originally starting as a one-page flyer, this publication has a unique feature: the front page can be flipped upside down for the activities section.

In addition, Tamarac University offers a seven-week curriculum in which the manager of each department of the city presents a history of his or her department, an update on the department's plans, and how different duties are performed. This program is invaluable; Tamarac University appears on the resume of two city commissioners.

Neighborhood meetings also keep residents up-to-date. At the meetings, each department gives a presentation and then answers questions from the audience. No question goes unanswered, even if it needs to be researched first. Finally, residents are encouraged to attend commission meetings; even there, any resident has three minutes to speak on any subject they like.

The mayor and city commissioners govern Tamarac with this mission: "Committed to Excellence . . . Always."

One

City Beginnings

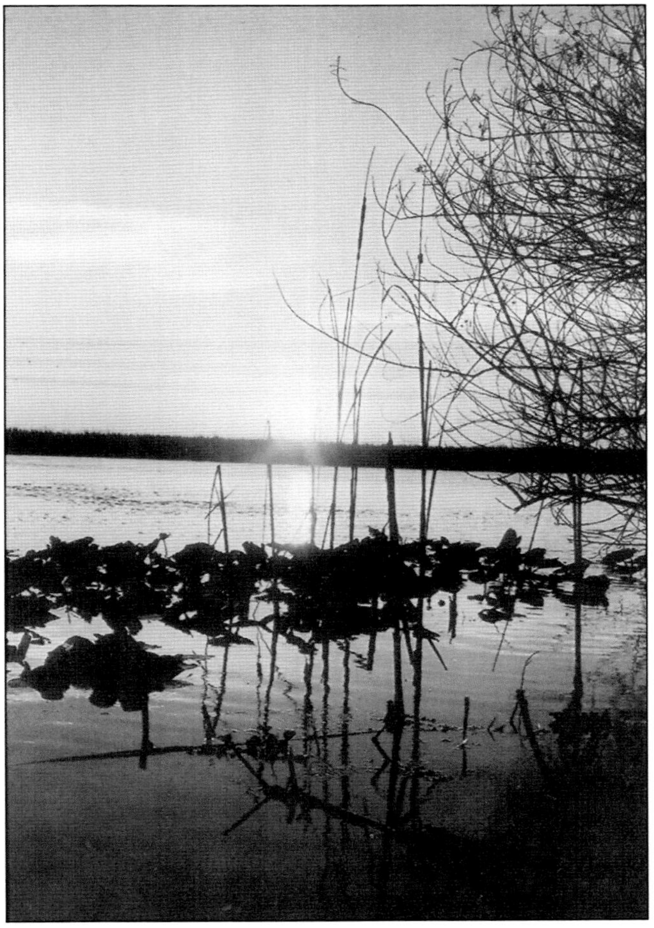

The Florida Everglades. The land Kenneth E. Behring acquired to develop the city of Tamarac was part of a rich Everglades ecosystem comprised of sawgrass marshes, lush green cypress hammocks, and cow pastures. The city is located on the semitropical ridge between the Everglades and the Atlantic Ocean. (Courtesy of Susan Buzzi.)

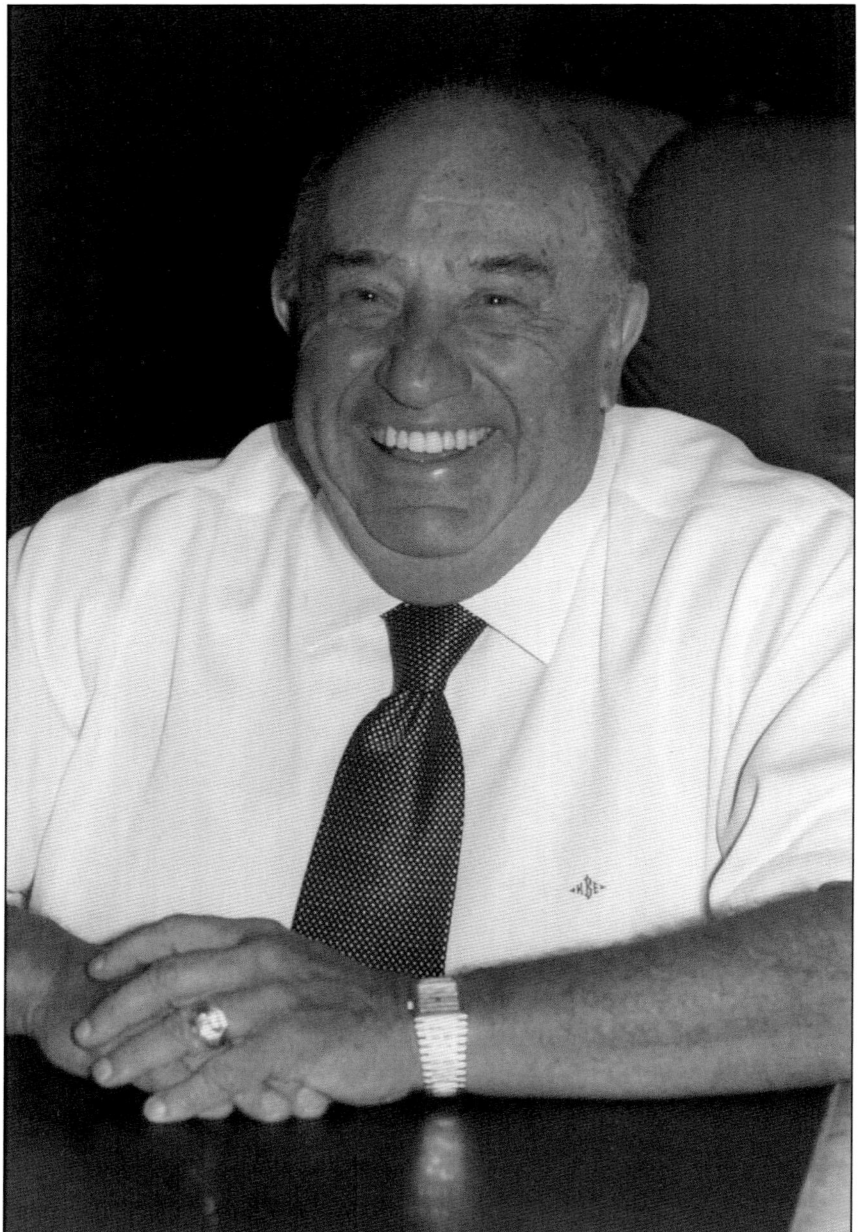

Ken Behring. Behring was born on June 13, 1928, to poor parents in Illinois. He moved to Wisconsin when he was four years old. Growing up, he held many jobs. Behring worked all through school while playing football, and he played well enough to receive a partial football scholarship to the University of Wisconsin, but he eventually dropped out. Behring started out selling cars and eventually owned a dealership. He then married his wife, Pat, whose father, an avid golfer, moved to Florida. Behring saw a new way of life in the Sunshine State. At the age of 27, and with $1 million in assets, he started building apartments in South Florida. This was the beginning of a career that led to the creation of cities, a life of philanthropy (including the Wheelchair Foundation), and a sports team. (Courtesy of Kenneth E. Behring.)

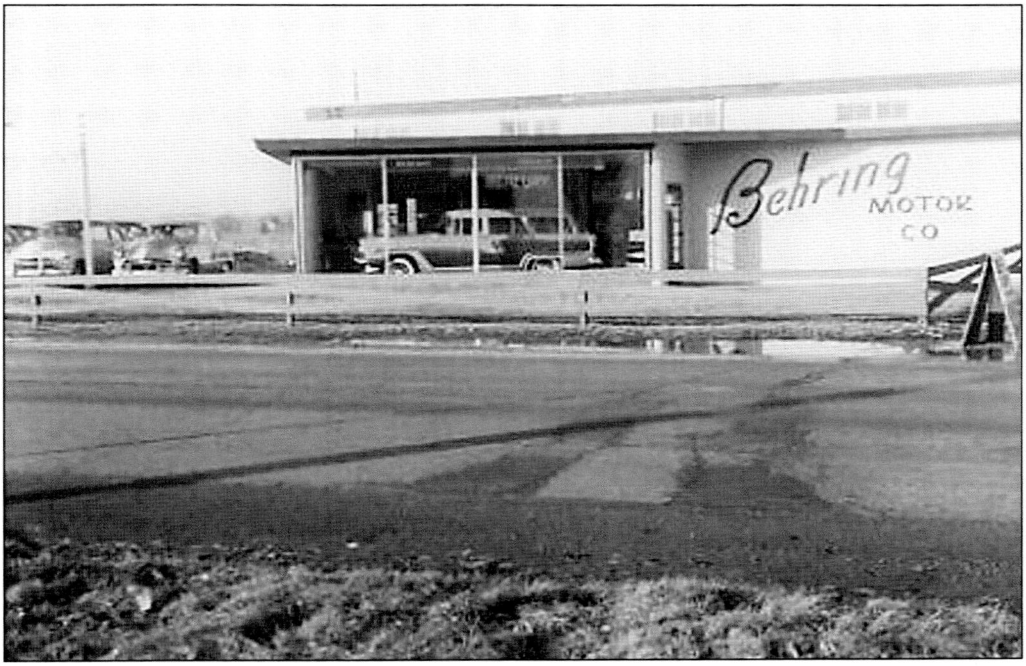

BEHRING THE CAR SALESMAN. As a young man, Ken Behring was a go-getter. Out of college, he worked as a car salesman, and soon owned a Lincoln-Mercury dealership (above). As a salesman, he made $100 for each car sold. (Courtesy of Kenneth E. Behring.)

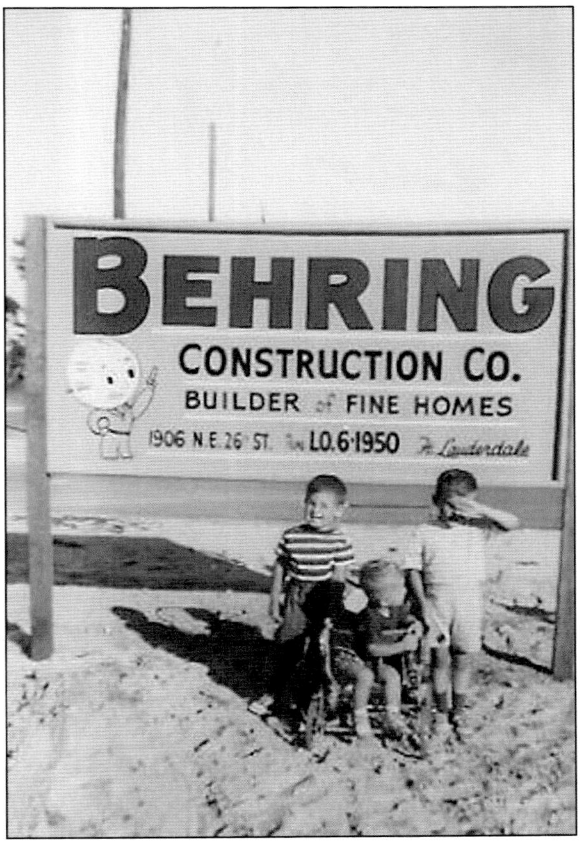

BEHRING THE BUILDER. Behring's idea was to build single-family retirement homes with maintenance and recreation facilities. His father, a carpenter, joined him in this venture. He also began asking his friends from back home to be part of this new opportunity in Florida. In 1963, Tamarac was realized and the boom began. (Courtesy of Kenneth E. Behring.)

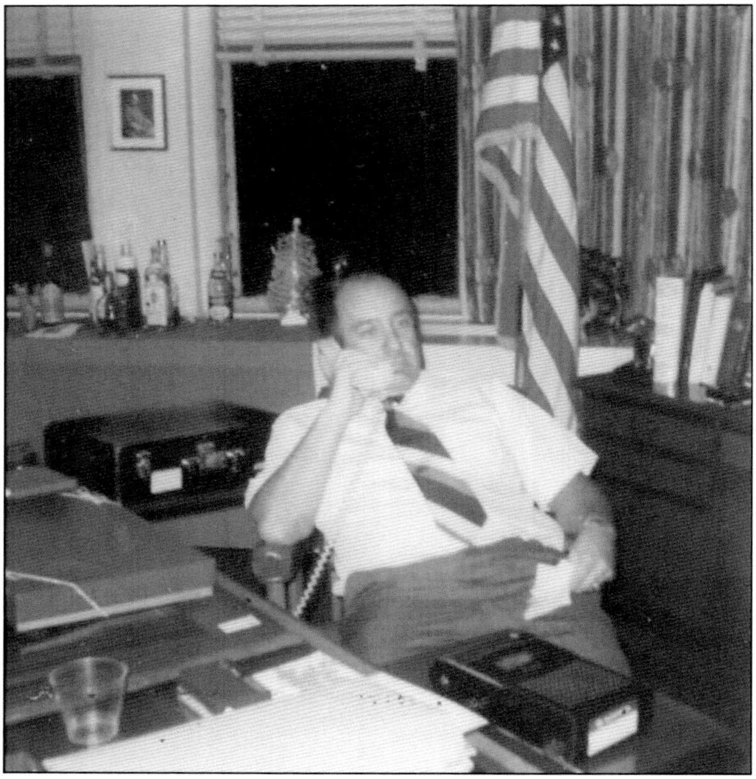

Behring Makes a Deal. At his peak, Behring was managing several properties at a time. Many of his friends from his early days would help him continue to succeed. (Courtesy of Kenneth E. Behring.)

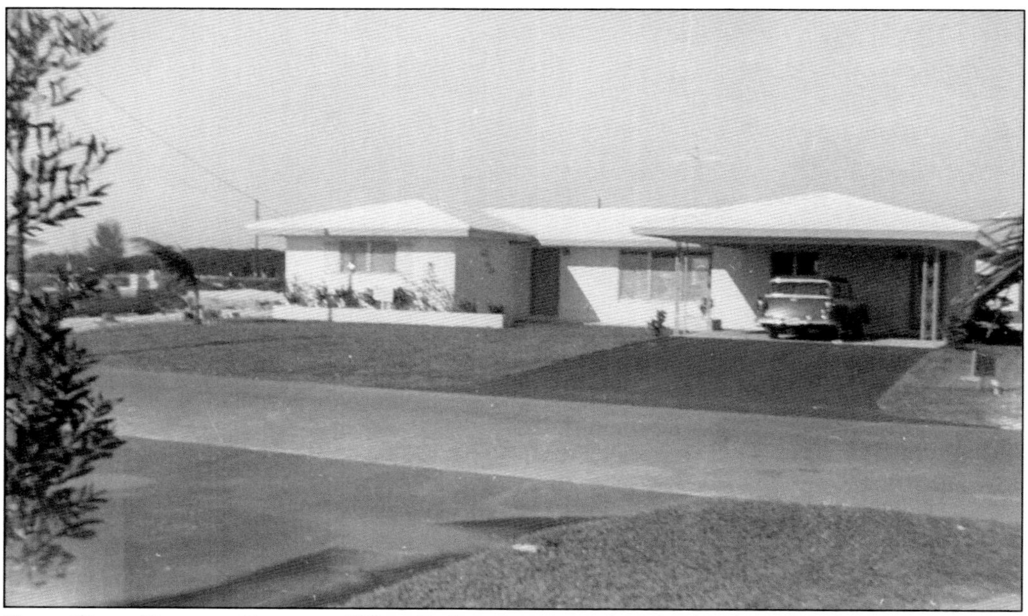

First Home Built in Florida. When Behring came to South Florida to build a home that was to be his own, he was offered more than the cost of the home, so he sold it. This convinced him that single-family home construction was going to be a new career path. (Courtesy of Kenneth E. Behring.)

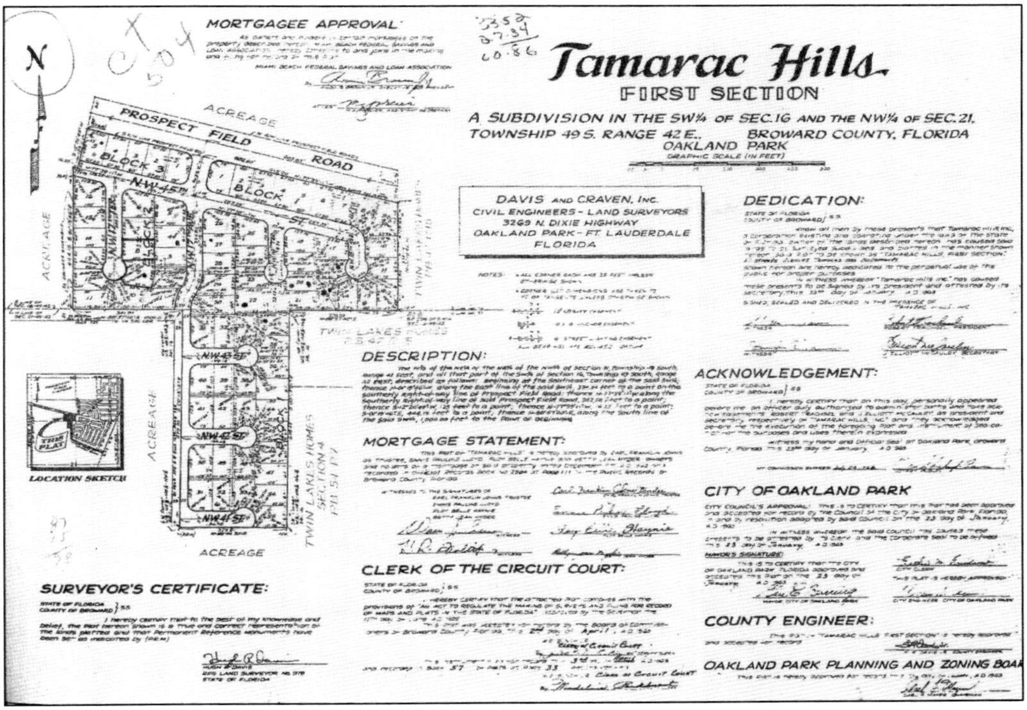

Plat Map. Above is the plat map of the first property Behring purchased to build his city. Purchased from Earl Franklin Johns (trustee), Ennis Pauline Lloyd, Floy Belle Haynie, and Betty Jean Hyder, the land was part of Tamarac Hills, Oakland Park, and Broward County. (Courtesy of the Broward County Public Records.)

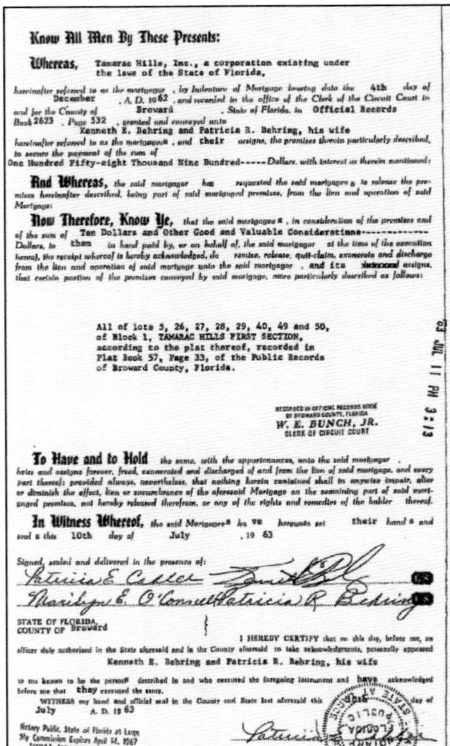

Know All Men By These Presents:

Whereas, Tamarac Hills, Inc., a corporation existing under the laws of the State of Florida,

hereinafter referred to as the mortgagor, by Indenture of Mortgage bearing date the 4th day of December, A. D. 1962, and recorded in the office of the Clerk of the Circuit Court in and for the County of Broward, State of Florida, in Official Records Book 2623, Page 532, granted and conveyed unto Kenneth E. Behring and Patricia R. Behring, his wife hereinafter referred to as the mortgagees, and their assigns, the premises therein particularly described, to secure the payment of the sum of One Hundred Fifty-eight Thousand Nine Hundred----- Dollars, with interest as therein mentioned:

And Whereas, the said mortgagor has requested the said mortgagees to release the premises hereinafter described, being part of said mortgaged premises, from the lien and operation of said Mortgage:

Now Therefore, Know Ye, that the said mortgagees, in consideration of the premises and of the sum of Ten Dollars and Other Good and Valuable Considerations------------ Dollars, to them in hand paid by, or on behalf of, the said mortgagor at the time of the execution hereof, the receipt whereof is hereby acknowledged, do remise, release, quit-claim, exonerate and discharge from the lien and operation of said mortgage unto the said mortgagor, and its assigns, that certain portion of the premises conveyed by said mortgage, more particularly described as follows:

All of lots 5, 26, 27, 28, 29, 40, 49 and 50, of Block 1, TAMARAC HILLS FIRST SECTION, according to the plat thereof, recorded in Plat Book 57, Page 33, of the Public Records of Broward County, Florida.

'63 JUL 11 PM 3:13

RECORDED IN OFFICIAL RECORDS BOOK OF BROWARD COUNTY, FLORIDA
W. E. BUNCH, JR.
CLERK OF CIRCUIT COURT

To Have and to Hold the same, with the appurtenances, unto the said mortgagor, heirs and assigns forever, freed, exonerated and discharged of and from the lien of said mortgage, and every part thereof; provided always, nevertheless, that nothing herein contained shall in anywise impair, alter or diminish the effect, lien or encumbrance of the aforesaid Mortgage on the remaining part of said mortgaged premises, not hereby released therefrom, or any of the rights and remedies of the holder thereof.

In Witness Whereof, the said Mortgagees have hereunto set their hands and seals this 10th day of July, 1963

Signed, sealed and delivered in the presence of:
Patricia E. Cable
Marilyn E. O'Connell
Patricia R. Behring

STATE OF FLORIDA,
COUNTY OF Broward

I HEREBY CERTIFY that on this day, before me, an officer duly authorized in the State aforesaid and in the County aforesaid to take acknowledgments, personally appeared Kenneth E. Behring and Patricia R. Behring, his wife to me known to be the persons described in and who executed the foregoing instrument and have acknowledged before me that they executed the same.

WITNESS my hand and official seal in the County and State last aforesaid this 10th day of July A. D. 1963

Notary Public, State of Florida at Large
My Commission Expires April 14, 1967

Return: Tamarac Hills, Inc.
1941 W. Oakland Park Blvd.,
Fort Lauderdale, Fla.

First Property. The first property secured by Ken Behring was property owned by Earl Franklin Johns and others. The property known as Tamarac Hill, Inc., was deeded to Behring on December 4, 1962, which became the original homes that are today Tamarac Lakes. The mortgage on this property was $158,900. The location on Prospect Road, in Broward County, had a minimum lot size requirement of 60 by 100 feet. If he adhered to the established size requirement, it would have raised the cost for maintenance and higher water bills. William Morse, Behring's attorney, joked that they should form their own city and that way they could regulate their own lot sizes. Behring was criticized for having small lots but was determined to give the home owner more green space. The City of Tamarac was incorporated on July 19, 1963. (Courtesy of the Broward County Public Records.)

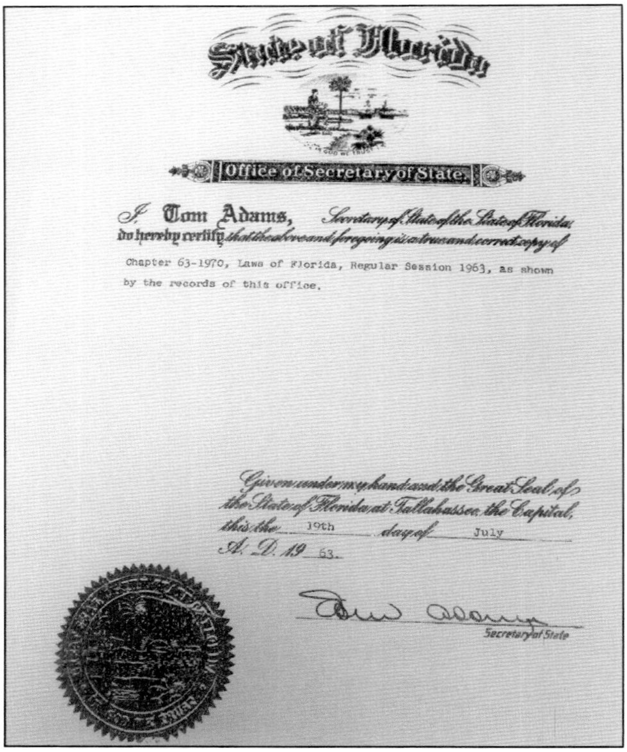

State of Florida

Office of Secretary of State.

I, Tom Adams, Secretary of State of the State of Florida, do hereby certify that the above and foregoing is a true and correct copy of Chapter 63-1970, Laws of Florida, Regular Session 1963, as shown by the records of this office.

Given under my hand and the Great Seal of the State of Florida at Tallahassee, the Capital, this the 19th day of July A.D. 19 63.

Tom Adams
Secretary of State

TAMARAC INCORPORATED. On July 19, 1963, Tom Adams, then secretary of the state, signed the incorporation papers, making Tamarac a city within Broward County. Kenneth Behring declares in his book *Road to Purpose* that this was awarded for raw land, until then only communities that were already built out qualified. (Courtesy of the City of Tamarac.)

WHAT'S IN A NAME? The origin of the name Tamarac has long been up for debate. In 2012, Ken Behring explained that when he purchased the first 13 acres for the city, Tamarac Country Club (later known as the Oak Tree Country Club) was located next door, so he took that name for the city. (Courtesy of the Tamarac Historical Society.)

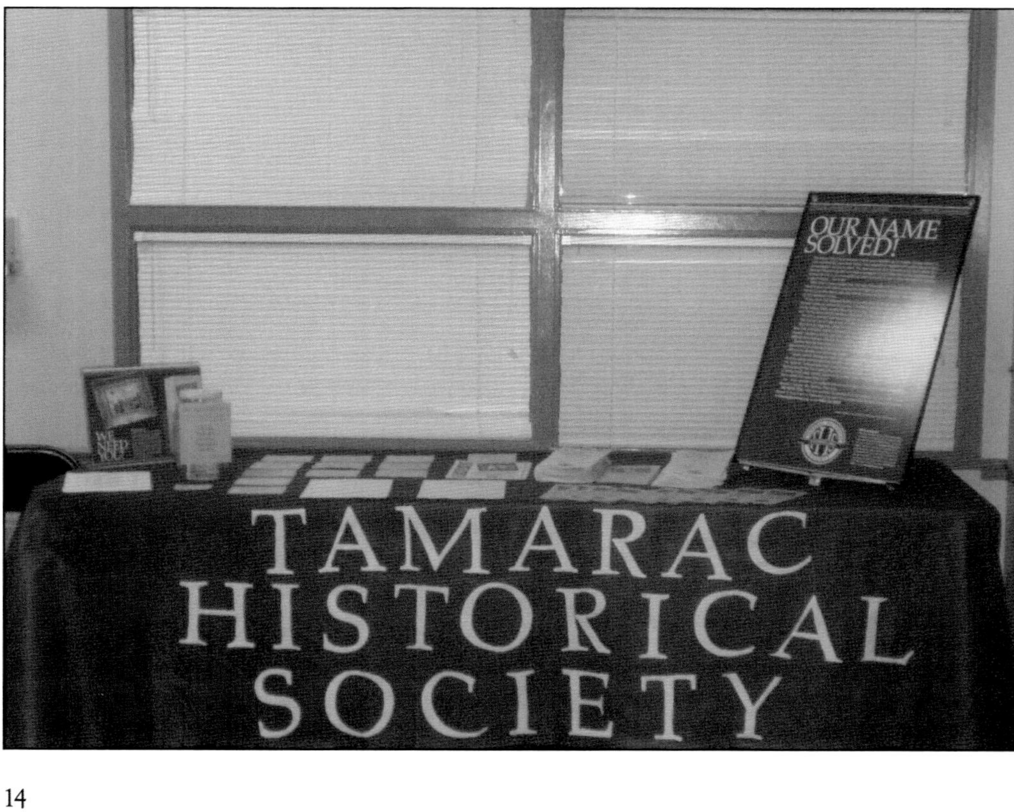

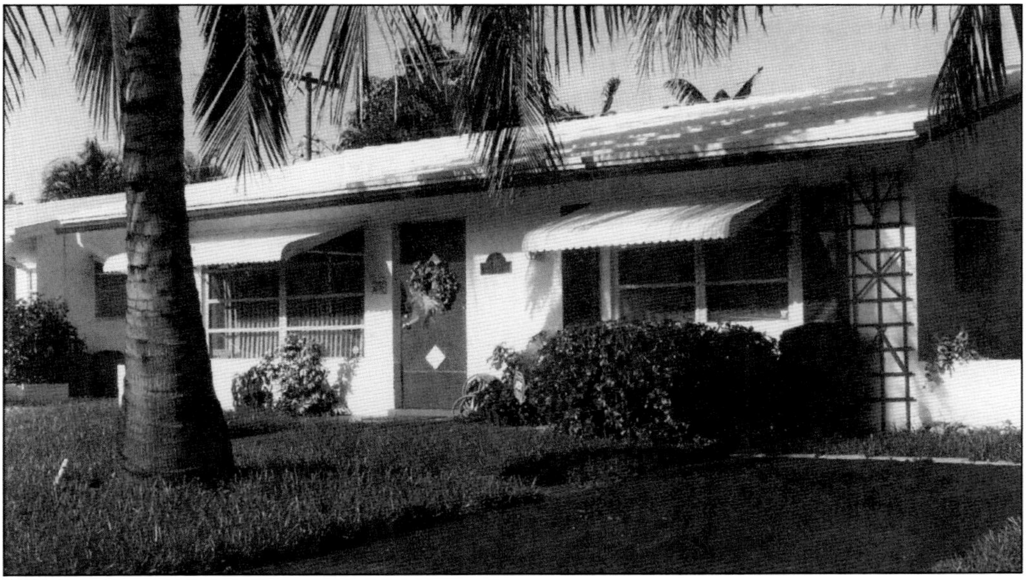

FIRST HOMEOWNERS. Jack and Margaret Hardy and Peter and Bernetha Nyce purchased the first two homes in Tamarac Lakes in 1964. The Hardys came from Queens, Long Island in New York, where Jack was a banker, and his wife, Margaret, was a nurse. Margaret became the first librarian at Tamarac Lakes. Peter and Bernetha Nyce arrived at the same time. Peter was also in banking in Geneva, New York, while Bernetha was a private secretary. The Nyces were very involved in the early community, writing articles for the *Tamarac News Bulletin*. (Courtesy of the City of Tamarac.)

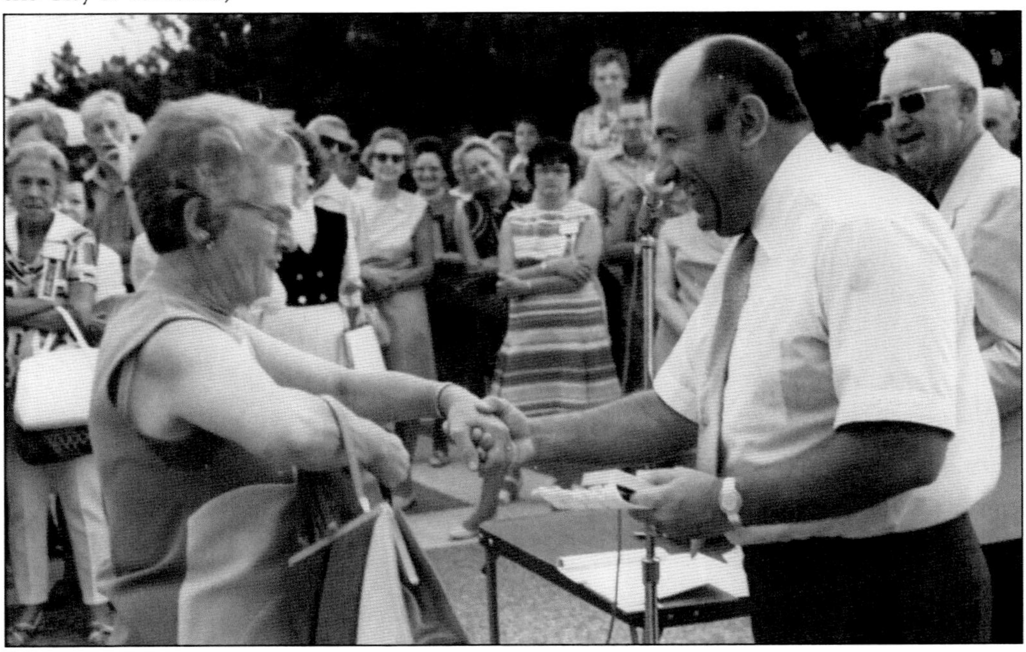

GIFTS AND A HANDSHAKE. Shaking hands and giving gifts was a feature at each gathering held in the city in the early days. Here, at a city barbecue, winning a small gift from Ken Behring himself added to the excitement of the event. (Courtesy of Kenneth E. Behring.)

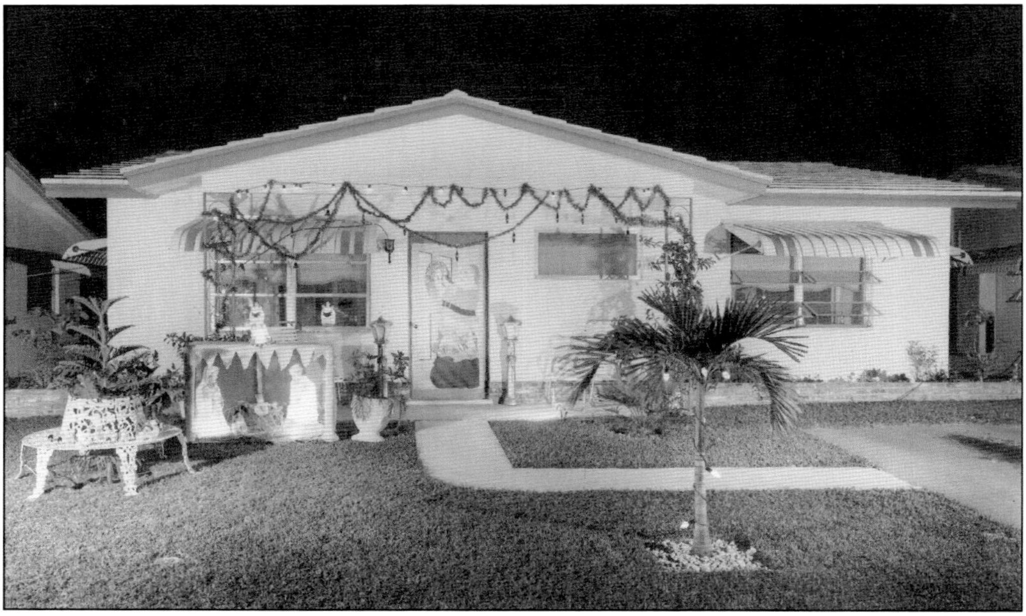

House Decorations. Be it an angel or a Santa, a Christmas tree or a palm tree, tinsel or bells, each resident was an artist when it came to holiday decorations. Decorating the clubhouse was a community affair of spectacular merriment and cheer. (Courtesy of the City of Tamarac.)

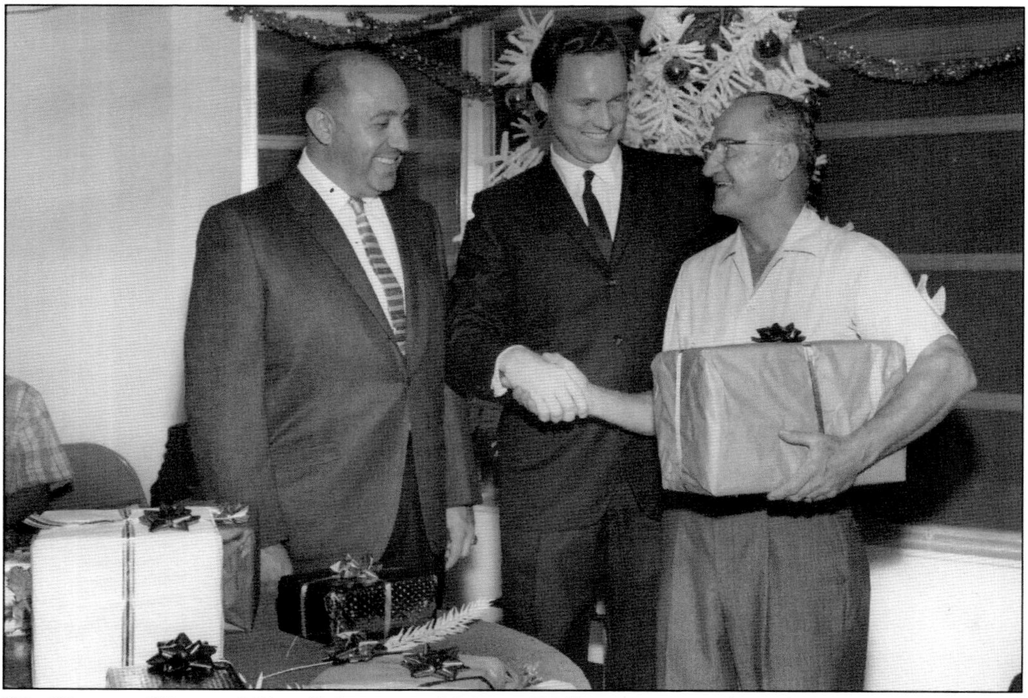

We Have a Winner! Ken Behring and Mayor William Morse selected the most beautifully decorated home and handed out the top prize. A sense of community was shared through the enthusiasm of decorating for the first Christmas. Tamarac lit up the sky. (Courtesy of the City of Tamarac.)

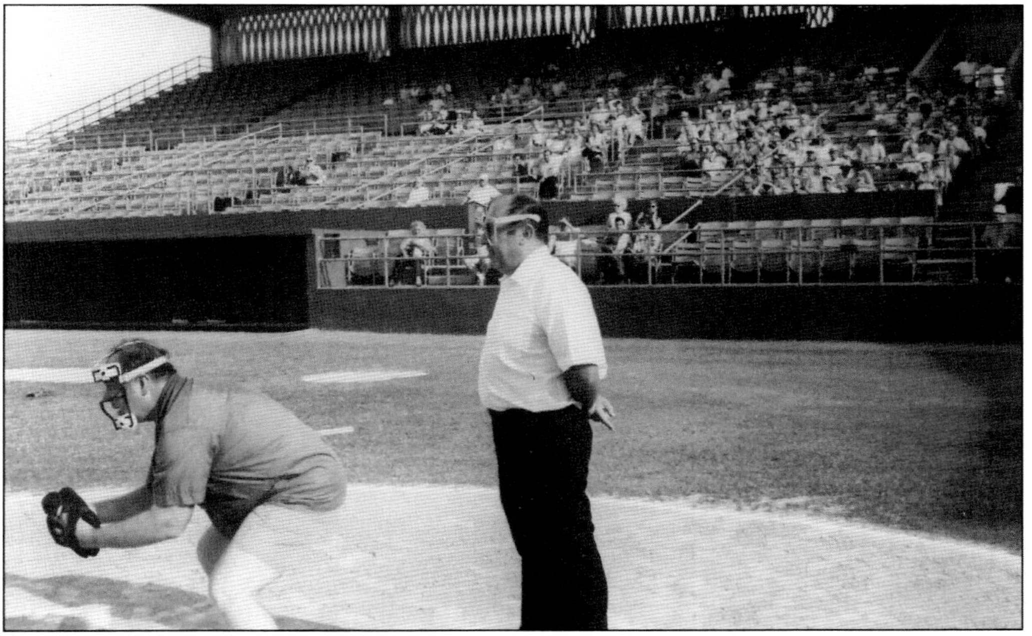

Baseball, the Nation's Pastime. Tamaracans loved baseball so much that they often formed teams to play each other for fun and, of course, competition. Ken Behring playfully donned a large pair of glasses to make sure all pitches were in the strike zone. (Courtesy of Kenneth E. Behring.)

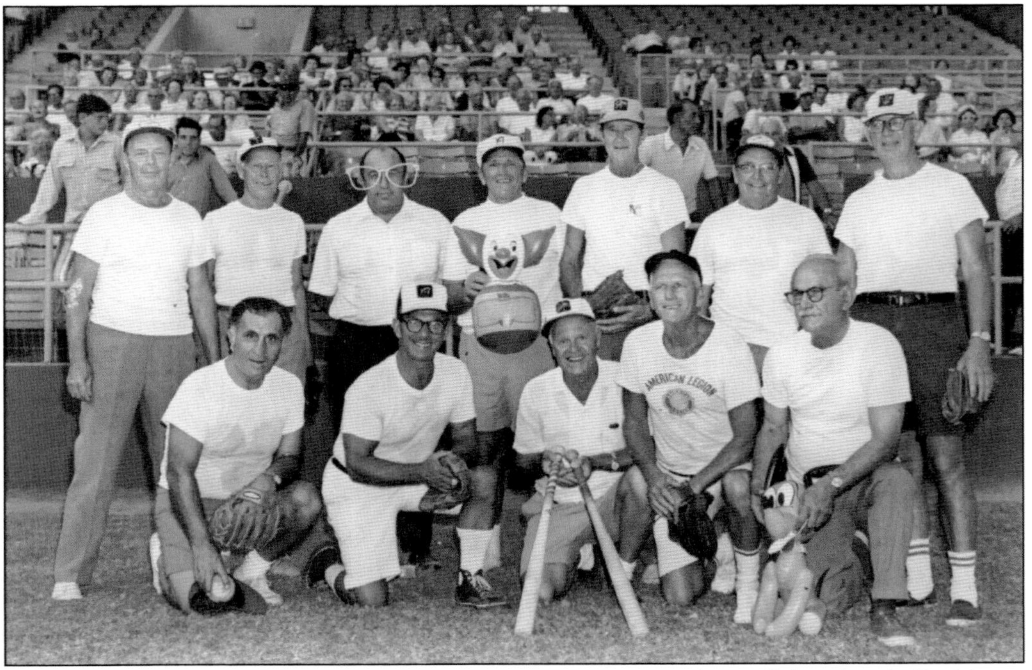

This was the Team. Residents of all ages and skills came out to show off their baseball athletics to a nice crowd. The team mascot is pictured in the lower right. Later, when Behring built on the west coast of Florida, the games matched east coast against west coast, with one side traveling to the other side. (Courtesy of Kenneth E. Behring.)

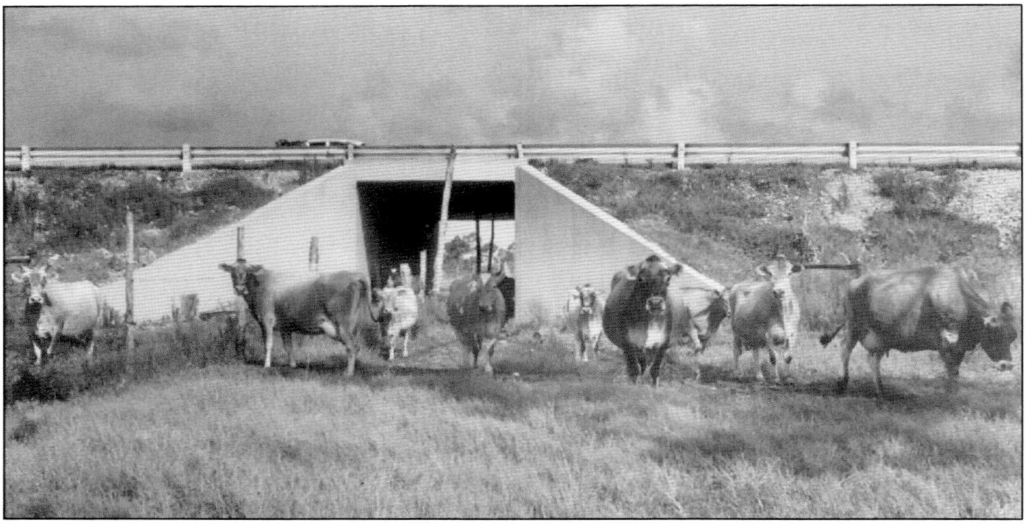

THE STOCK TUNNEL. Behring wanted to expand westward, but the only means to cross the Sunshine State Parkway was through a stock tunnel meant for moving cattle that grazed freely in the area. Only one car could pass through at a time. Behring petitioned the state to build an overpass at Commercial Boulevard, but the state denied the request since there was no reason to travel to a place where nothing existed. Behring petitioned again but included a donation of 29 acres of land to the state in exchange for the overpass, later dubbed Behring Overpass. (Courtesy of Florida's Turnpike Enterprise.)

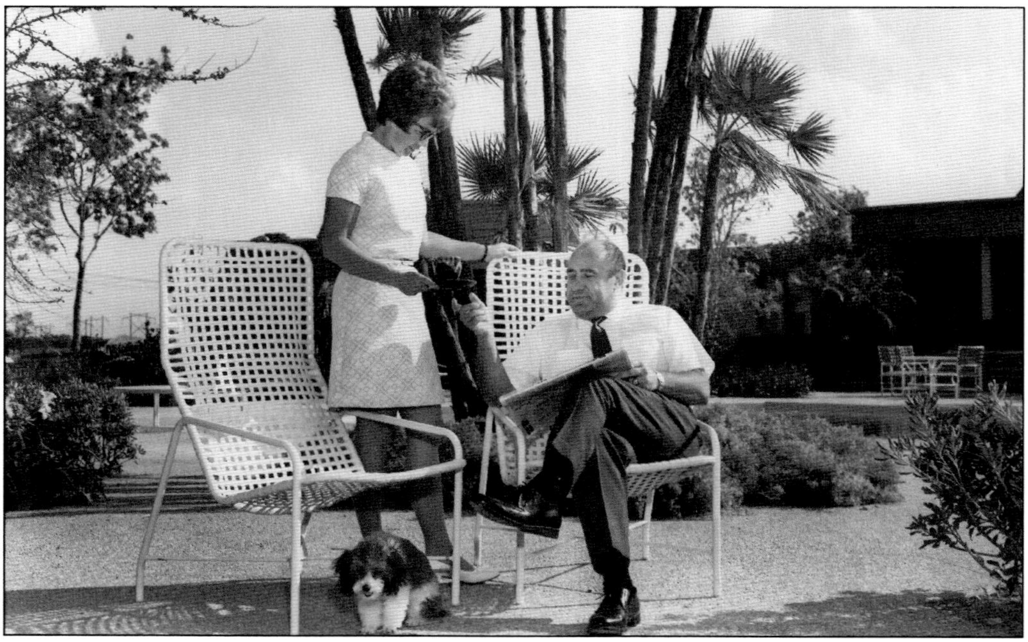

BEHRING'S HOME IN THE WOODLANDS. Finding success in his first two developments, Behring knew larger, more upscale homes could sell as well. Buying land west of the Sunshine State Parkway allowed him to create Vista Villas (now the Woodlands), where he finally built his own estate. This property would include a private country club carved out of land that once was the R Bar Ranch, owned by the Daniels Family. (Courtesy of Kenneth E. Behring.)

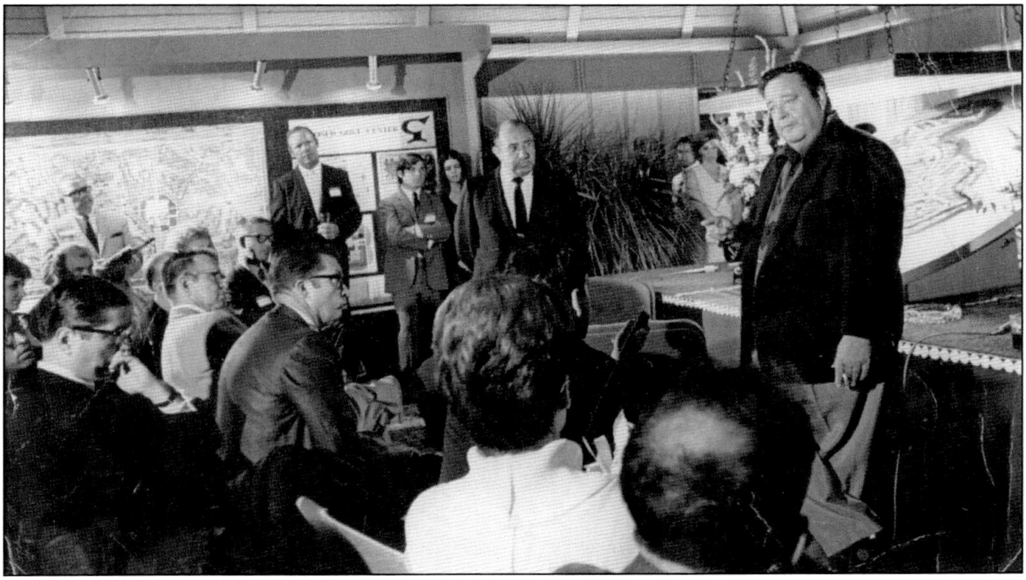

The Great One. Jackie Gleason (pictured), an avid golfer, wanted to have a tournament of his own like fellow celebrities Bob Hope and Bing Crosby. The colorful Jackie Gleason had a 10-year dream, all he needed was someone with "money and guts," and that was Behring. They ventured into an agreement to build a golf course that would be able to feature a PGA golf tournament. Gleason's dream complex called "The Great One" would include six courses, with all the amenities possible served by moving walkways. Included was a home for Gleason, costing $500,000, surrounded by water and accessible via a tunnel from the course. Course designer Robert Von Hagge envisioned viewing terraces, the forerunner of stadium golf. Gleason would have his tournament. Gleason and Behring eventually parted ways due to the project's costs being over a billion dollars and Behring felt he could not make the project profitable. Gleason went to Inverrary Country Club where the Jackie Gleason Inverrary Classic remained from 1972 to 1983. This tournament became the Honda Classic. (Courtesy of Kenneth E. Behring.)

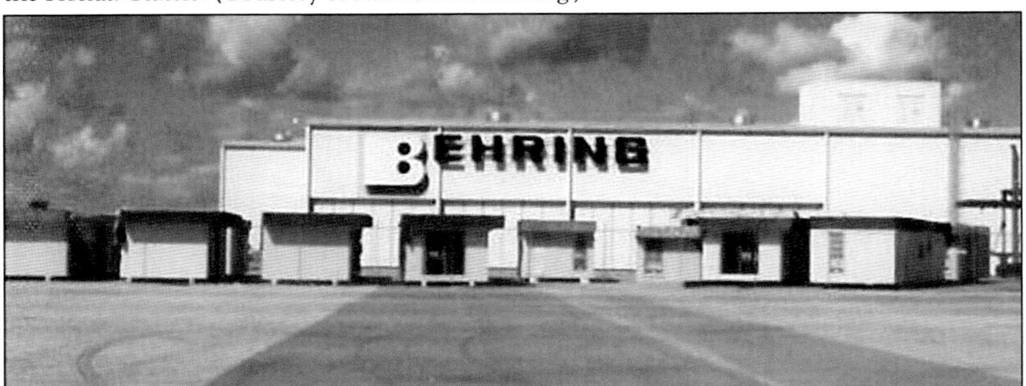

Behring's New Business. Having secured another 5,000 acres to continue his empire, Behring embarked on a new business venture, Modiflex, and built a modular home processing plant on the western end of the city. A Modiflex prefabricated home could be delivered in a week after purchase. In addition, Modiflex was accepted by the Federal Housing Administration, thus adding another financing choice along with cash sales and conventional bank financing. (Courtesy of Kenneth E. Behring.)

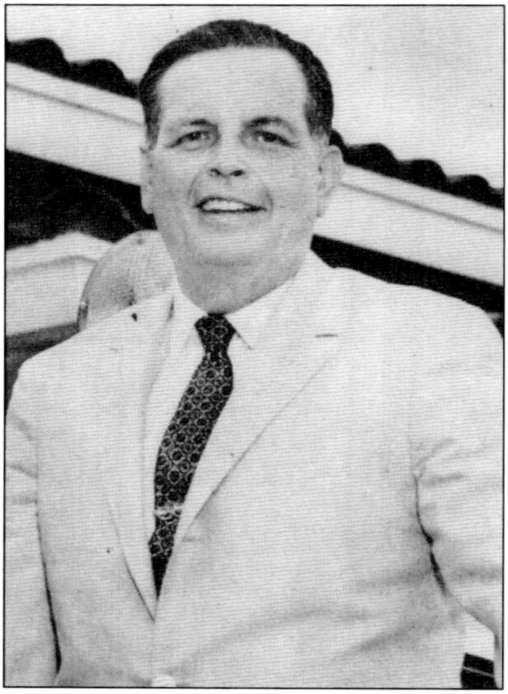

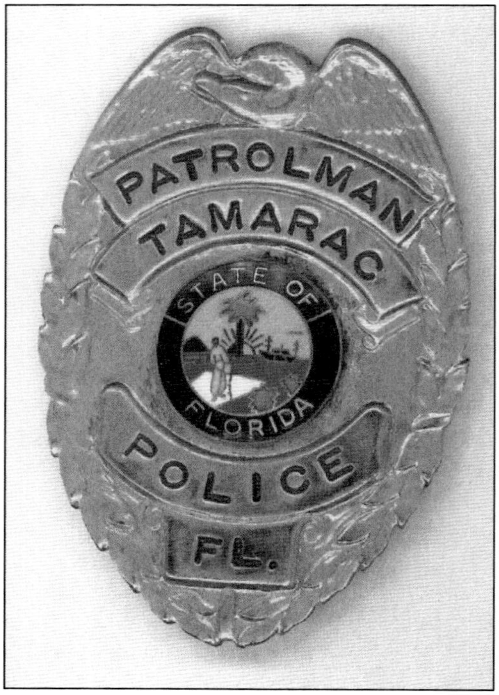

The First Chief. Chief Ellis DeVoe was hired to head up the Tamarac Police Force, modeled after his former force in Lighthouse Point, Florida. The police were a welcome sight on the streets of Tamarac. Chief DeVoe's new patrolmen were proud to wear their badges, which displayed the State of Florida seal. (Both, courtesy of the City of Tamarac.)

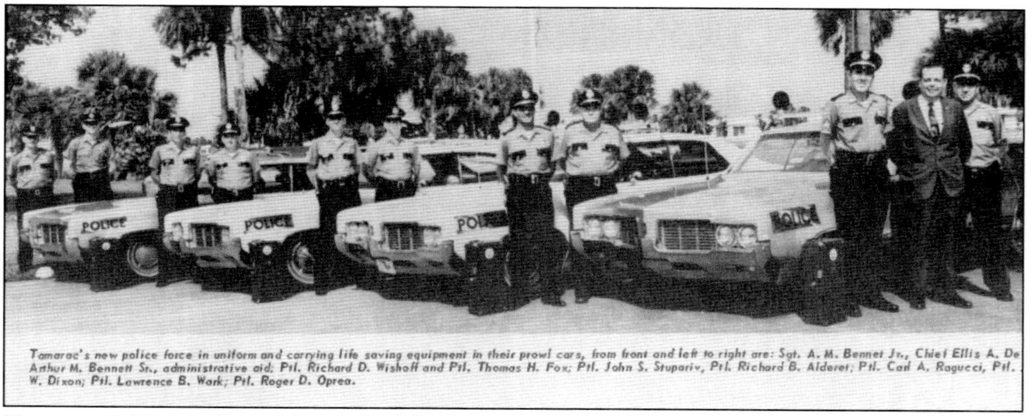

Tamarac's Police Force. Prior to 1969, city security was left to private firms hired by Behring. The new force consisted of 10 officers and four patrol cars. Police headquarters was part of the farmhouse converted into city hall on Rock Island Road. (Courtesy of the City of Tamarac.)

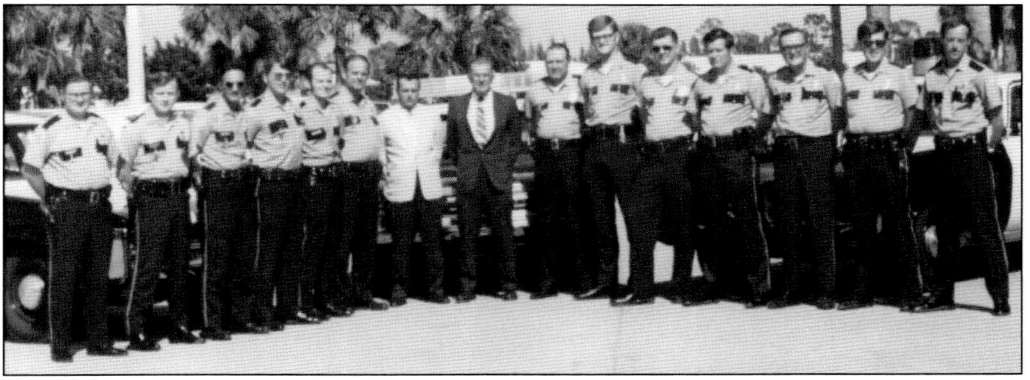

Larger Force. Chief Milton F. Stocker joined the Tamarac Police Force in 1970 and was named chief in 1971. With the explosion of residents, a larger police force (30 officers) was necessary. The crime rate was very low, but the population was expected to hit 30,000. With new families, including many children, moving in, the chief wanted to create a juvenile division. (Courtesy of Sgt. Robert Logan.)

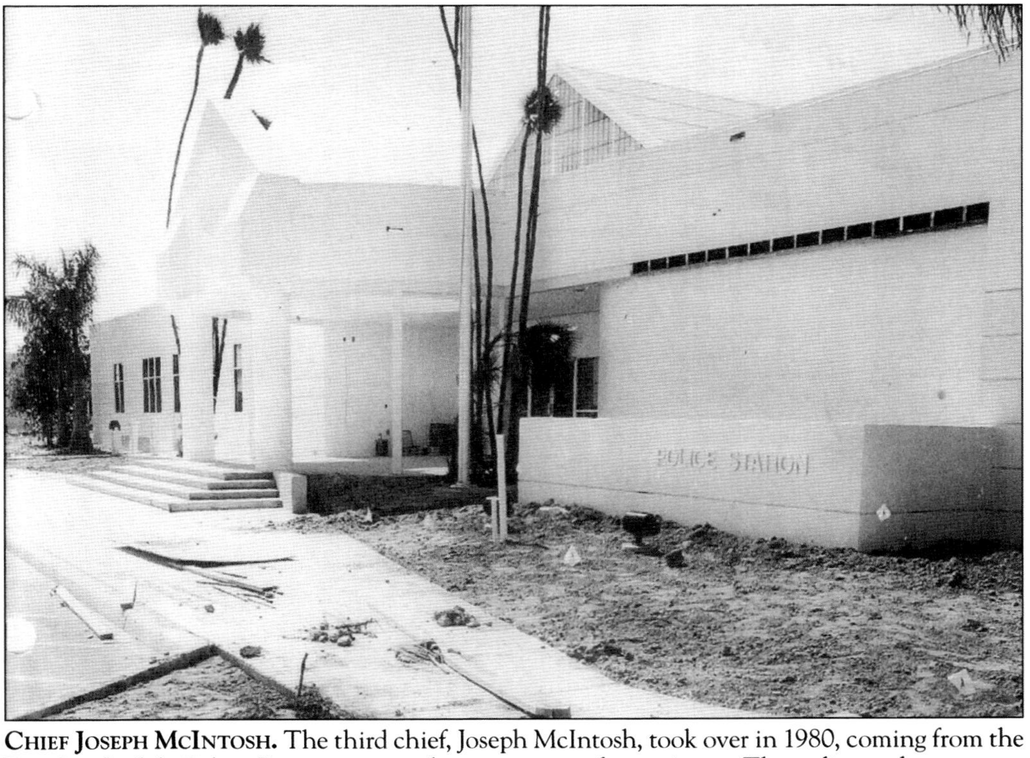

Chief Joseph McIntosh. The third chief, Joseph McIntosh, took over in 1980, coming from the Fort Lauderdale Police Department with many years of experience. The police cadet program was well underway with 15- to 19-year-old individuals that wanted to be on the force getting first-hand working knowledge. Cpl. David Harris visited the school to teach children about safety issues and trust of the police. During McIntosh's tenure, the force numbered 64 and the city's population hit 30,000, and changes were still needed, including more space and equipment that required to be repaired or replaced. McIntosh worked with the city to get what the force needed, including working on a new building. Depicted here is the new police station under construction. (Courtesy of the City of Tamarac.)

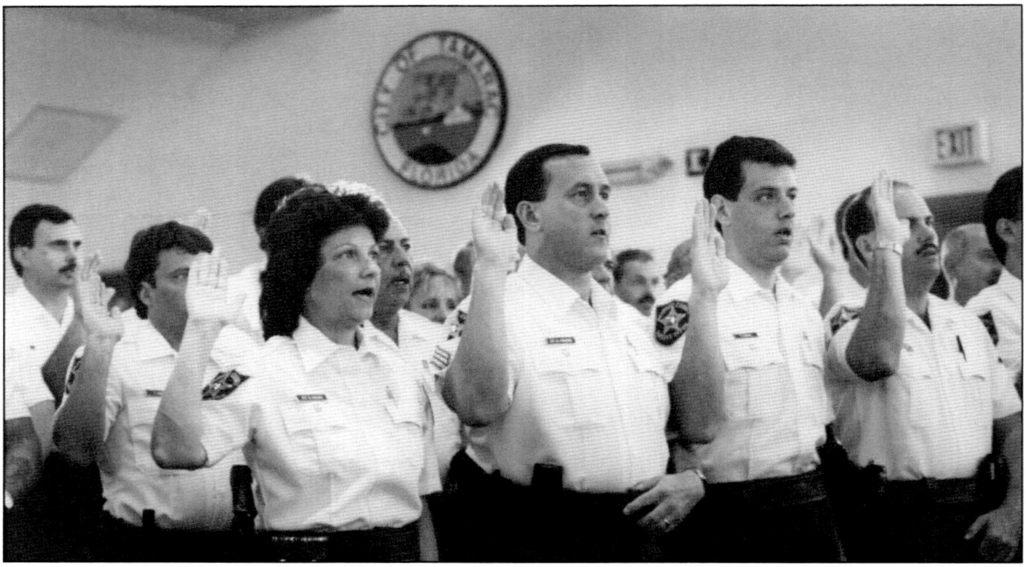

The Broward Sheriff's Office. After several failed attempts at a merger between the Tamarac Police Force and the Broward Sheriff's Office, and despite the city acquiring 16 new patrol cars and new radios, the Tamarac Police Force became part of BSO on June 29, 1989. The city population was now 60,000-plus, and the BSO force included 92 personnel. (Courtesy of *Sun Sentinel* staff photographer Lou Toman.)

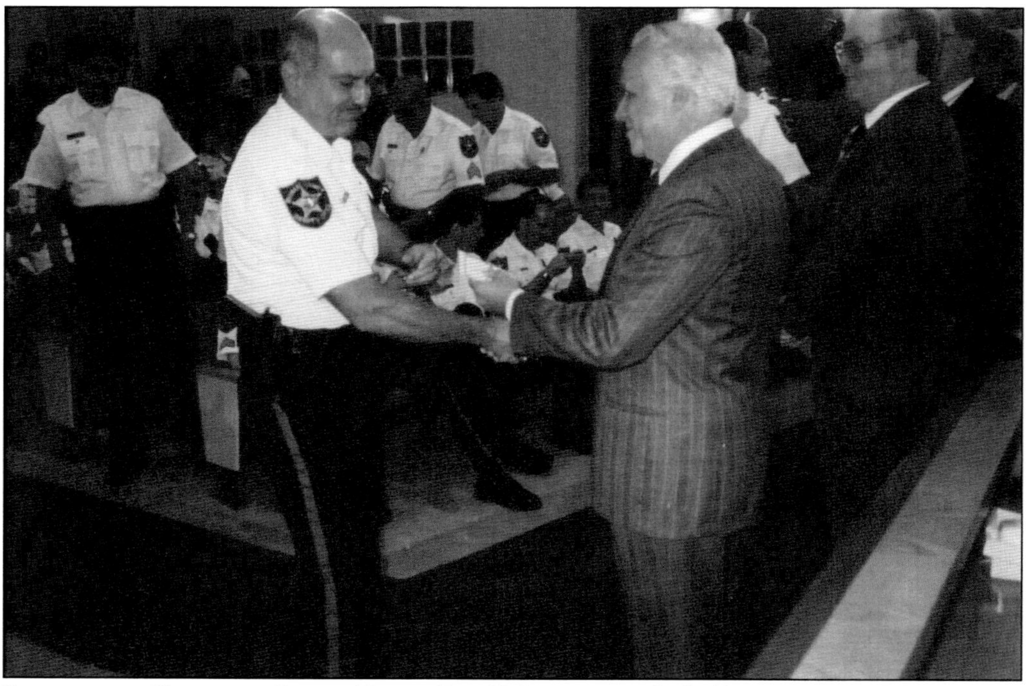

Swearing-in Ceremony. Pictured here is Ron Holt, a nine-and-a-half-year veteran of the Tamarac Police Force, being sworn in as a Broward Sheriff Office deputy by Sheriff Nick Navarro. On Holt's first tour of duty, as a deputy, he was astounded at the many residents who stopped to wave and welcome him in the newly painted BSO patrol car. (Courtesy of personal collection of Ron Holt.)

Two

City Neighborhoods

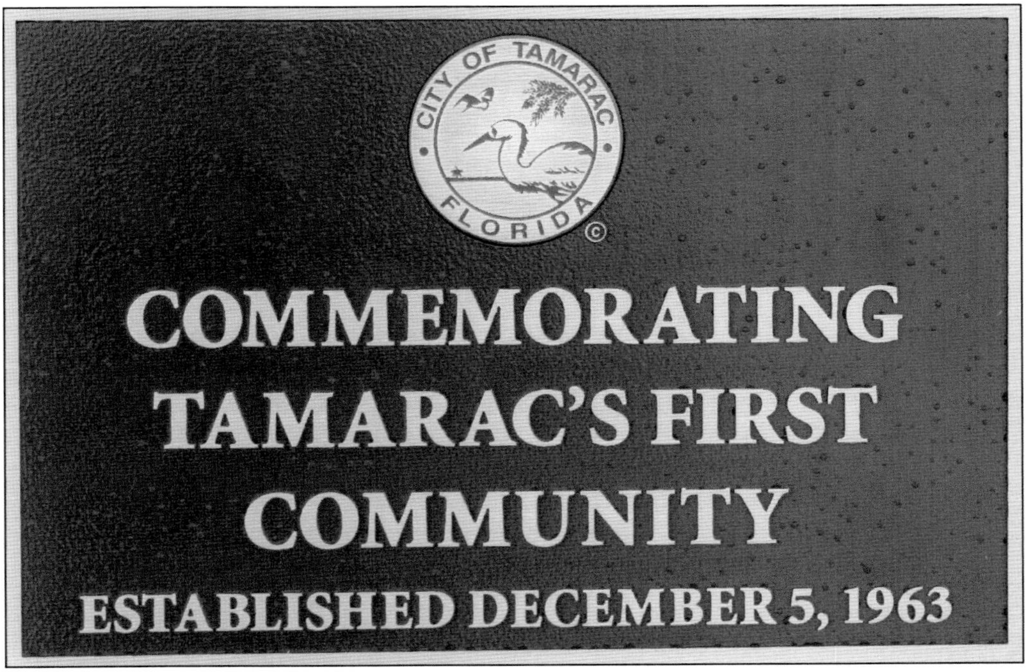

Forever Plaque. A Tamarac Lakes plaque was presented by the city to ensure that this Behring first is forever designated. (Courtesy of the City of Tamarac.)

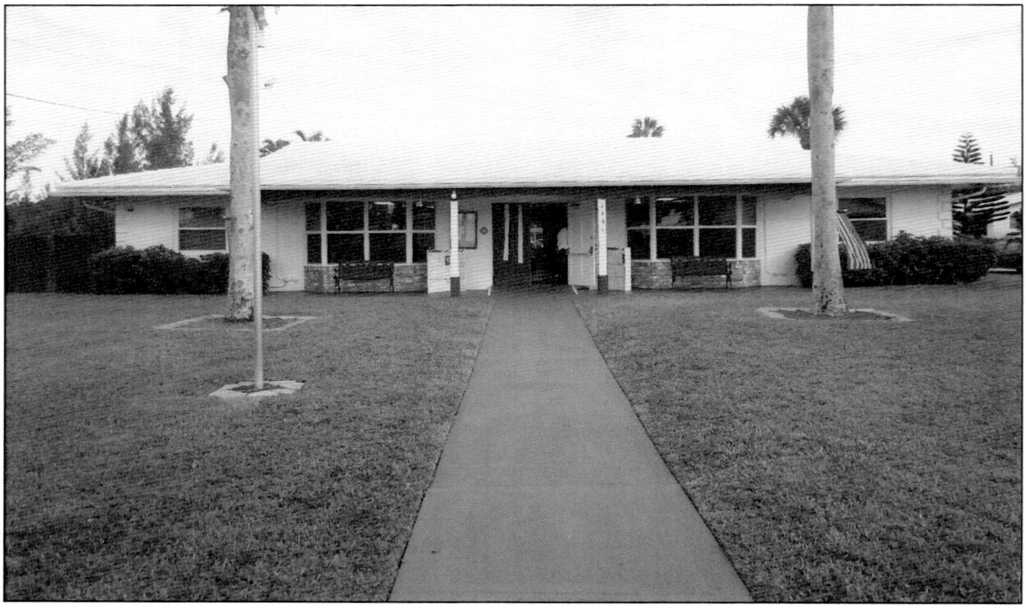

The First Clubhouse. The model Behring established included a clubhouse—the center of activity for 250 homes. Pictured here is the first clubhouse built in Tamarac Lakes. It quickly became the center of everything: parties, dances, holidays, and events Behring sponsored to promote his homes. As the community developed, residents provided prospective buyers with coffee and dessert at the clubhouse. (Courtesy of Marian Daly.)

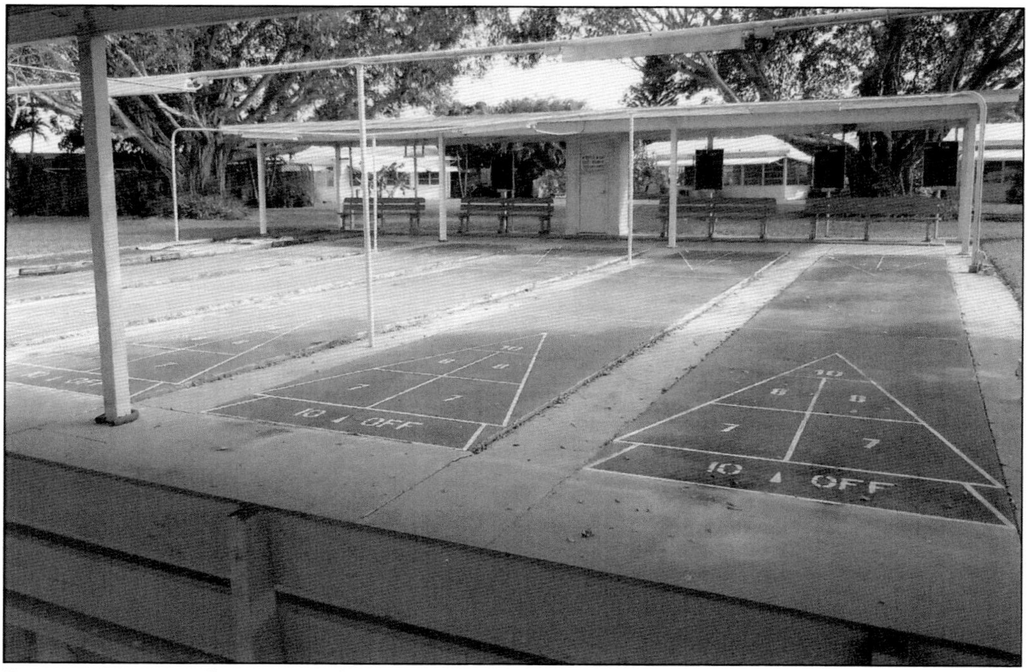

Shuffleboard. A fun pastime became a fierce competition among the different developments. A shuffleboard court was built in each clubhouse area, and tournaments were frequently held. (Courtesy of Marian Daly.)

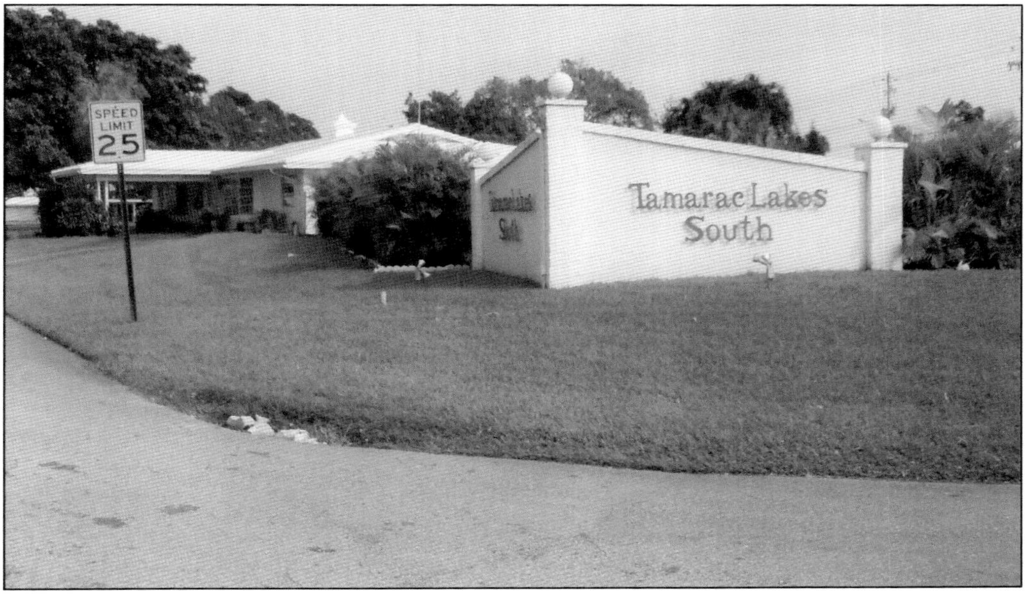

Tamarac Lakes South. This Behring community, which followed the model of clubhouse, pool, and recreational facilities, had one additional amenity: a nine-hole, par-three golf course nestled among the homes. New homeowners who golfed could not believe that they would have their own course on which to hone their skills each and every day. (Courtesy of Marian Daly.)

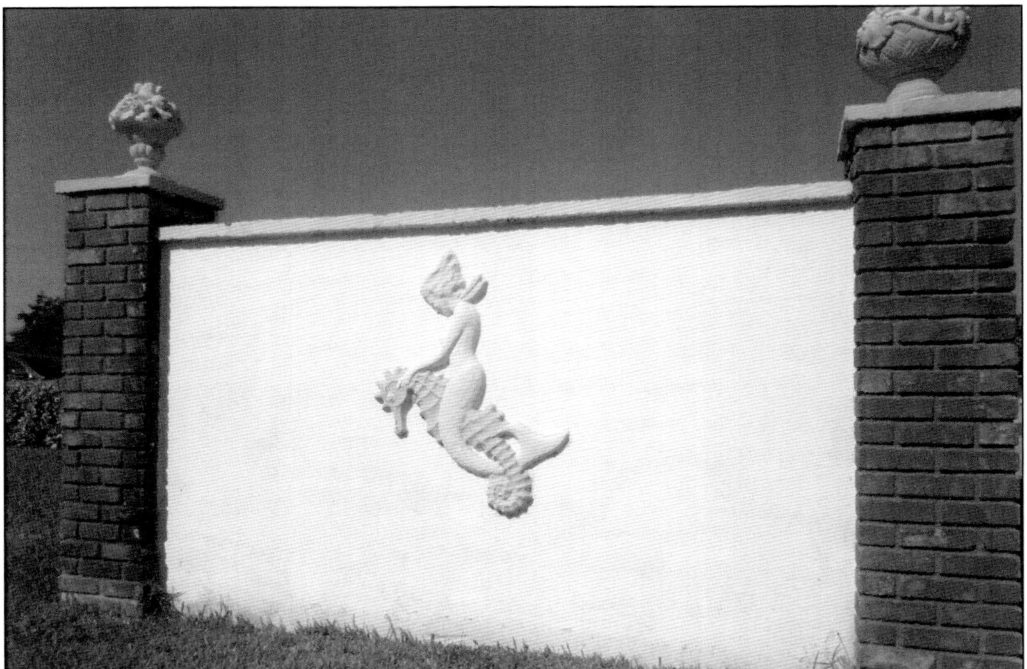

Mermaid on a Sea Horse. The original entrance sign of Tamarac Lakes North has stood since the early 1960s, welcoming residents to their dream homes built on land that was once an orange grove. Pictured here is the back of that sign: a mermaid on a sea horse in bas-relief. (Courtesy of Marian Daly.)

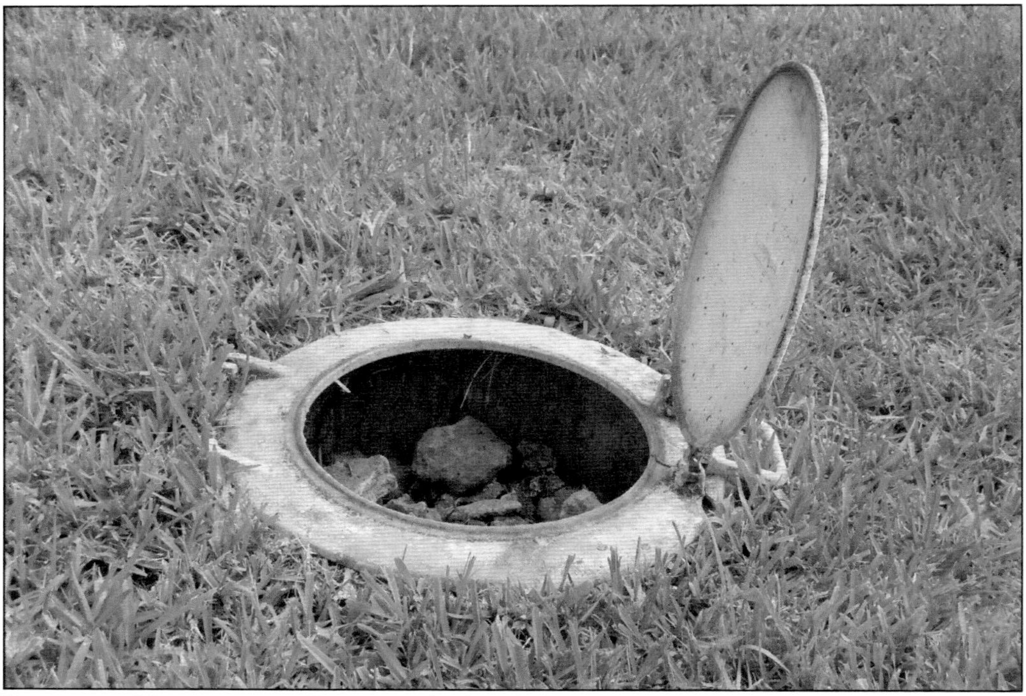

Preserving Neighborhood Beauty. A built-in, below-ground, solid waste can was located in the backyard of each home constructed in the early days of Tamarac. This preserved neighborhood beauty, prevented trash cans from blowing around, and discouraged wildlife scavenging. (Courtesy of Marian Daly.)

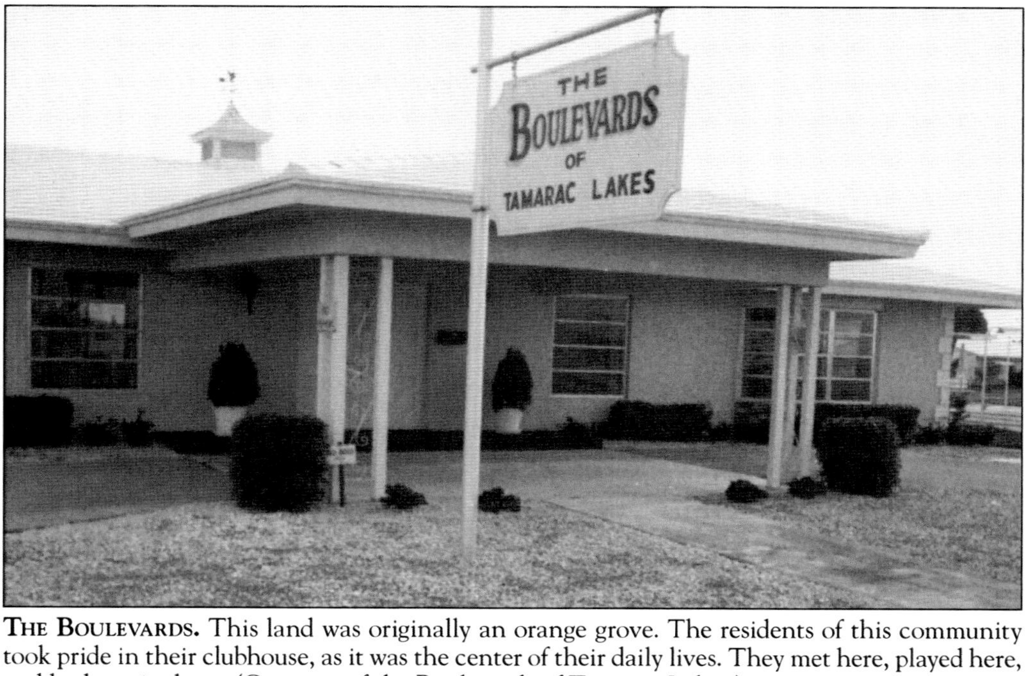

The Boulevards. This land was originally an orange grove. The residents of this community took pride in their clubhouse, as it was the center of their daily lives. They met here, played here, and had parties here. (Courtesy of the Boulevards of Tamarac Lakes.)

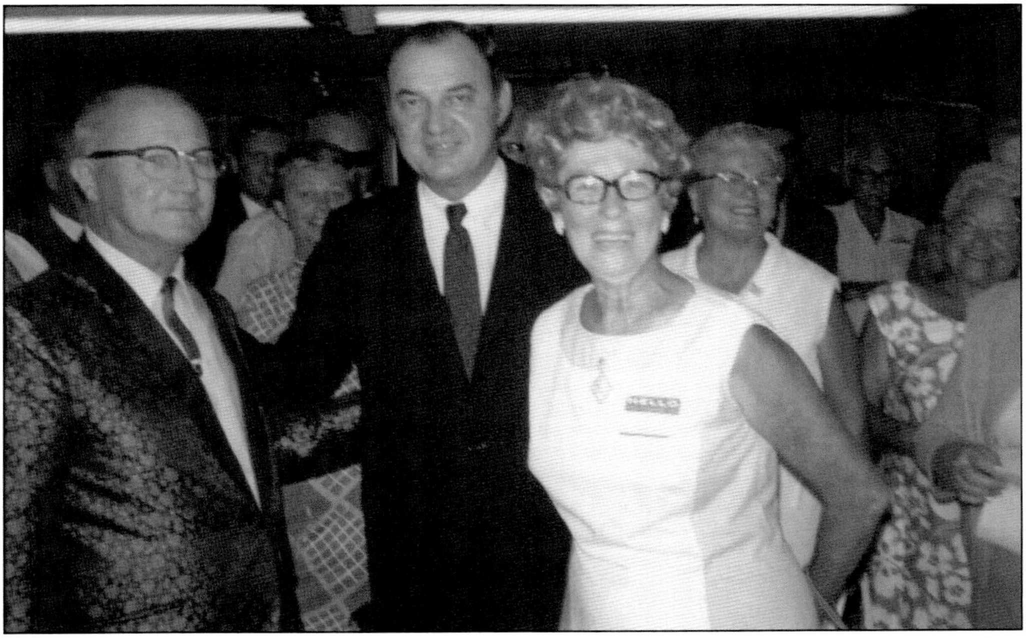

A Celebrity in Tamarac. Gov. Claude Kirk, center, served from 1967 to 1971. He was the first Republican governor elected in Florida in the 20th century. Governor Kirk was instrumental in drafting the current Florida Constitution, he signed the legislation that brought Walt Disney World to Florida, and he was very interested in the environment. He even made time for public appearances, here with residents of the Boulevards of Tamarac Lakes. (Courtesy of the Boulevards of Tamarac Lakes.)

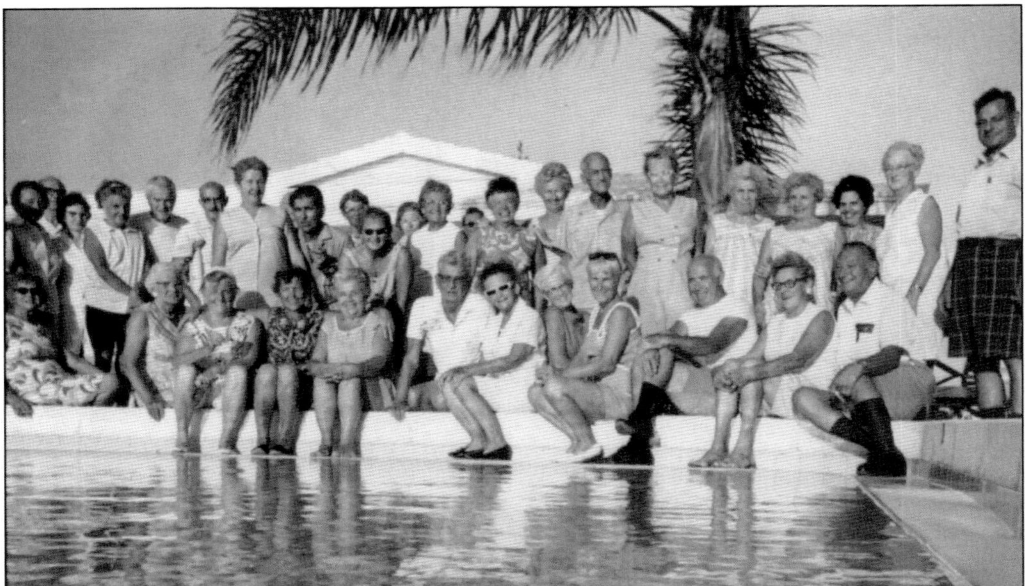

Boulevards of Tamarac. Early citizens of Tamarac came to the city for its comfortable, carefree lifestyle year-round. Residents from the Boulevards of Tamarac Lakes enjoyed a day at their community's swimming pool. (Courtesy of the Boulevards of Tamarac Lakes.)

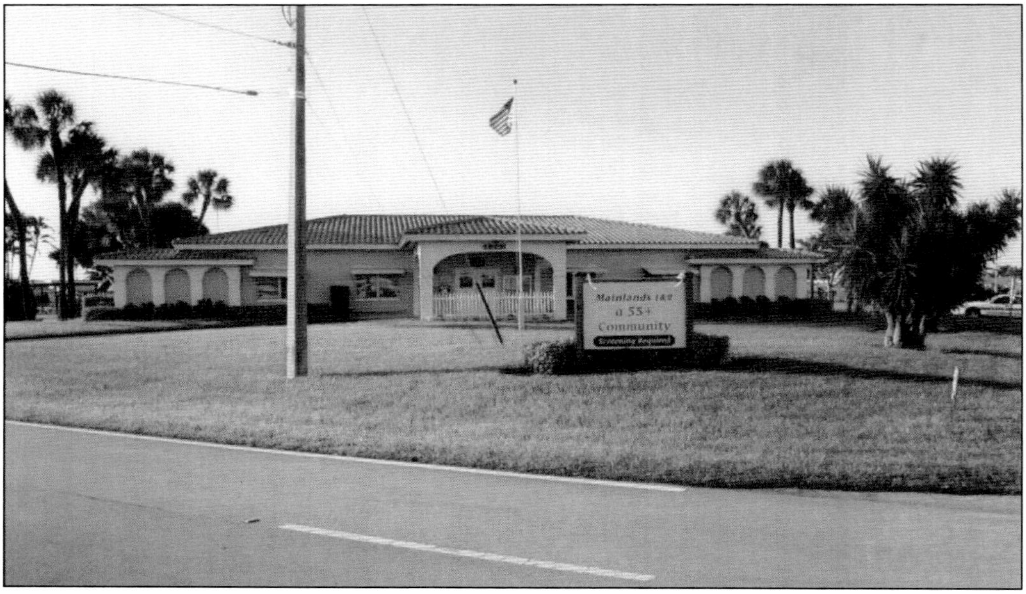

THE MAINLANDS. The Mainlands is an adult community of single-family homes located at Commercial Boulevard and State Road 7 (Route 441). Development began late in 1967 with homes priced in the range of $9,990 to $13,990. However, the most attractive features of the community were the services provided by the city, including full lawn care, house painting, roof cleaning, and lawn sprinkling, allowing residents to enjoy the clubhouse, swimming pools, shuffleboard courts, golf courses, and waterways for fishing. (Courtesy of the City of Tamarac.)

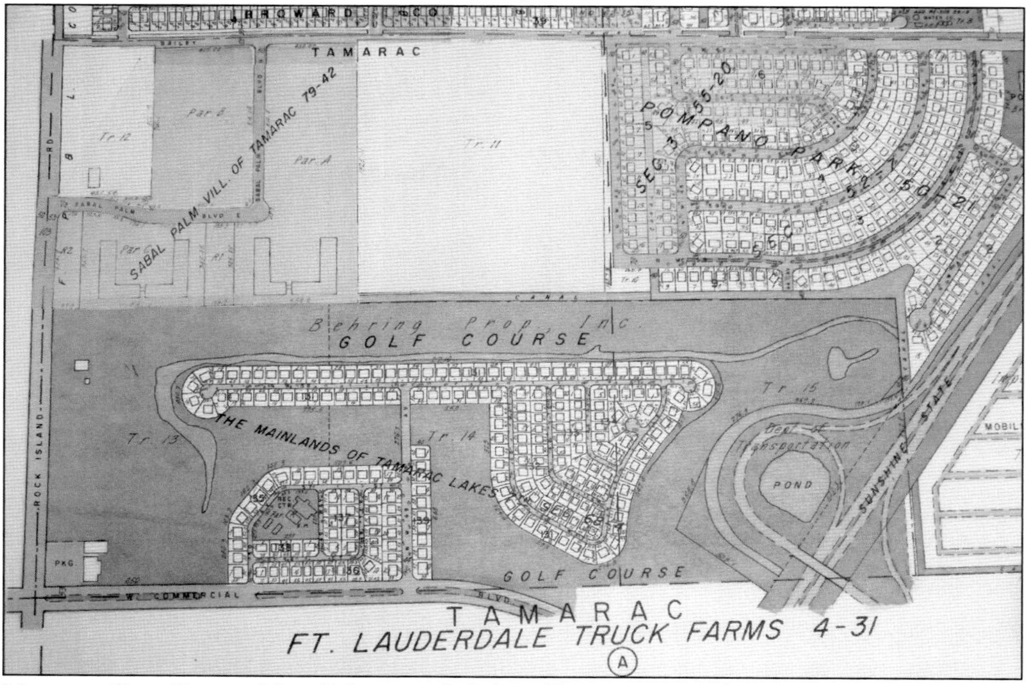

MONTERY GOLF COURSE MAP. Behring included a golf course among the amenities he built into his design for the Mainlands in 1967. (Courtesy of the Broward County Historical Commission.)

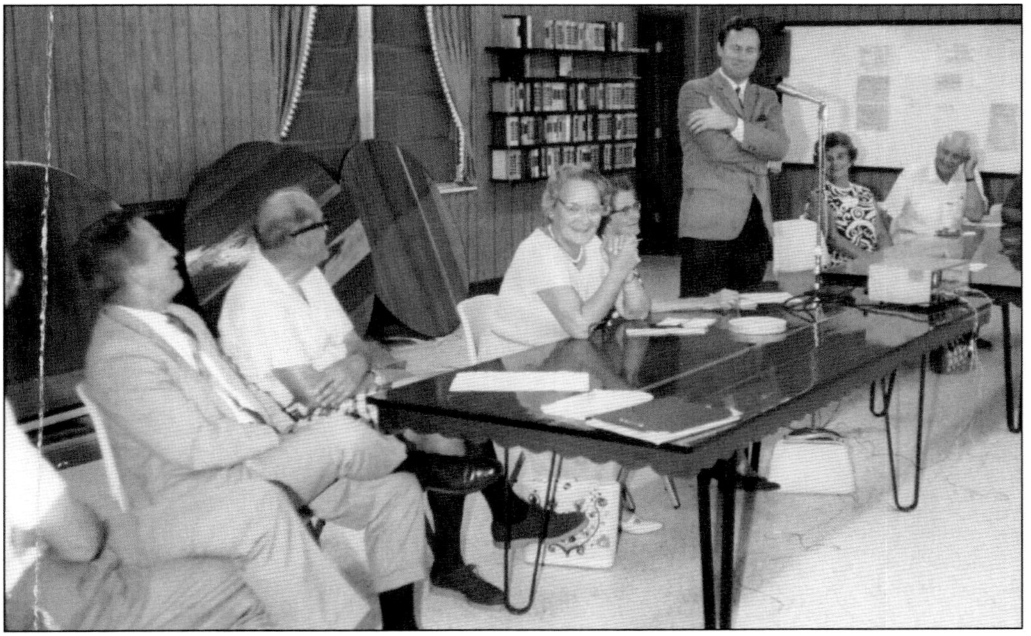

MAINLANDS 3 CLUBHOUSE. Prior to 1969, Tamarac's city hall was located outside city limits. City council meetings were held monthly on a rotating basis at the various clubhouses located in the city. Pictured standing is Tamarac's first mayor, William A. Morse, officiating at a meeting at the Mainlands 3 Clubhouse. An advisory committee, made up of the civic chairman from each neighborhood, met monthly to make recommendations to the city council. (Courtesy of Mainlands 3.)

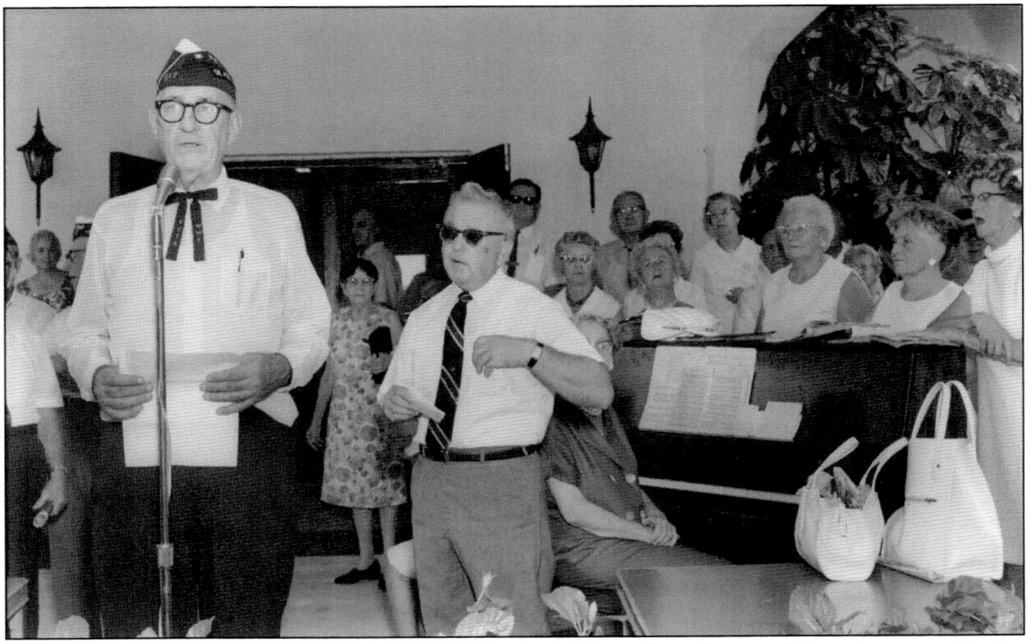

RAISING THE FLAG. In 1969, the Mainlands 3 community gathered around the piano outside the clubhouse at a ceremony dedicated to the American flag. (Courtesy of Mainlands 3.)

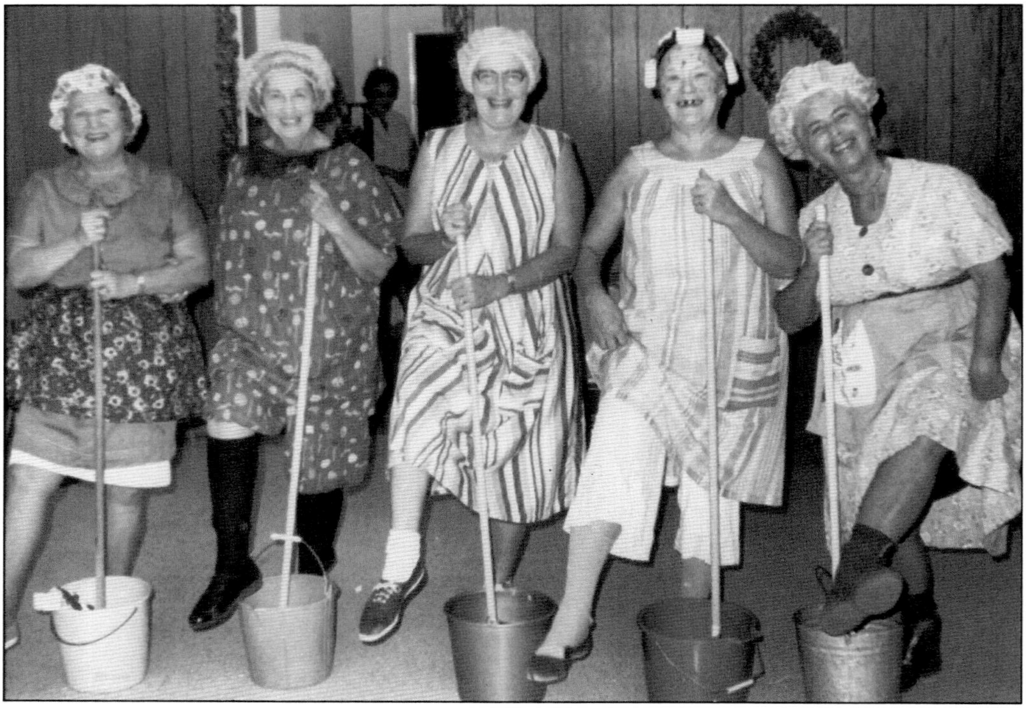

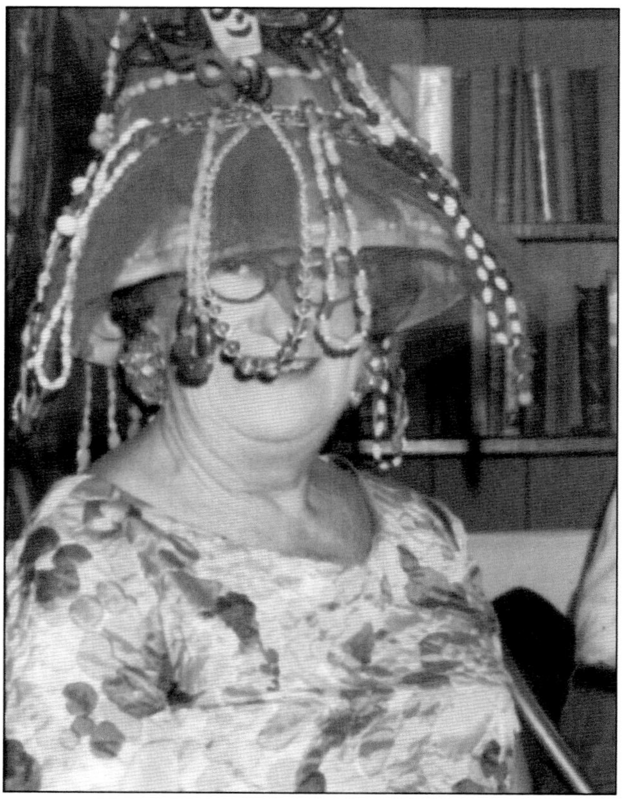

SHOWTIME. Above, the talented women of the Mainlands 3 Women's Club created a comedy show for the community in 1969 at the clubhouse. It was a tremendous success. (Courtesy of Mainlands 3.)

EASTER HAT. This resident donned her Easter hat for the clubhouse celebration. (Courtesy of the Boulevards of Tamarac Lakes.)

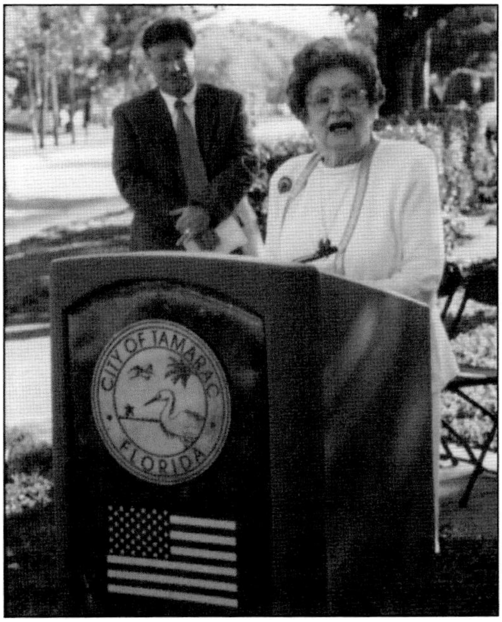

HELEN SIVELLE RECEIVES HONOR. City manager Jeff Miller presented Helen Sivelle with an honor bestowed on her deceased husband. In 2005, the city named Northwest Seventieth Street "Charles Sivelle Street" for his work on the beautification of the medians of the Woodmont neighborhood. (Courtesy of the City of Tamarac.)

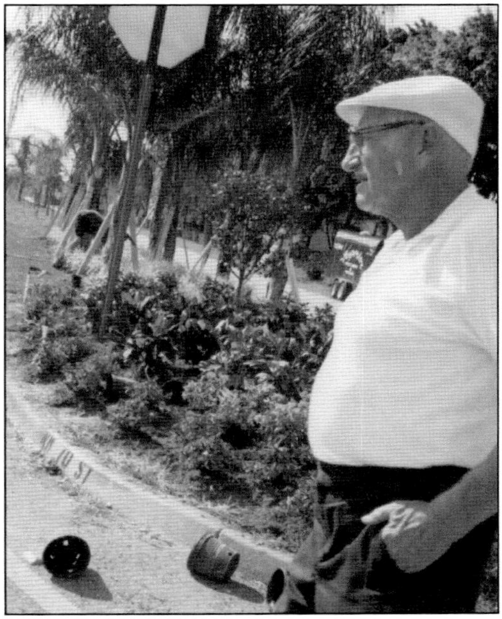

NEW PLANTINGS. Charles Sivelle oversees the beautification of the medians. Plants compatible with warm weather and a sprinkler system enabled the medians to thrive for a long time to come. (Courtesy of the City of Tamarac.)

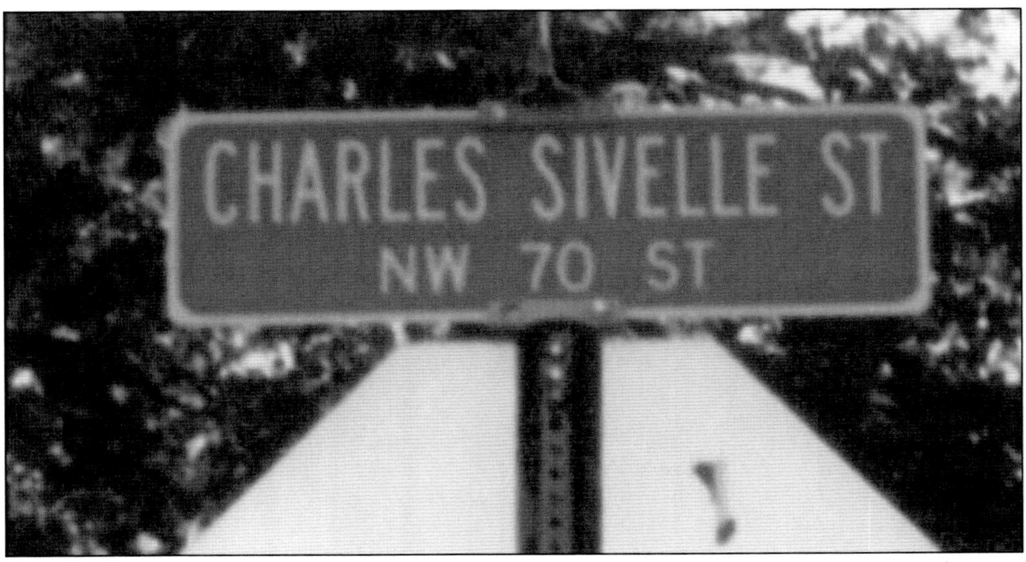

CHARLES SIVELLE STREET, TAMARAC. This is the only street named for a person in the city. (Courtesy of the City of Tamarac.)

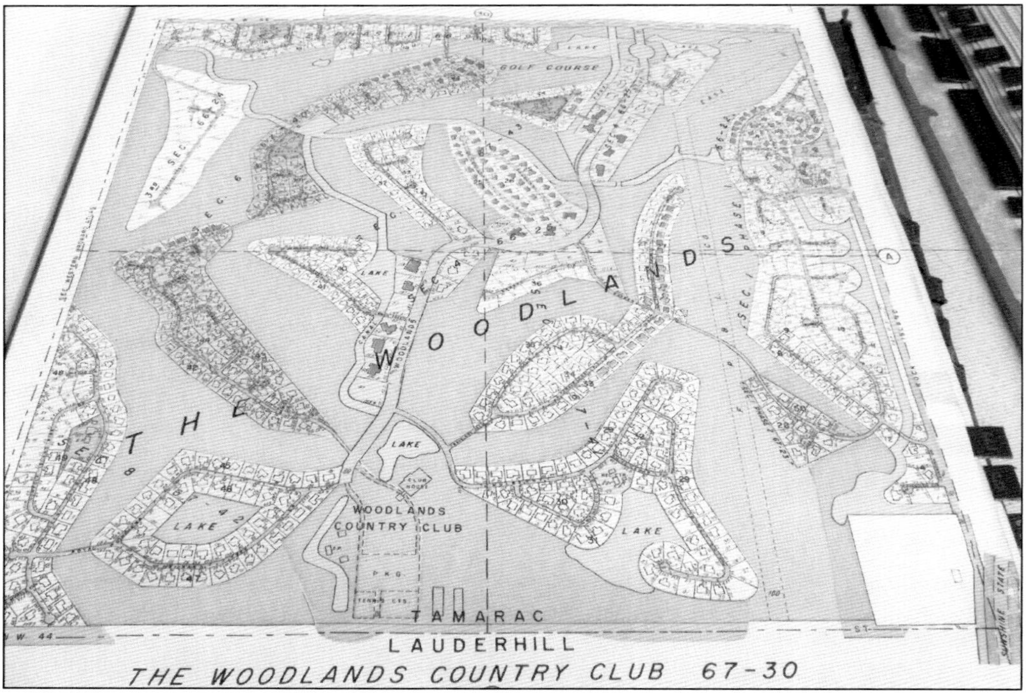

A Country Club Community. In the spring of 1968, Kenneth E. Behring launched Woodlands Community acres, located off Commercial Boulevard, southwest of Rock Island Road. Vista Villas luxury, custom-built homes ranged in price from $19,900 to $27,900. The community features two golf courses designed by Robert Von Hagge. The country club's facilities include a contemporary clubhouse and championship tennis courts with spectator stands for tournament games. Originally, there was an initiation fee of $2,000 to join the country club with annual dues set at $660. (Courtesy of the City of Tamarac.)

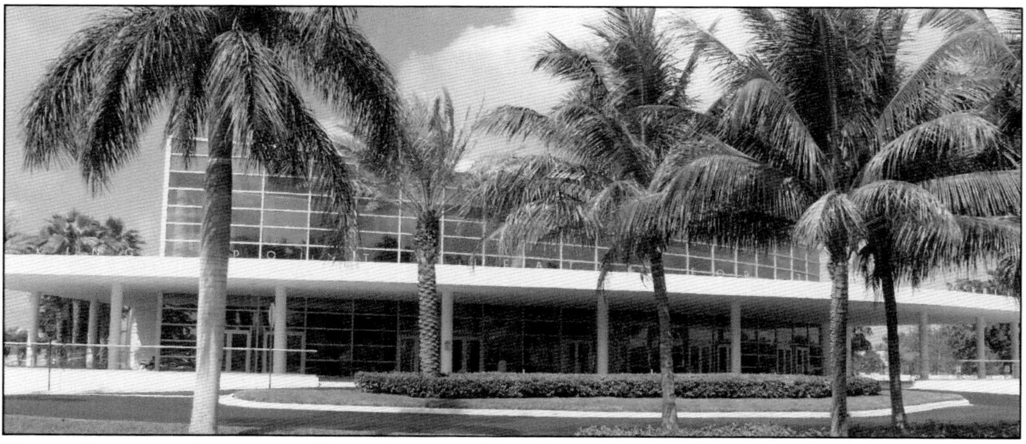

Kings Point in Tamarac. Kings Point in Tamarac consists of 13 neighborhoods and more than 4,000 condos, villas, and homes. The theater was designed to meet accessibility needs of the Kings Point senior communities and provide its patrons with a venue to experience musical artists, revues, dramas, and films. The clubhouse located across from the theater features a fully equipped exercise room, indoor pool with spa, and rooms for social club meetings, classes, and events. (Courtesy of the City of Tamarac.)

Three

City Facilities

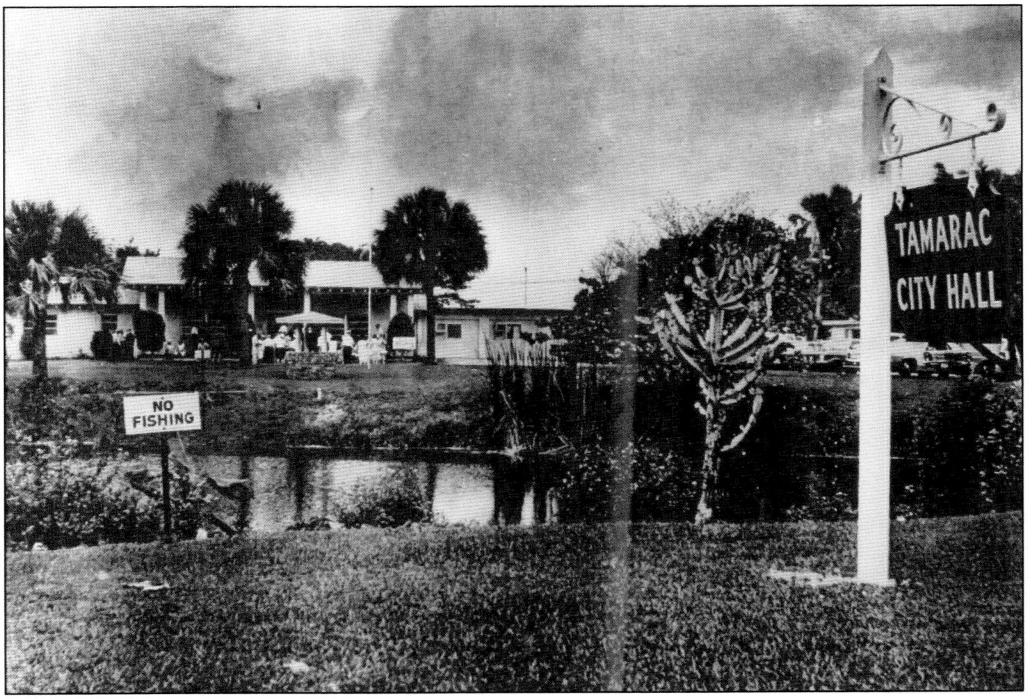

Rock Island Road City Hall. From 1969 through November 1975, Tamarac's city hall was located at 5000 Rock Island Road. City officials and residents were happy to finally have a city hall located within the city limits. This Rock Island property was formerly the site of a ranch. The various ranch structures housed the city's departments. The public works department was located in the yard; the city council took up chambers in the big, old barn; and the police department worked out of a two-car garage. Due to the deterioration of the structures, city hall had to be relocated. Today, all traces of the ranch are gone, and the property is now the site for several Tamarac homes. (Courtesy of the City of Tamarac.)

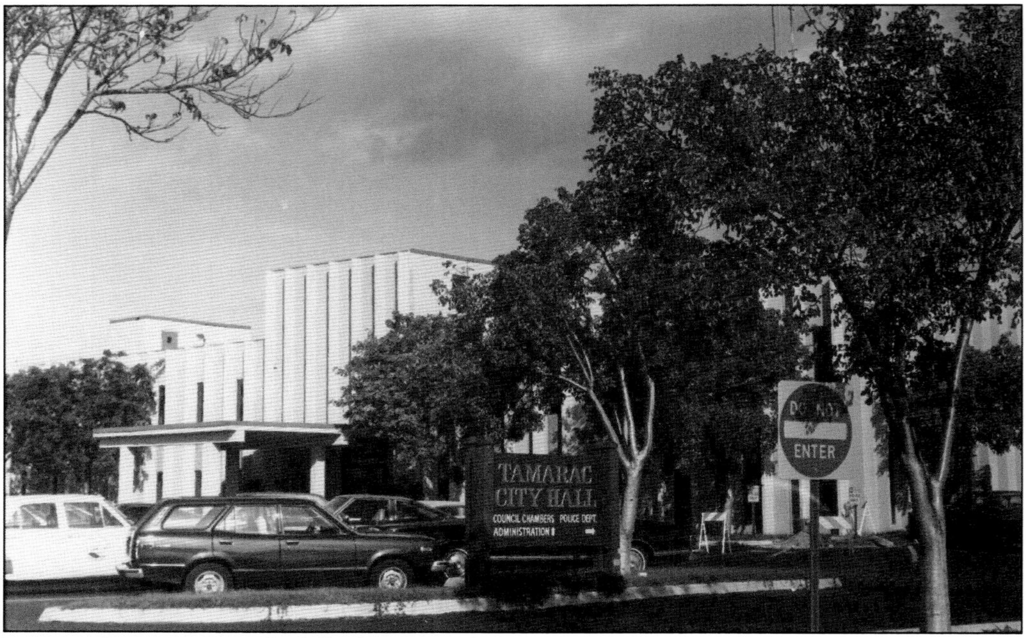

LUXURY CITY HALL. In the fall of 1975, city hall was moved to 5811 Pine Island Road. Originally the building was to be the site for luxury executive office suites, however, builder S. Marcus Rosenblatt was having difficulty finding enough tenants. At this city hall were all city departments, conference rooms, a fireproof vault for city records, and two jail cells each with toilet facilities. Public city council meetings were held every other week. In 1991, the city sold the building to the Tamarac Congregation of Jehovah's Witnesses. (Courtesy of the City of Tamarac.)

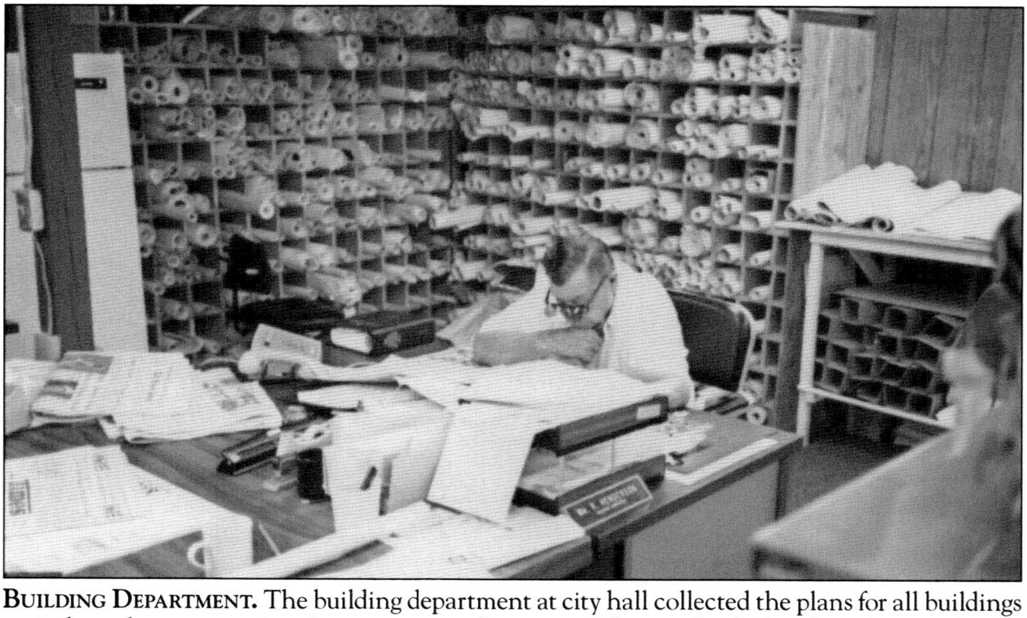

BUILDING DEPARTMENT. The building department at city hall collected the plans for all buildings actively under construction. It was personnel's responsibility to check the plans for compliance and schedule and carry out site inspections during the building process. Mr. Henderson is pictured here. (Courtesy of the City of Tamarac.)

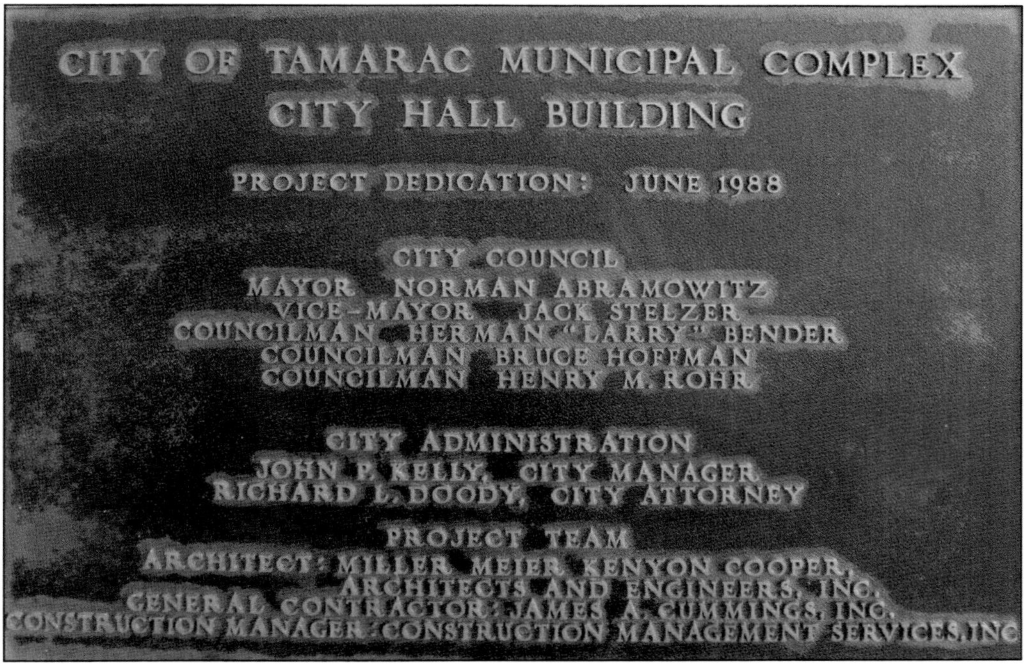

CITY HALL DEDICATED. Mayor Norman Abramowitz dedicated the current city hall, located at 7525 Northwest Eighty-eighth Avenue, in 1988. City hall houses the mayor and commission offices, financial services, the city clerk, human resources, community development, code compliance, housing administration, the city manager's office, and a council chamber. In October 2006, the city rededicated its city hall to Mayor Abramowitz. (Both, courtesy of the City of Tamarac.)

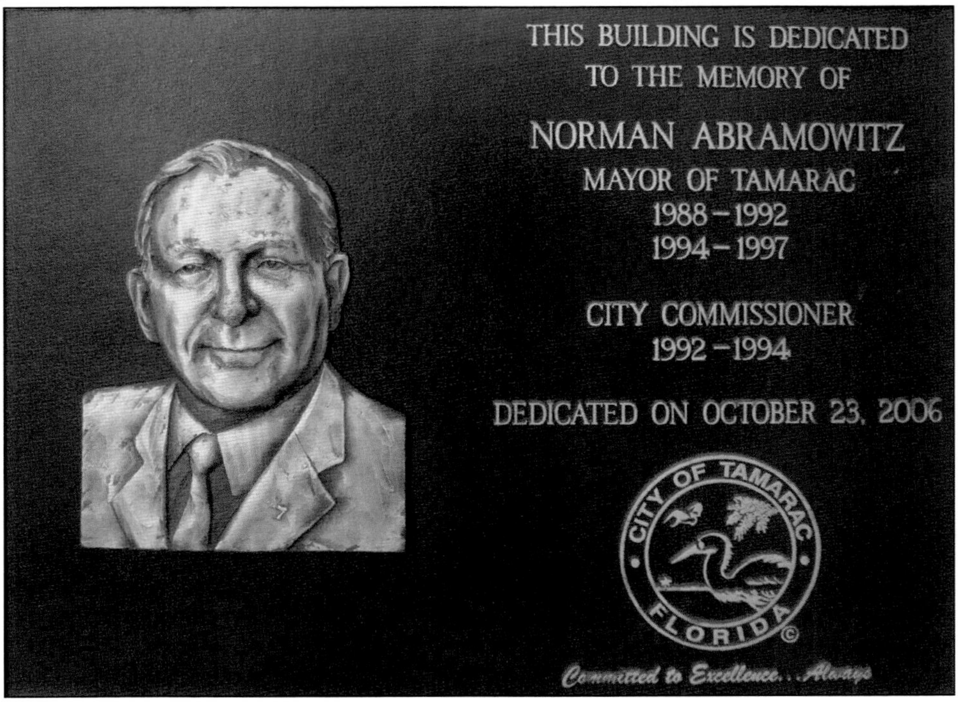

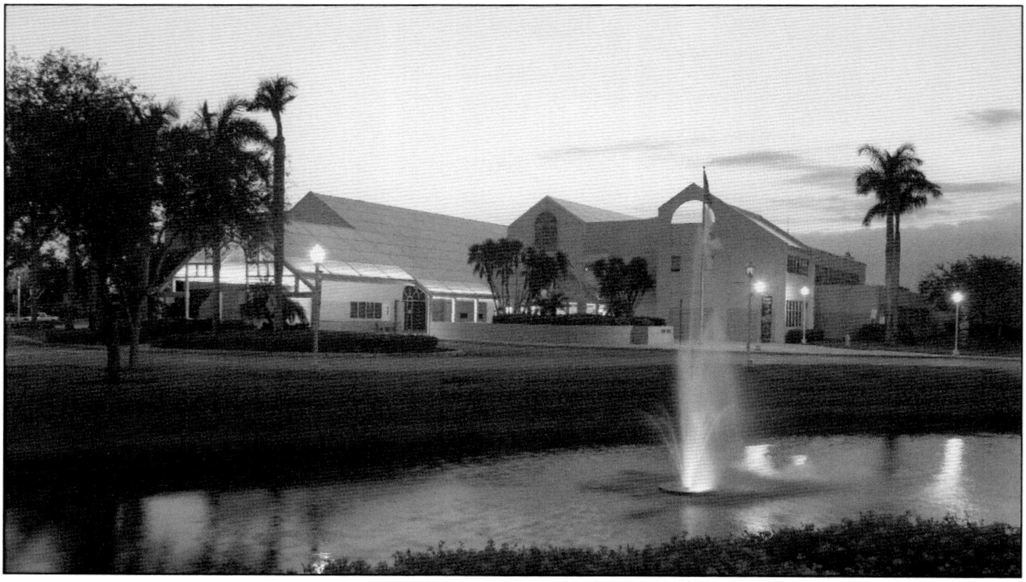

Current City Hall. Tamarac's city hall is a stucco structure, which peaks 40 feet at the clear, Plexiglas skylight that overlooks the two-story lobby with a second-floor walkway and glass-encased elevator. The bright and spacious 47,924-square-foot building was designed in the Post-Modern tradition by the Fort Lauderdale architectural firm Miller, Meier, Kenyon & Cooper. Construction of the building was awarded to James A. Cummings, Inc. The structure won an award of excellence in architecture from the Broward County Chapter of the Florida Association of the American Institute of Architects. (Courtesy of the City of Tamarac.)

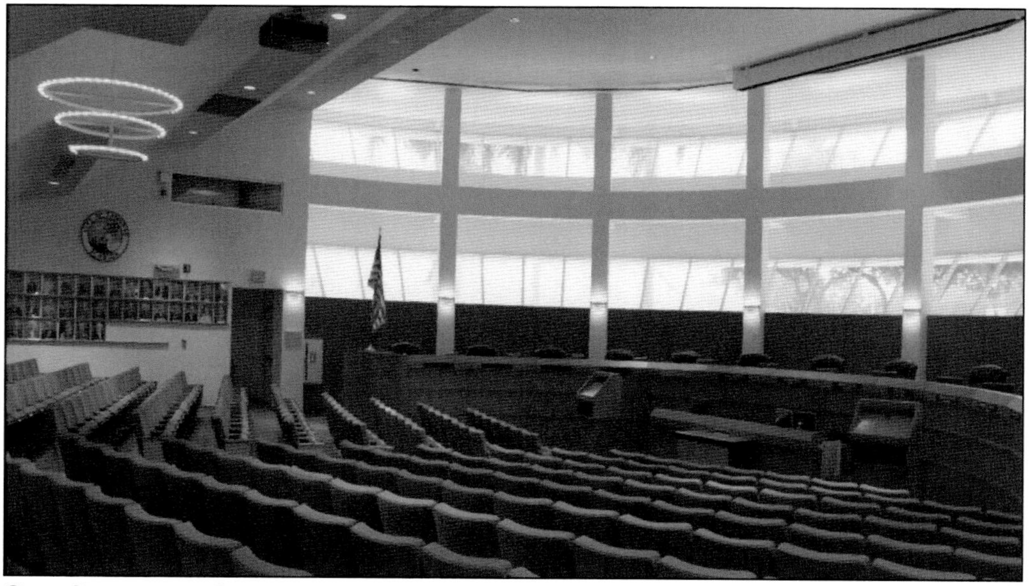

City Commission Chamber. Tamarac's city hall has a state-of-the-art commission chamber. Residents are encouraged to attend commission meetings that are held on the second and fourth Wednesday of each month. The meetings are open to the public where during public participation anyone can sign up to speak before the commission on any subject for three minutes. (Courtesy of the City of Tamarac.)

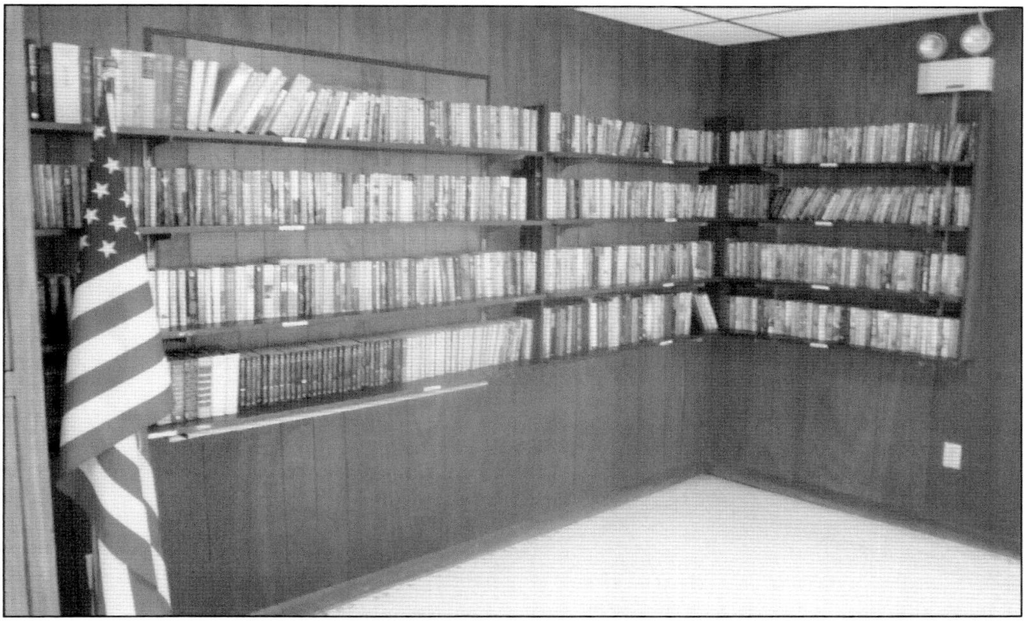

CLUBHOUSE LIBRARY. As the city became more populated and the clubhouses became the center of everyone's daily routine, amenities were added by the residents. In many clubhouses, a library was started from a few paperbacks but rapidly grew to many volumes. Here is a great example of a well-maintained library in the clubhouse of the Boulevards of Tamarac Lakes. (Courtesy of the Tamarac Historical Society.)

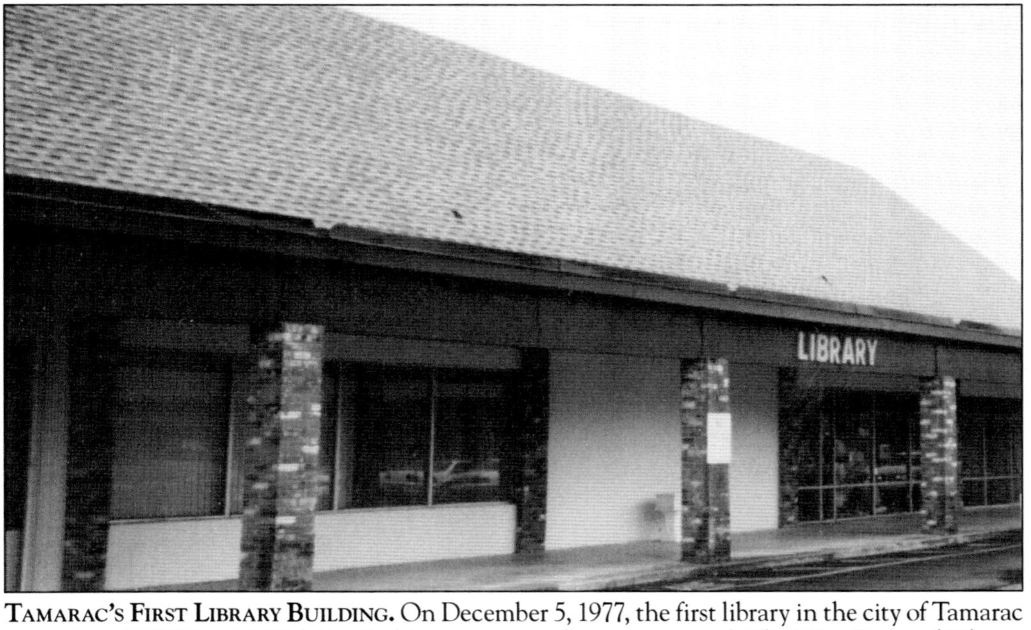

TAMARAC'S FIRST LIBRARY BUILDING. On December 5, 1977, the first library in the city of Tamarac opened on 8601 West McNab Road; this event went almost unnoticed. The West Broward Library opened with 10,000 volumes, and during its first 30 days, 1,263 library cards were issued. The most-requested titles were books on arts and crafts. (Courtesy of *Broward Times/South Florida Times*, Julie Calsi, staff writer, January 13, 1978.)

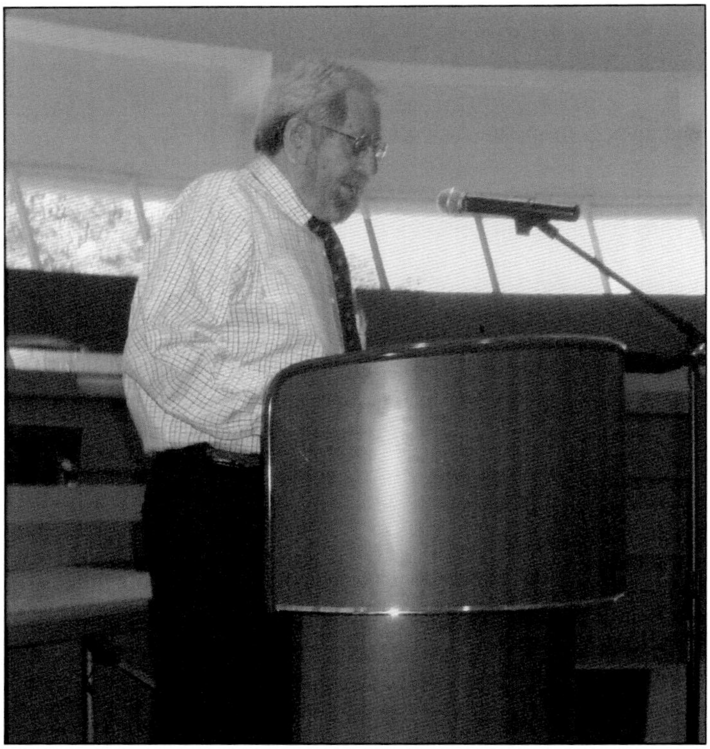

FORMER FLORIDA STATE LIBRARIAN. Cecil Beach is best known for his work with the Broward County Library System, which began in 1977. He was hired as director of the newly created county library, and his task was to pull the system together, gain the support of the cities, plan and institute a building program, build a collection, hire a competent staff, prepare and defend adequate budgets for operation, and plan for the future. He presented "A Funny Thing Happened on the Way to the Library" to invited guests and the Tamarac Historical Society, on July 13, 2010, in Tamarac City Hall chambers. (Courtesy of the City of Tamarac.)

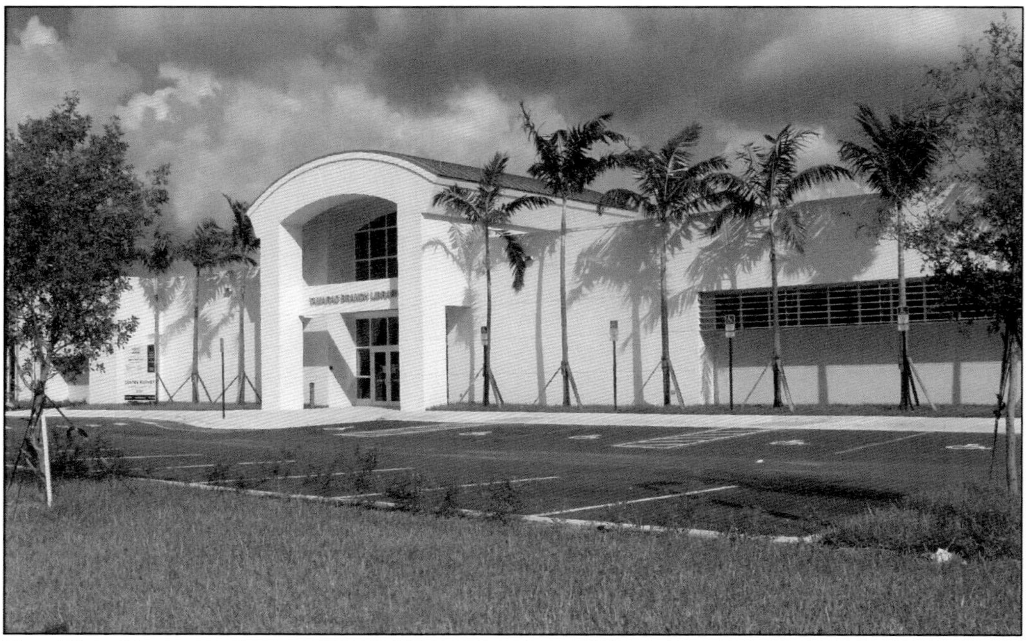

THE NEW TAMARAC LIBRARY. In 2003, a new, larger library opened next to the community center. This Tamarac Library has amenities the old library did not: computer banks, spaces for DVDs and videos, a multipurpose room, and an expanded children's area. (Courtesy of the City of Tamarac.)

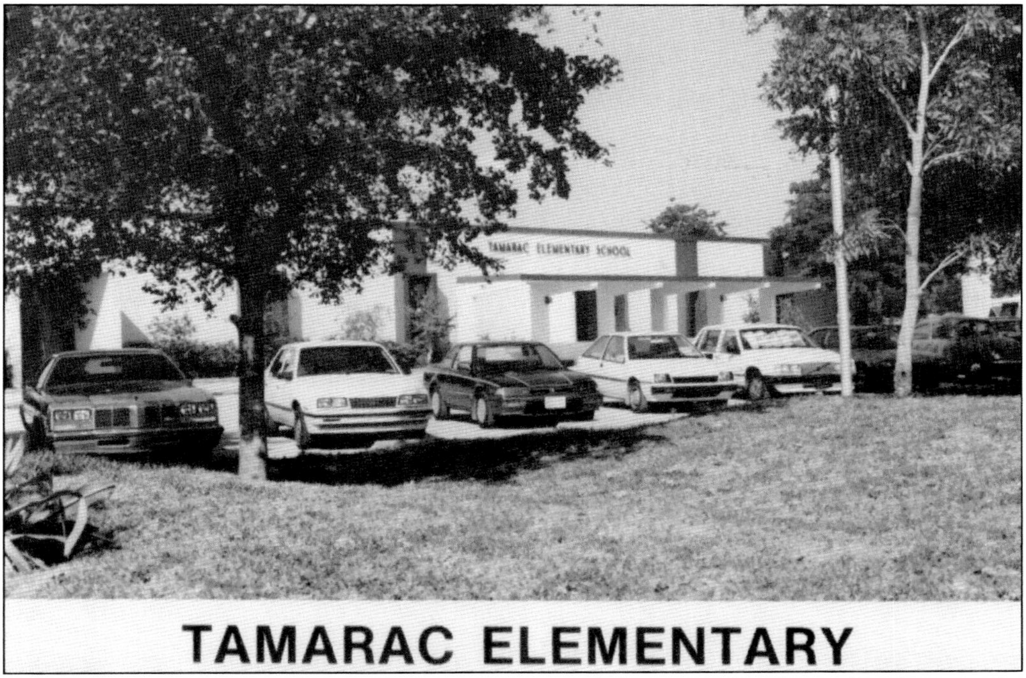

The First School. In the fall of 1974, James H. Henschel, principal, welcomed students to the city's first school, Tamarac Elementary School, located on North University Drive. Designed by architect Charles F. McAlpine, the school was constructed on land donated by Leadership Housing, Inc. Parents from the Heathgate neighborhood vigorously campaigned for a city school so their children would not have to be bussed long distances to other county schools. The school's motto is "Show me what you can become. There's a dream for everyone." (Courtesy of Tamarac Elementary School.)

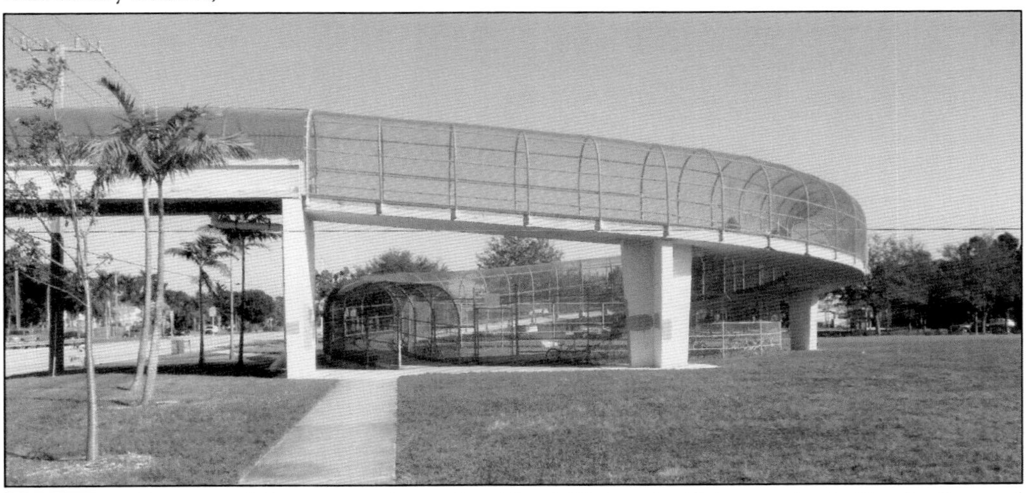

University Overpass. The overpass located on North University Drive was funded by the Broward County Department of Transportation and designed by Yohalem Engineering Inc. Completed in 1979, the structure is a free-standing bridge and provides safe east-to-west access for students attending Tamarac Elementary School and for residents accessing facilities at Tamarac Park. (Courtesy of the Tamarac Historical Society.)

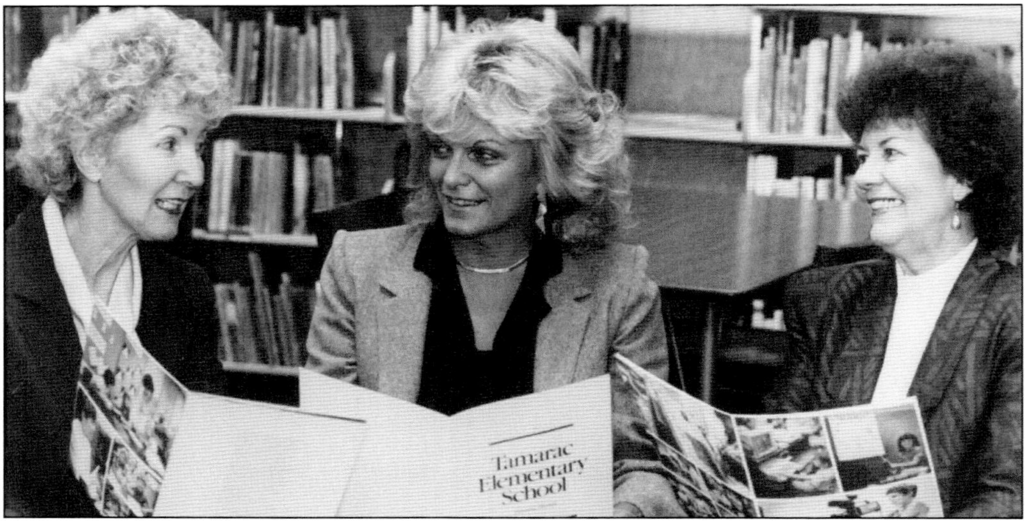

A Public Relation Plan for Tamarac Elementary School. The Tamarac Elementary School built in 1974 was still a little known entity in 1987. The school administrators teamed with the Woodmont Corporation, the school's Partner in Excellence, in a public relations campaign to attract more families to Tamarac. With the brochure the partnership created in hand, (from left to right) Principal Pat Rancati, Doris Olds, and Kay Patenti Busch researched businesses that catered to children and would be interested in moving to Tamarac. They felt the brochure would help attract families and also show how well the school was meeting the needs of it children. (Courtesy of the *Sun Sentinel* and staff photographer Eliot J. Schechter.)

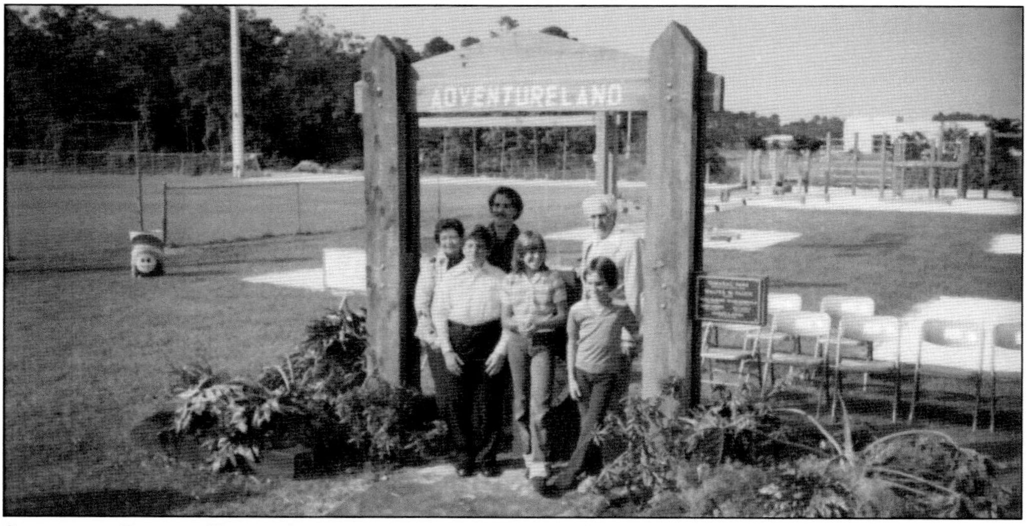

Students Design Their Own Park. The Tamarac Elementary School fifth-grade enrichment program class began designing a park as a local government project. Diane Lade, staff writer for the *Sun Sentinel,* reported how the class teamed up with Tamarac City Planner Dick Rubin, who gave the class a course in city development. After taking a survey, students decided they wanted a playground specially designed for preteens. They chose the equipment and determined the placement in the park via an architectural drawing. In order to make presentations to the city council, the class joined the Junior Toastmasters. Adventureland Park was dedicated in November 1979. (Courtesy of the City of Tamarac.)

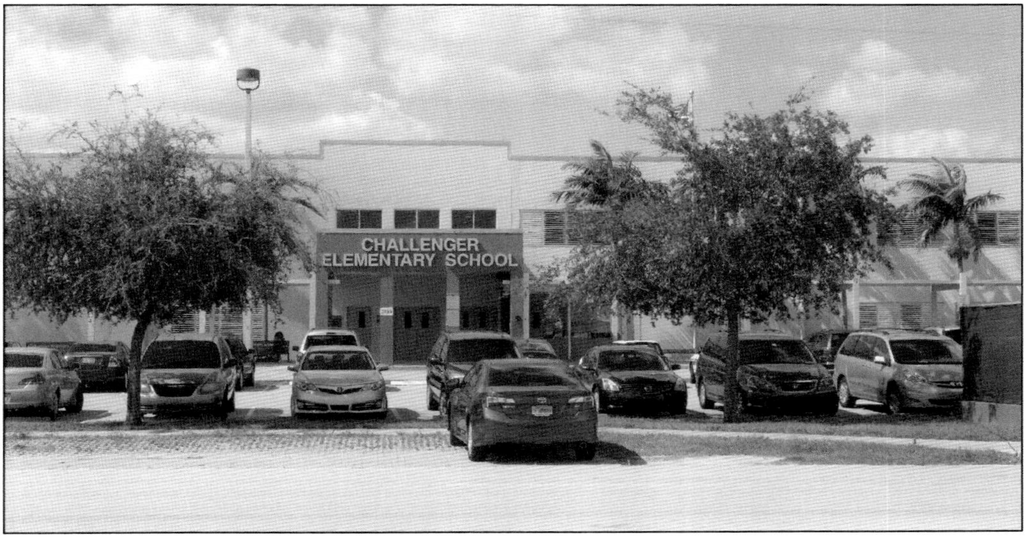

Challenger Elementary School. Challenger Elementary School opened in 2001 to meet the city's increasing student population. Zyscovich, Inc., was the architect for the building constructed by James B. Pirtle Construction Company Inc. The school's mission is "To ensure that all students will meet the highest standards and will achieve their greatest potential in a respectful and safe environment." Committed to a greener environment, the school recycles electronic equipment. Funds raised are used to update classrooms with the latest technology. (Courtesy of the City of Tamarac.)

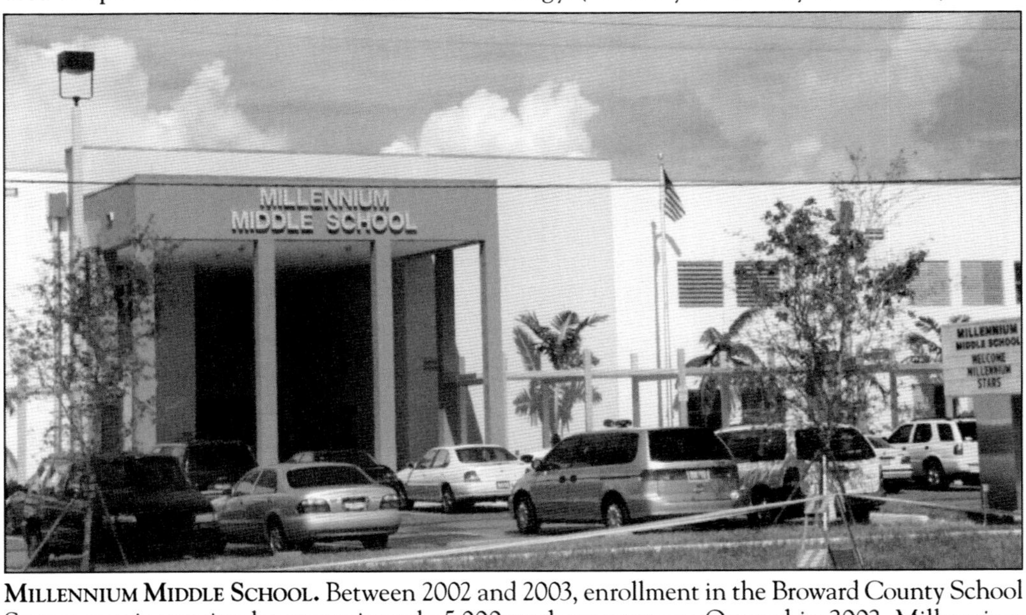

Millennium Middle School. Between 2002 and 2003, enrollment in the Broward County School System was increasing by approximately 5,000 students per year. Opened in 2002, Millennium Middle School was one of seven new schools constructed to meet this increase. Zyscovich, Inc., was the architect for the building constructed by James B. Pirtle Construction Company, Inc. This school's mission is "To provide a stimulating and safe learning environment where each student's diversified needs are challenged and social needs are met creating productive citizens and lifelong learners." The county also uses the school facilities as an emergency shelter during hurricanes. It is the only pet-friendly shelter in the county. (Courtesy of the City of Tamarac.)

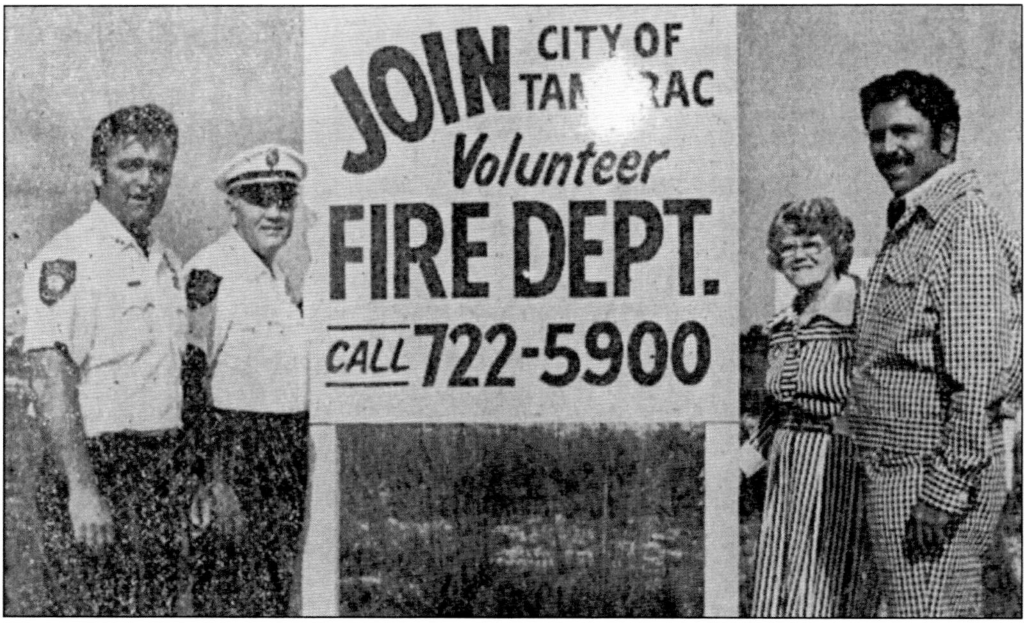

The Department Needs You. The Tamarac Fire Department had six volunteer firemen and is conducting a drive to recruit at least 20 more. From left to right are assistant fire chief Raymond Briant, chief of volunteers Frank Lawler, Vice Mayor Helen Massaro, and city manager Edward Gross. (Courtesy of the City of Tamarac.)

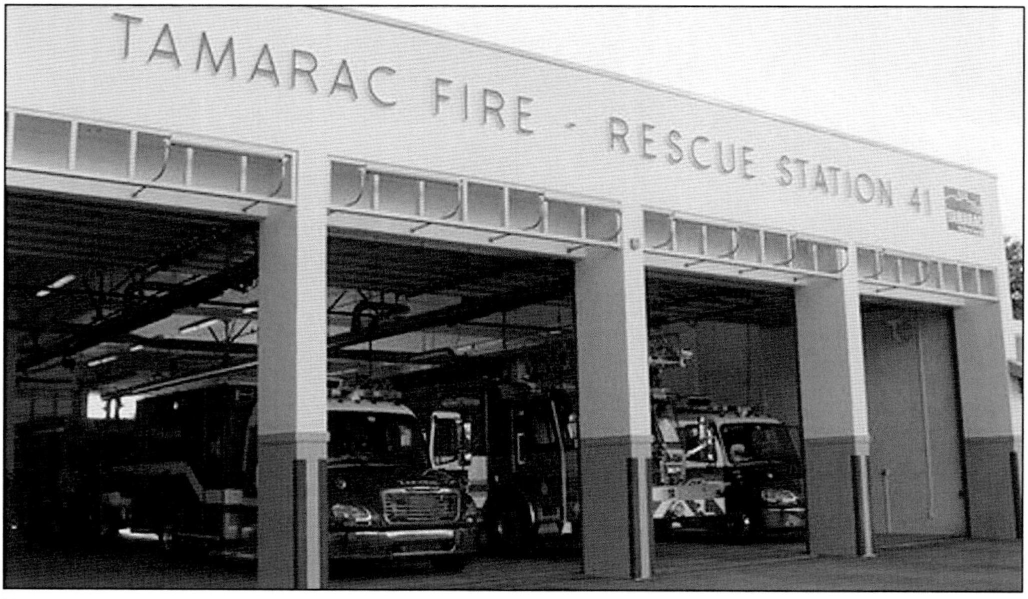

Early Tamarac Fire Department. Prior to the fire department, fire rescue was managed by the North Andrews and Sunrise Fire Departments. The Tamarac Fire Department began in 1977 when it was housed at the then city hall at 5811 Northwest Eighty-eighth Avenue. Chief Bernie Simon was the first to head this rescue department, where the firemen slept on the floor of the council chamber to be ready for any emergency. This early department included volunteer firemen who supported Chief Simon's team. (Courtesy of Rudy Hoffman.)

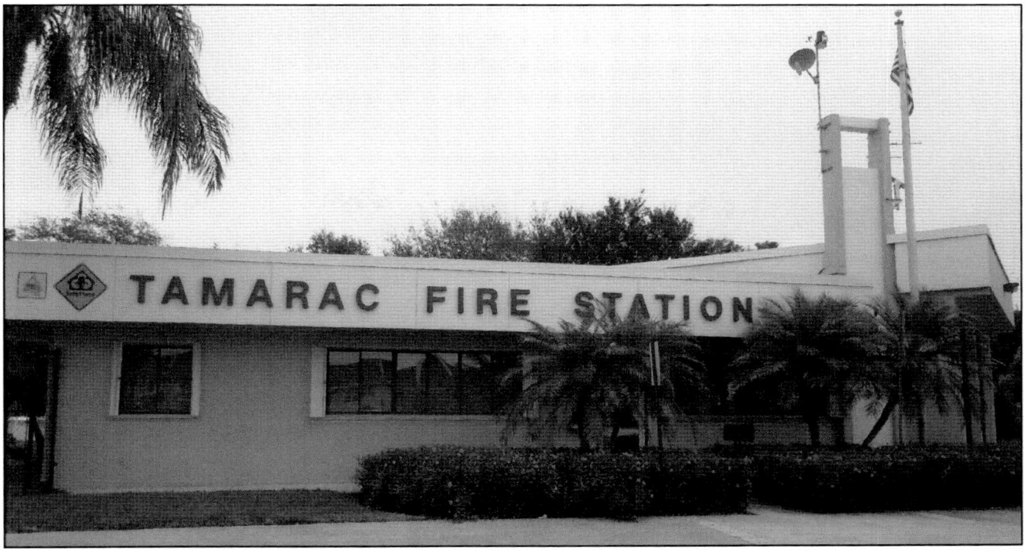

What Do the Numbers Mean? Prior to 1990, each city could number their stations as they pleased. The first two stations were numbered 32-1 (7501 Northwest Eighty-eighth Avenue) and 32-2 (4801 West Commercial Boulevard). When Broward County Chief's Association decided to link all county fires stations, the numbers changed based on when they were built. The first two stations became No. 41 and No. 78. The newest fire department and headquarters was built in 1995 and was assigned No. 15, a fire station that was closed in the county and whose number was available. (Courtesy of Paul Kelly, retired Fire Fighter.)

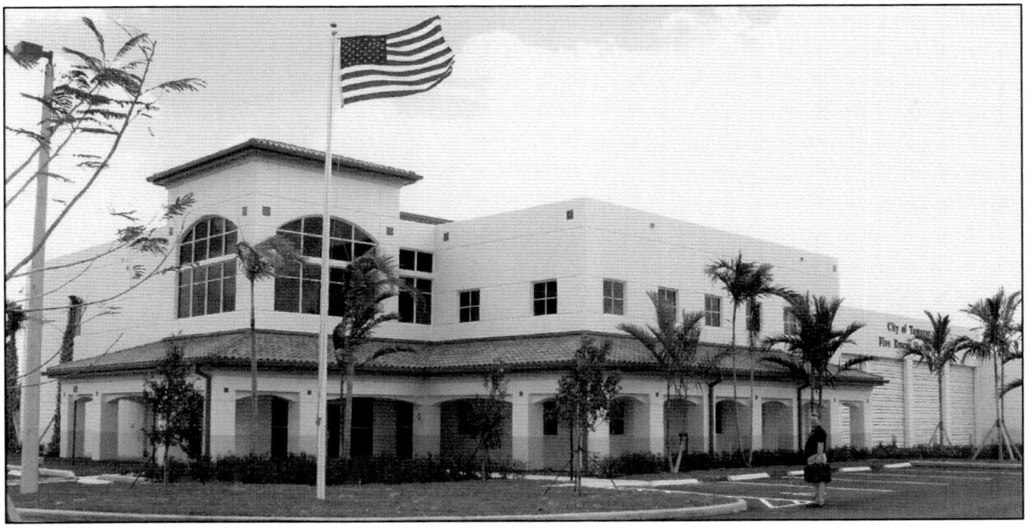

Fire Rescue Headquarters. In 2004, the fire rescue department moved into its new headquarters, Station No. 15. It provided the following services: fire prevention; fire suppression; Emergency Medical Services (EMS), including advanced life support and transport; public education; and emergency preparedness. This organization of career firefighters and paramedics is fully equipped to handle all emergency responses in the city. The department includes a Community Emergency Response Team (CERT) training for residents that want to be ready to help in case of a disaster. Training continues to the cadets, who are working alongside the firefighters to determine if they are headed for a career in fire rescue. (Courtesy of the City of Tamarac.)

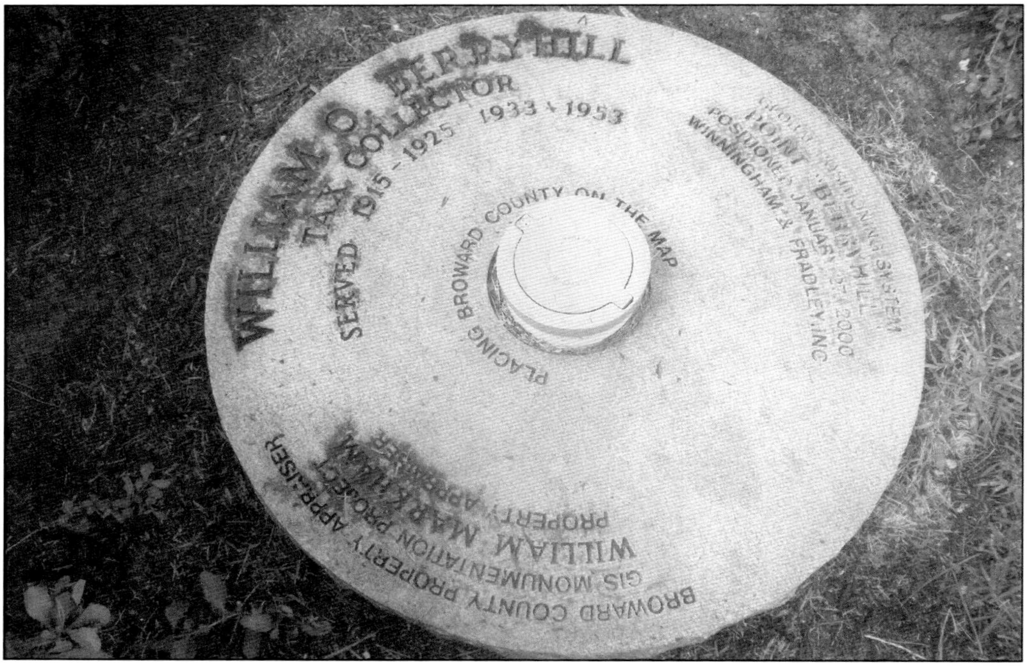

SATELLITE MAP. Among shrubs on the grounds of the city hall is a GPS satellite marker. The monument was erected to mark the GPS mapping as part of the 440 square miles of Broward County, precisely marking property lines and placement of underground utilities, along with listing underground soil and water data. There are 62 monuments in the county that honor William Oscar Berryhill, Broward County's first tax collector. (Courtesy of the City of Tamarac.)

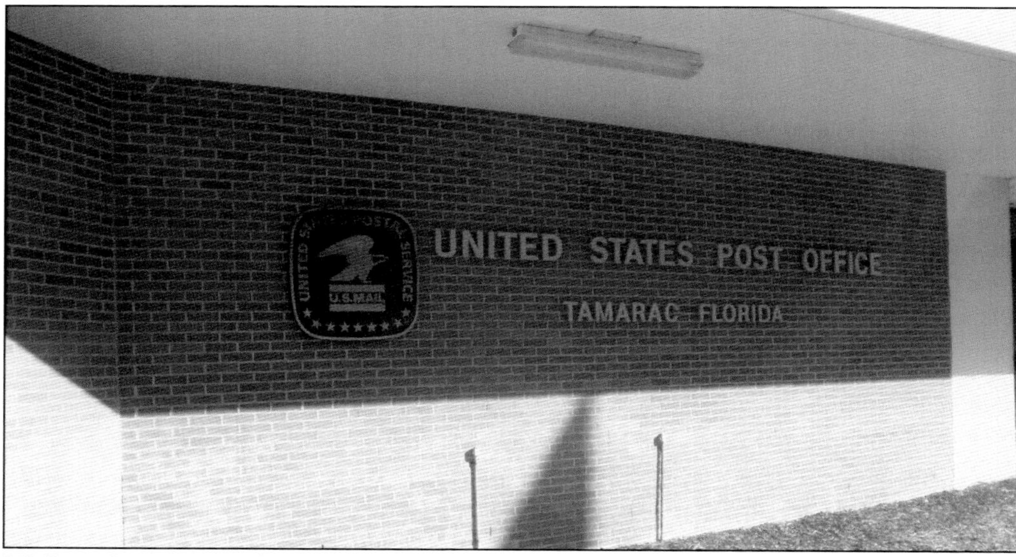

US POST OFFICE. On July 1, 1963, the post office implemented a new program aimed at speeding up mail delivery. A five-digit code was assigned to every address in the country, but that did not help many Tamarac residents. It seemed like no one ever heard of Tamarac. Mail intended for Tamarac residents was addressed, more often than not, to Fort Lauderdale. (Courtesy of the Tamarac Historical Society.)

Four

City Spirit

The First City Logo. Tamaracʼs first logo showed a clubhouse in the background, a golf green, and a flag in the foreground. A branch from a tamarack tree hung symbolically in the image. According to Lynn Demerest, staff writer at the *Miami Herald*, the original logo served the city until 1990, when it was replaced by an updated logo. (Courtesy of the City of Tamarac.)

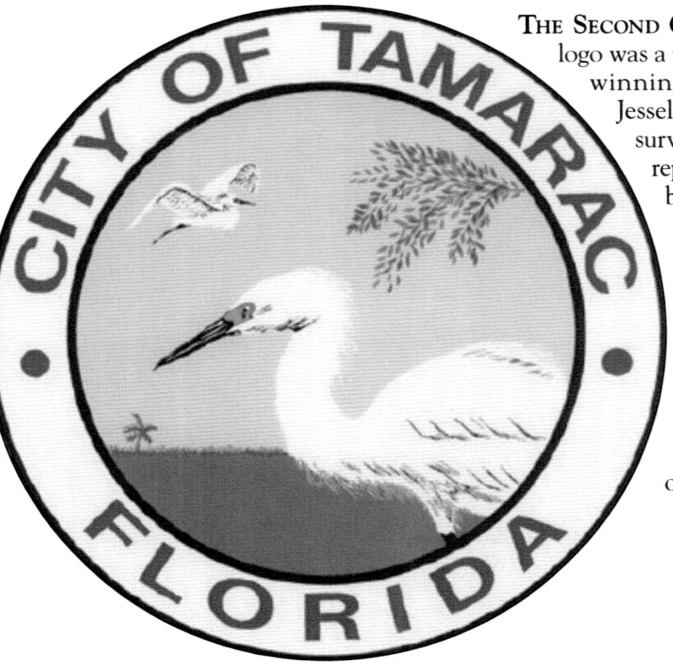

The Second City Logo. Tamarac's second logo was a result of a citywide contest; the winning logo was designed by Trish Jesseli. It displayed two snowy egrets surveying the sawgrass. The scene is representative of how Tamarac was becoming more aware of the birds, waterways, and environment. The logo was used by the city from 1990 through 2008. Interestingly, Trish's original design incorporated a recycling symbol that did not become a part of the final design, as reported in the *Miami Herald* on December 6, 1990. (Courtesy of the City of Tamarac.)

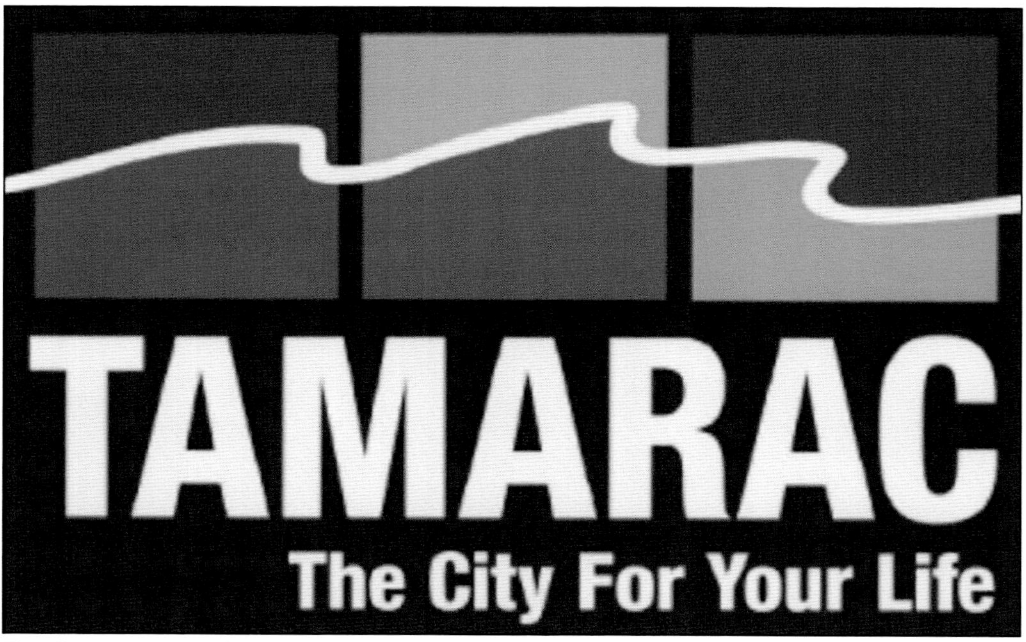

The Current Logo. Tamarac's current logo, its third, reflects the changes in the city's demographics over the years. The green space represents the abundant green space in Tamarac and the community's sensitivity for the environment. The bright colors represent Tamarac's reputation as a friendly city with growing diversity and a commitment to arts and culture. The three boxes represent three distinct groups: youthful singles, growing families, and retired seniors. This logo evolved out of focus groups and the 2007 Community Survey. (Courtesy of the City of Tamarac.)

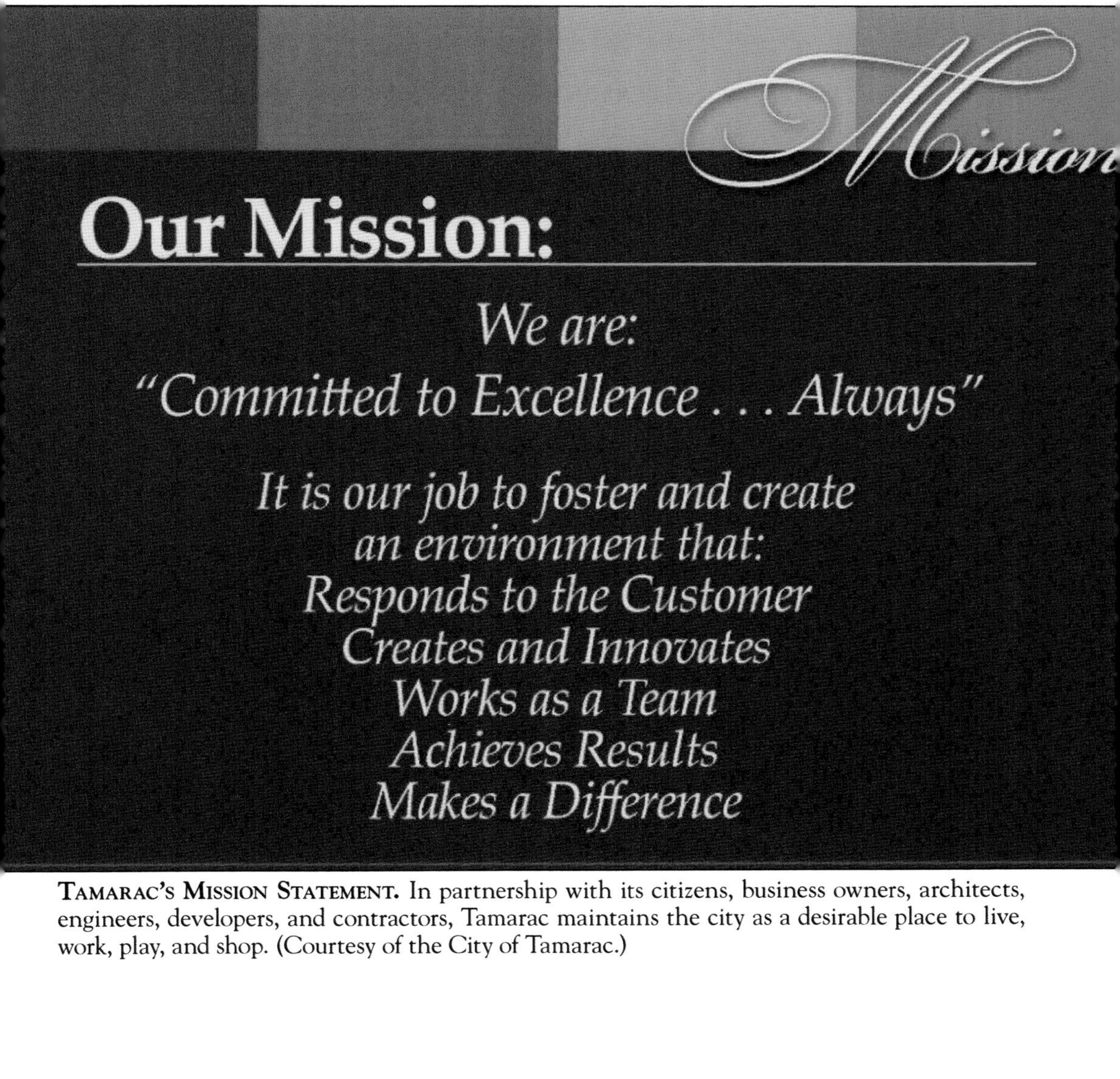

TAMARAC'S MISSION STATEMENT. In partnership with its citizens, business owners, architects, engineers, developers, and contractors, Tamarac maintains the city as a desirable place to live, work, play, and shop. (Courtesy of the City of Tamarac.)

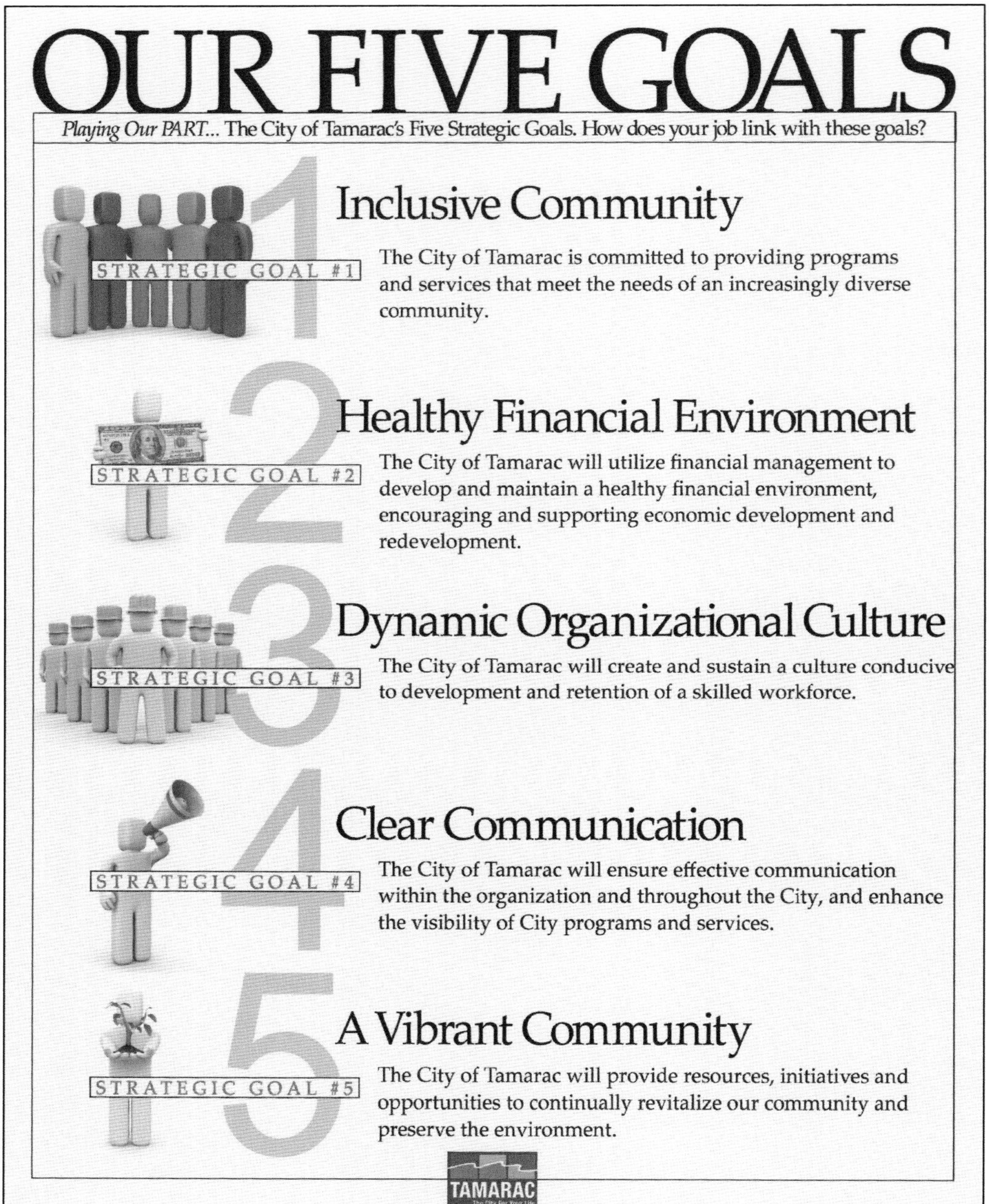

City of Tamarac has Strategic Goals. To answer the issues important to residents, the city sets priorities for the future. In addition to the city's mission statement, it is guided by five strategic goals. (Courtesy of the City of Tamarac.)

CITY OF TAMARAC
PROCLAMATION

Requested by Mayor Joe Schreiber

WHEREAS, *Sid Feffer resided in Tamarac from 1977 – 2001, and was active in community affairs; and*

WHEREAS, *Sid Feffer is a member of the American Society of Composers, Authors and Publishers (ASCAP); and*

WHEREAS, *Sid Feffer's years in Tamarac and love for this wonderful City have inspired him to write song lyrics for the City of Tamarac.*

NOW, THEREFORE, *I, Joe Schreiber, Mayor of the City of Tamarac, Broward County, Florida, do hereby honor*

MR. SID FEFFER

For his contributions to the City of Tamarac, and express our grateful appreciation to Sid Feffer for commemorating the City of Tamarac in song.

Tamarac

Lyrics by Sid Feffer
(Sung to the tune of Cornell University Alma Mater)

Nestled in the west of Broward
From Commercial back
There's a green expanse of beauty
Known as Tamarac.

Smiling mornings, glowing sunsets
Blue skies in between
Where good neighbors dwell together
Happy and serene.

Pound the drums and sound the trumpets
Celebrate with us
This fair city let's all call it
TAMARACULOUS

IN WITNESS WHEREOF, I have hereunto set my hand and caused the Seal of the City of Tamarac to be affixed this 22nd day of December 2004.

Joe Schreiber, MAYOR

THE CITY'S SONG. In 2004, the city commission honored Sid Feffer for his contributions and for commemorating the city of Tamarac in song. A proclamation requested and signed by Mayor Joe Schreiber was issued. Sid Feffer lived in Tamarac from 1977 to 2001 and was active in community affairs. The tune is sung to the theme of his alma mater, Cornell University. (Courtesy of the City of Tamarac.)

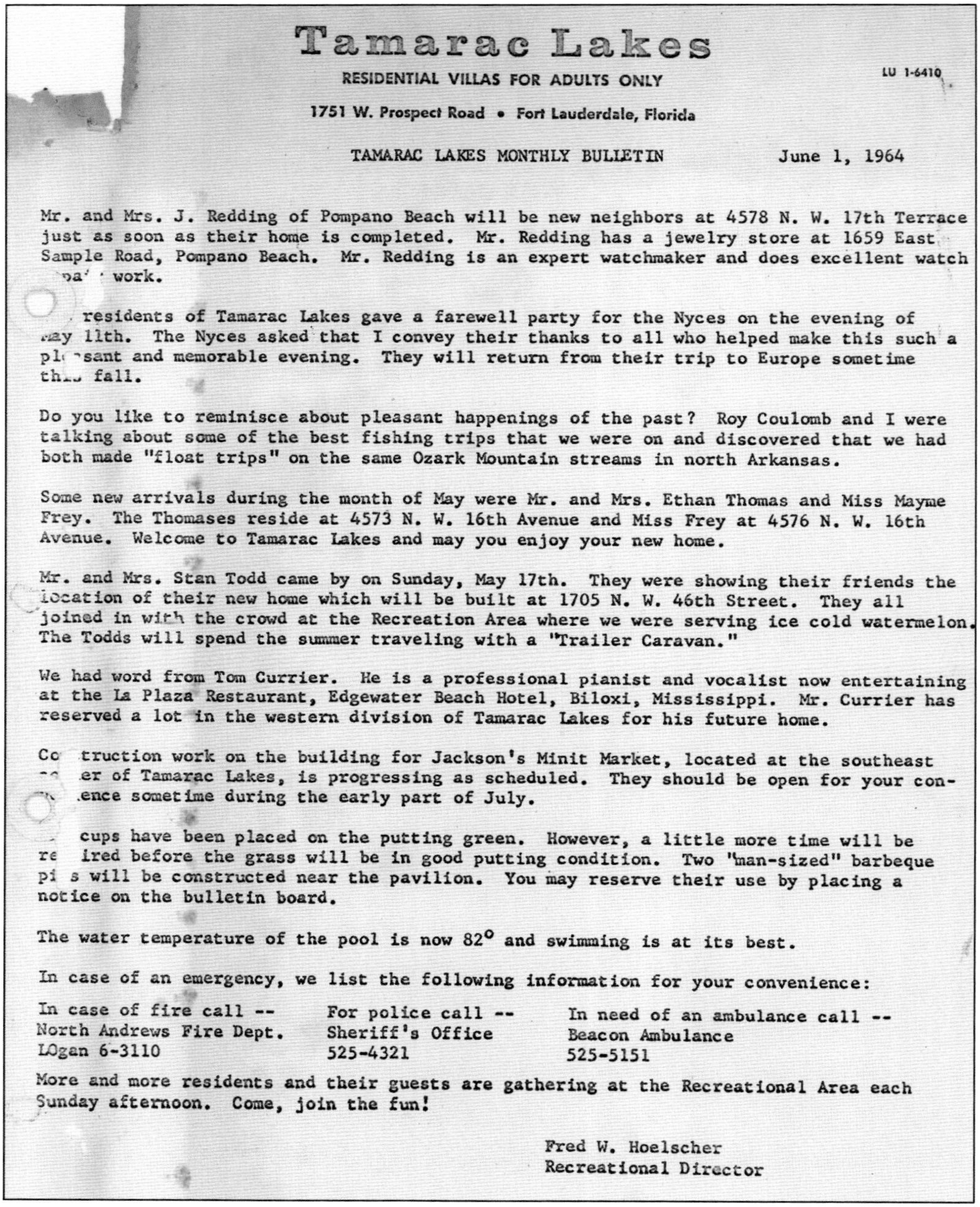

Tamarac Lakes

RESIDENTIAL VILLAS FOR ADULTS ONLY

LU 1-6410

1751 W. Prospect Road • Fort Lauderdale, Florida

TAMARAC LAKES MONTHLY BULLETIN June 1, 1964

Mr. and Mrs. J. Redding of Pompano Beach will be new neighbors at 4578 N. W. 17th Terrace just as soon as their home is completed. Mr. Redding has a jewelry store at 1659 East Sample Road, Pompano Beach. Mr. Redding is an expert watchmaker and does excellent watch repair work.

The residents of Tamarac Lakes gave a farewell party for the Nyces on the evening of May 11th. The Nyces asked that I convey their thanks to all who helped make this such a pleasant and memorable evening. They will return from their trip to Europe sometime this fall.

Do you like to reminisce about pleasant happenings of the past? Roy Coulomb and I were talking about some of the best fishing trips that we were on and discovered that we had both made "float trips" on the same Ozark Mountain streams in north Arkansas.

Some new arrivals during the month of May were Mr. and Mrs. Ethan Thomas and Miss Mayme Frey. The Thomases reside at 4573 N. W. 16th Avenue and Miss Frey at 4576 N. W. 16th Avenue. Welcome to Tamarac Lakes and may you enjoy your new home.

Mr. and Mrs. Stan Todd came by on Sunday, May 17th. They were showing their friends the location of their new home which will be built at 1705 N. W. 46th Street. They all joined in with the crowd at the Recreation Area where we were serving ice cold watermelon. The Todds will spend the summer traveling with a "Trailer Caravan."

We had word from Tom Currier. He is a professional pianist and vocalist now entertaining at the La Plaza Restaurant, Edgewater Beach Hotel, Biloxi, Mississippi. Mr. Currier has reserved a lot in the western division of Tamarac Lakes for his future home.

Construction work on the building for Jackson's Minit Market, located at the southeast corner of Tamarac Lakes, is progressing as scheduled. They should be open for your convenience sometime during the early part of July.

The cups have been placed on the putting green. However, a little more time will be required before the grass will be in good putting condition. Two "man-sized" barbeque pits will be constructed near the pavilion. You may reserve their use by placing a notice on the bulletin board.

The water temperature of the pool is now 82° and swimming is at its best.

In case of an emergency, we list the following information for your convenience:

In case of fire call --	For police call --	In need of an ambulance call --
North Andrews Fire Dept.	Sheriff's Office	Beacon Ambulance
LOgan 6-3110	525-4321	525-5151

More and more residents and their guests are gathering at the Recreational Area each Sunday afternoon. Come, join the fun!

Fred W. Hoelscher
Recreational Director

The First Newsletter. First issued in June 1964, the *Tamarac Lakes Monthly Bulletin* informed Tamarac's retired citizens of important civic and social events. Fred W. Hoelscher was an editor and contributor. Known as "Mr. Tamarac," Hoelscher encouraged residents to enjoy "The Tamarac Way of Life," which included community barbecues, receptions welcoming new residents, fishing and golf tournaments, holiday parties, and bus excursions to Florida's attractions. (Courtesy of Tamarac Lakes.)

PAGE 3

Tamarac Topics

PUBLISHED MONTHLY FOR THE CITIZENS OF THE CITY OF TAMARAC, FLORIDA

Mailing Address: 1941 West Oakland Park Boulevard, Fort Lauderdale, Florida 33311

OCTOBER, 1966, ISSUE

TAMARAC TOPICS REPLACES BULLETINS

Combined News of All Tamarac Sections to be Published in Newspaper Format

This is the first issue of the Tamarac Topics, a tabloid size newspaper, designed to cover the news formerly printed in separate "section" bulletins. This publication will be printed and mailed, free, approximately once a month. It will go to all residents of the City of Tamarac, and their friends.

Correspondents have been appointed in each Tamarac section. News item boxes will be placed in each clubhouse. Residents are requested to report items of interest to a publicity chairman or drop it in a news box. Articles may be rewritten by the editors for publication, therefore no special talent is required. Just write the information in your own words. Or you may phone it to a publicity chairman.

They are:
Tamarac Lakes -- Mrs. Peter Nyce, phone 565-0295
Tamarac North -- Mrs. George Weston, phone 565-8296

We Will Mail Topics

Many residents of Tamarac have been sending copies of the Monthly Bulletin to friends and relatives. They have found this to be an easy method of keeping them posted of the many things that they enjoy here. We will gladly include these people in our regular mailing of TAMARAC TOPICS if you will list their names and addresses in the spaces provided. Send this list to TAMARAC TOPICS, 1941 West Oakland Park Blvd. Fort Lauderdale, Fla. 33309. (Be sure to list zip code no.)

NAME ______________

ADDRESS ______________

ZIP CODE ______________

NAME ______________

ADDRESS ______________

ZIP CODE ______________

Photographer Needed Here

The Topics would welcome the services of a local - on the spot - photographer to take extemporaneous "shots" for use in this publication. Anyone interested please contact your Recreation Director.

MORSE RALLY SCHEDULED

Residents of all sections are invited to attend a special rally for Mayor Morse, to be held in the "North" club-

THE NAME NEED NOT BE THE SAME

Tamarac Topics - the name appearing on this masthead need not be the official name of the publication. It was used, just to get things started. Residents of the City of Tamarac are invited to suggest their choice for a name.

Please send your suggestions, in writing, to Mr. Fred Hoelscher, 1941 W. Oakland Park Blvd, Fort Lauderdale, Florida.

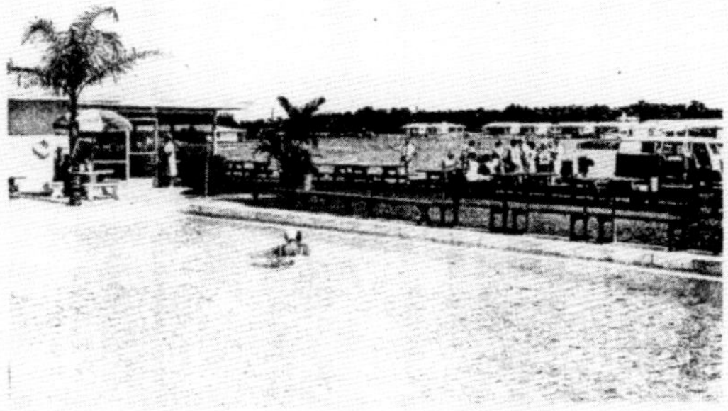

Tamarac Lakes North...recreation area, with the pool clubhouse and barbeque facilities in use. One of the lakes is in the background. This activity is typical of the outdoor opportunities offered here year 'round.

Country Fair

The First Annual Tamarac Country Fair will be held on January 22, 1967. The committee to help plan this event will have its first meeting on Tuesday Oct 11 at the Tamarac North clubhouse. Meeting time 10:00 A. M. This event will be open to residents of all sections of Tamarac. The first committee meeting will be devoted to the listing of categories and games in which you may compete. Please attend this meeting if you think that you may have some suggestions that will help make this event a real success.

Xmas Bazaar in November

A Christmas Bazaar will be held at Tamarac Sections no. 1 and no. 2 clubhouses on November 12th and 13th, at 1 P.M. Featured will be homemade articles for your Christmas lists. Members of the committee have been preparing items for this Bazaar during the summer and have everything from art objects to ordinary but useful household necessities. There will be crafts, Christmas decorations, a 'Green Thumb' table, white elephant section, goodies from the gourmet table, door prizes and refreshments if you wish a snack. This is the first event of this type to be undertaken and we feel the neighborliness enjoyed and getting to know

Building 'Chickee'

A group of energetic residents of Tamarac Lakes North are in the process of building a "chickee" shelter over their barbeque pit.

This will not only make the barbeque pit more functional but will do much to enhance the beauty of their picnic grounds. Rather than try to describe this type of shelter, we are inviting you to come and see it. Barbeques are a very popular form of recreation at Tamarac Lakes North. A pork steak barbeque on Sept. 11 was well attended. A Chicken Barbeque is scheduled for the afternoon October 16 and preparations are being made to serve 200 people.

Tickets must be purchased in advance and will cost $1.00 each. Serving will start at 4:30 P.M. and will continue until 5:30 P.M.

Vote For Morse

The general election will be on November 9. Let's do all that we can to elect our Mayor William Morse to the state legislature. Voter registration will be open up to Oct. 8. You may register if you become eligible before election day. You become eligible one year from the date that you made a firm contract to purchase

TAMARAC GETS GOOD NEIGHBORS

Two of Tamarac Lakes residents were lauded recently in a letter to Mr. Fred W. Hoelscher, Recreation Director of the City of Tamarac. The letter is reprinted here.

Dear Mr. Hoelscher:

I had the privilege of reading your monthly bulletin for September and noticed the remarks with regard to Mrs. Lillia Lloyd and her sister Mrs. Iva Oppenheimer.

Your short stores about Iva and Lillia were very interesting but what you failed to state was that they make excellent neighbors. For many years my home backed up to their home in Hillside, New Jersey and I can only say that when it comes to being good neighbors, they should get a grade of A-plus. They are kind, considerate, gracious and, in short, the kind of neighbors everyone would like to have.

As a small token of my deep appreciation for having had these two wonderful neighbors I enclose check for $25.00 and hope that you will use the same for any worthwhile activity of your choice.

In closing I want to tell you how I envy all of you for having Iva and Lillia as your neighbors. If they treat you just half the way they treated their Hillside neighbors, you will be tickled to death that they moved to Florida.

With kindest regards and with best wishes to all of

And following is Mr. Hoelscher's reply. . . . .

Dear Mr. Goldhor:
Your wonderful letter regarding Mrs. Lloyd and Mrs. Oppenheimer certainly made the sun shine even brighter at Tamarac Lakes.

Your letter not only reminded us that Iva and Lillia are excellent neighbors but the fact that Tamarac Communities are filled with wonderful grade A-Plus people. This, more than all the physical attractions, makes it such a wonderful place to live.

Your kind words will be passed on so that all good neighbors may see them. I am sure that you would not object to our reprinting your letter in our monthly publication. I have not decided how to use your most generous gift but I will try to make it add to the enjoyment of all at Tamarac Lakes. And, I cannot help but remark that the lucky sisters also had a very good neighbor in you.

We are most grateful for your kindness in taking the time to write.

With sincere thanks from all at Tamarac.

TAMARAC TOPICS. *Tamarac Topics* replaced the *Tamarac Lakes Monthly Bulletin* in October 1966 and was mailed free to all residents. Correspondents from each community contributed articles to the tabloid-sized newspaper, featuring their social events and information on new homeowners. Also included were articles on issues facing the city's expansion and city elections, the formation of new businesses, and the development of Tamarac-By-The-Gulf, located on South Florida's west coast. (Courtesy of the City of Tamarac.)

TAM-A-GRAM

PUBLISHED BY THE TAMARAC PUBLIC INFORMATION COMMITTEE

VOL.1 ISSUE 1 JANUARY 1985

From the Mayor's Office

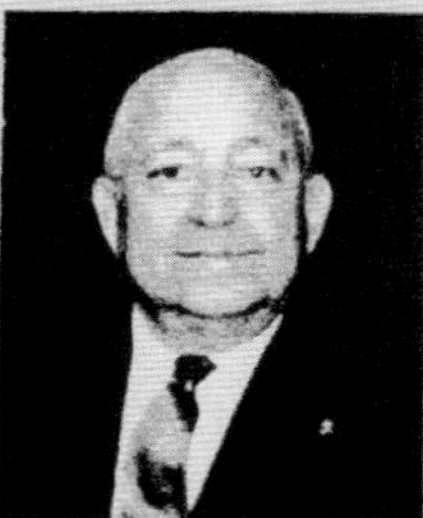

As we are approaching the end of 1984 and the beginnings of many innovations in our City for the year 1985, may I take this opportunity to wish everyone a very happy holiday--Chanukah and Christmas. One of the innovations is the Public Information Committees's Newsletter which has a new format and typeface. We hope it will give our citizens more information as to what our city is proposing for the betterment of all. Therefore I would encourage all citizens to obtain and read this newsletter. If there are any questions, suggestions or complaints, let either the Committee, Council or Mayor know your thoughts so that proper action be taken. Speaking for myself, I will listen and welcome this opportunity to be of service to the citizens of our community. I hope that the coming year brings to all in our City good health and prosperity!

Mayor Philip B. Kravitz

Low-Cost Tamarac Services

The News-Sun Sentinal on December 2nd published a survey on the cost of municipal services in twelve of the West Broward County areas. The costs of property tax; utility tax if any; water and sewer service and garbage collection were considered. Tamarac was the only City in which the residents do not pay individually for garbage collection; and only Tamarac, Parkland and Lauderdale Lakes have no Utility Tax. Our total bill was next to the lowest, only Parkland was lower BUT they provide NO water or sewer service! Four cities, CORAL SPRINGS, PLANTATION, COOPER CITY and MARGATE pay more than double the amount we pay.

Festival Of Lights

The Parks and Recreation Department did it again! The annual "Festival of Lights," was a smashing success! Several hundred parents and children attended the festivities. **Mayor Philip Kravitz** was the Master of Ceremonies, while Parks & Recreation Committee Chairperson **Doug Christy** presented welcoming remarks. The Invocation was delivered by Parks & Recreation Committee member **Irving Vitrofsky.** Traditional Hanukkah messages were delivered by **Rabbi Kurt Stone** of the Tamarac Jewish Center and Christmas messages were presented by **Pastor Joseph Kiser** of the All-Saints Lutheran Church. The Rabbi, along with **Cantor P. Hillel Brummer** and youth group lit the city Menorah and **Pastor Kiser** lit the city tree. Both are now on display at the entrance to Tamarac Park. A musical program was presented by the All-Saints Lutheran Choir; Cantor **P. Hillel Brummer,** and the Silver Lakes Middle School Band. At the conclusion of the program, wailing sirens were heard and Santa Claus arrived via fire engine with candy canes, coloring books and dreidels for all the children. What a heartwarming sight to behold!

Employee Service Awards

Five-year City Employees -**Paul Forsberg** - **William Fay** - **Steve Gotha** All of Tamarac Fire Department. Volunteer **Emil Beutner** member of Planning Commission **Dan Saale,** Deputy Finance Director, presented with Certificate of Conformance in Financial Reporting from Government Finance Office Association.

New Assistant City Manager

After checking 58 resumes, our City has hired David Wayne Heffner at a starting salary of $30,487.10 per annum, for a six-month probationary period. He will start work on January 2, 1985. We welcome him and wish him well.

TAM-A-GRAM. Published by the public information office, the Tamarac's current free publication is the *Tam-A-Gram*. The publication has evolved from a one-page issue into a quarterly magazine. The magazine provides information on city improvements, hurricane preparedness, safety alerts from the Broward County Sheriff's Office, green initiatives, youth and adult recreational activities, social services, and city-sponsored special events. (Courtesy of the City of Tamarac.)

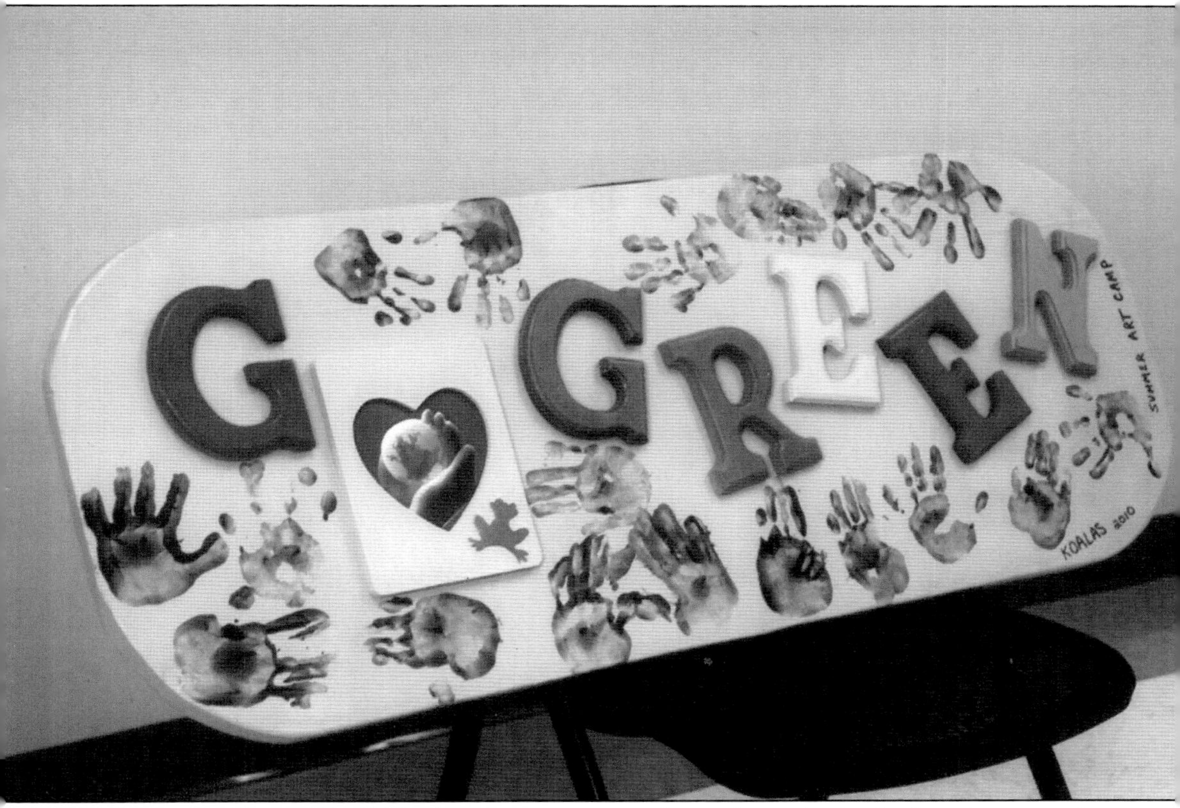

Go Green. In November 2007, the city commission deemed it to be in the best interest of Tamarac residents to support the Florida Green Building Coalition, Inc., (FGBC). Based on the FGBC's standards, the city of Tamarac received credit for many of the green initiatives that were already in place, such as its recycling program and water conservation efforts. In addition, the city received direction on how to implement additional green practices such as the expansion of the city's free/discounted product program, including faucet aerators, rain sensor devices, shower heads, leak detection tablets, rebates for ultra-low flow toilets, and other innovative green products. (Courtesy of Susan Buzzi.)

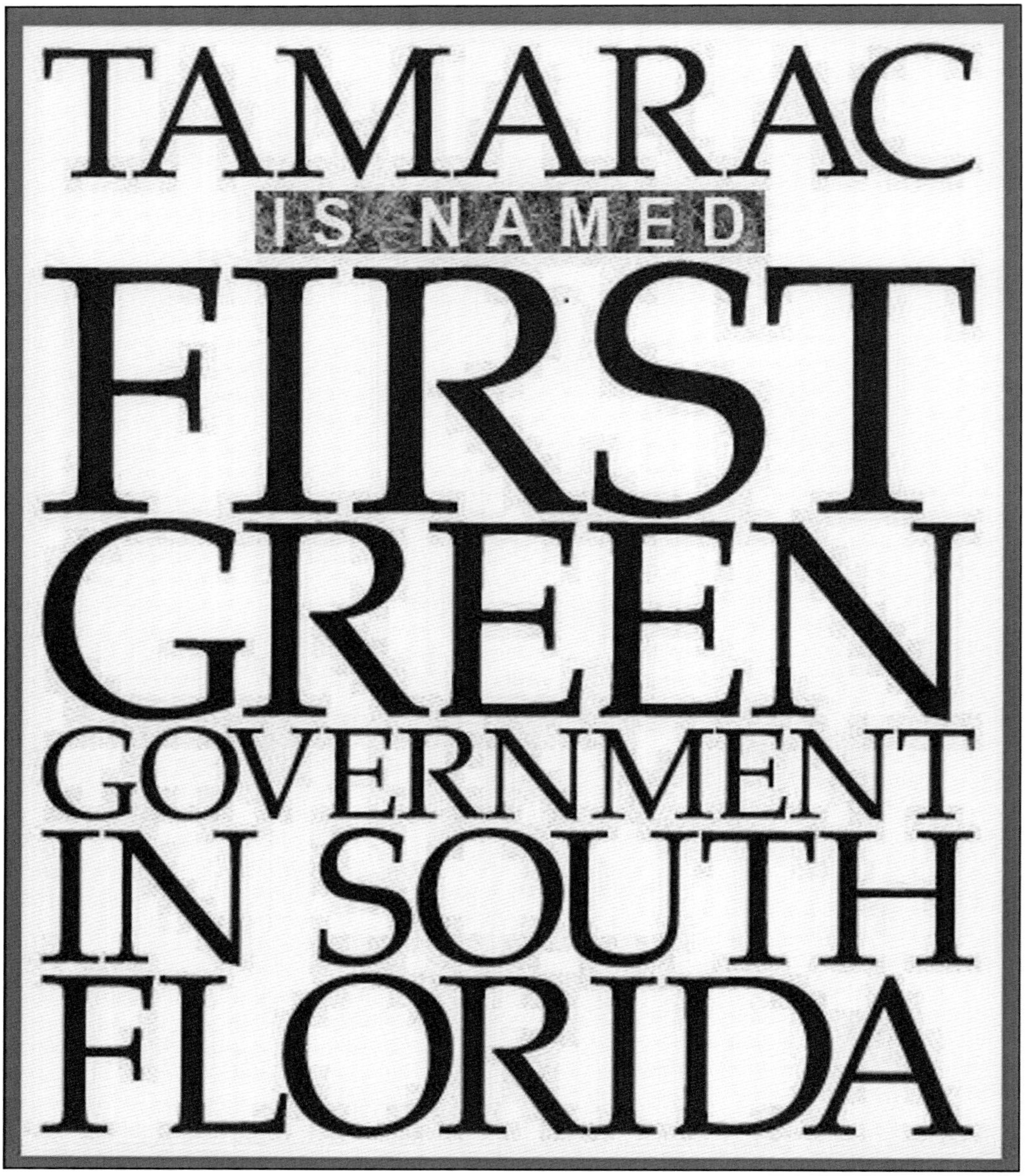

Silver Level Certification. Early in 2008, the FGBC designated the City of Tamarac as a Florida Green Local Government, and on May 19, 2008, the city was certified at the silver level, having earned 31 percent of the maximum applicable points. The FGBC acknowledged the city's commitment to the environment and praised innovative green practices such as BSO officers trained in crime prevention through environmental design, use of energy-saving computer equipment, the availability of a number of free and discounted green products, and a vast majority of the city medians, streetscapes, and facilities certified as "Florida Friendly" landscapes. More importantly, the city's designation had come at very little cost, since most of the items that Tamarac received points for were programs already in place. Tamarac was the first municipality in South Florida to be awarded this designation and also the first city in Broward County to win. (Courtesy of the City of Tamarac.)

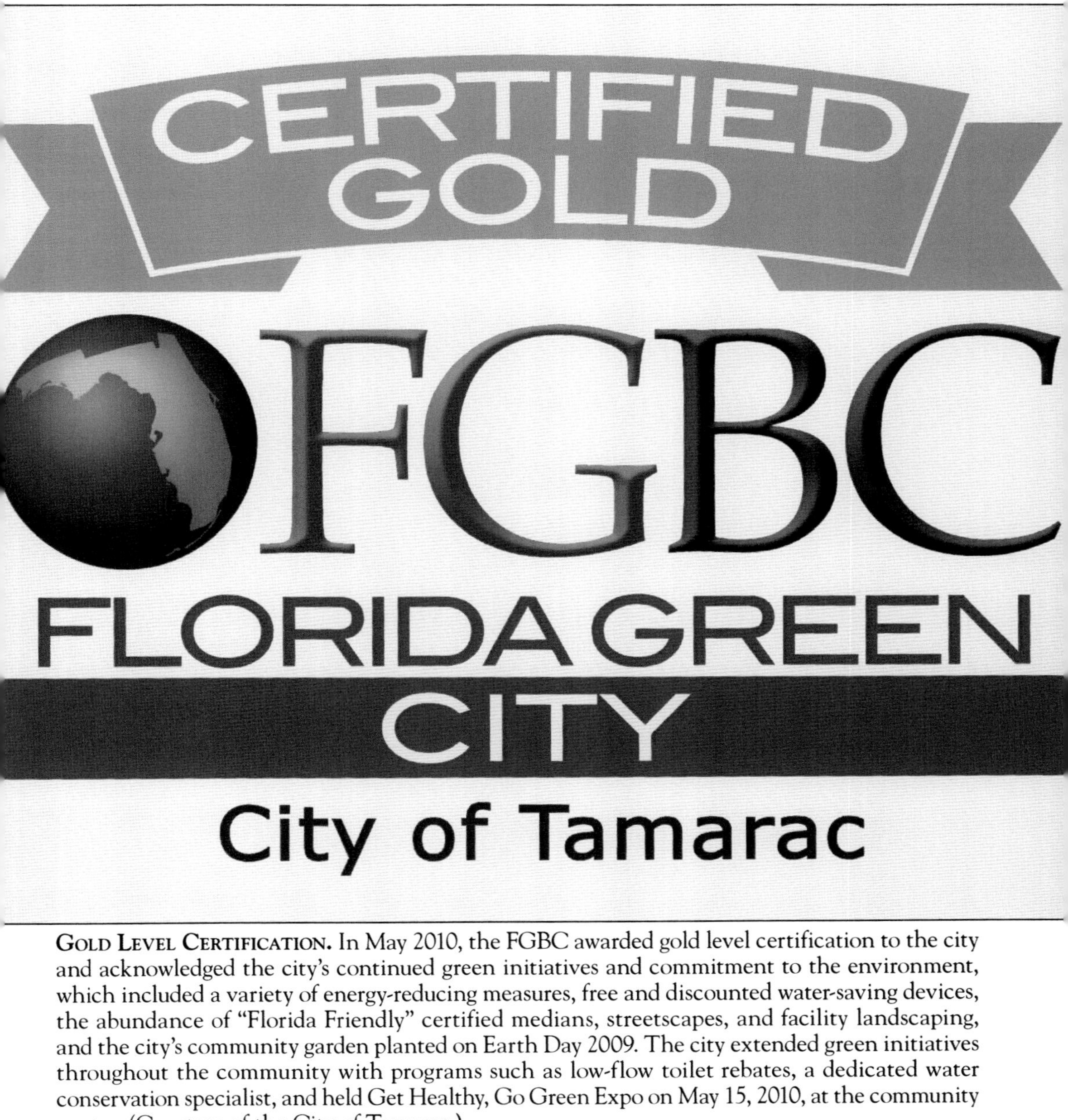

Gold Level Certification. In May 2010, the FGBC awarded gold level certification to the city and acknowledged the city's continued green initiatives and commitment to the environment, which included a variety of energy-reducing measures, free and discounted water-saving devices, the abundance of "Florida Friendly" certified medians, streetscapes, and facility landscaping, and the city's community garden planted on Earth Day 2009. The city extended green initiatives throughout the community with programs such as low-flow toilet rebates, a dedicated water conservation specialist, and held Get Healthy, Go Green Expo on May 15, 2010, at the community center. (Courtesy of the City of Tamarac.)

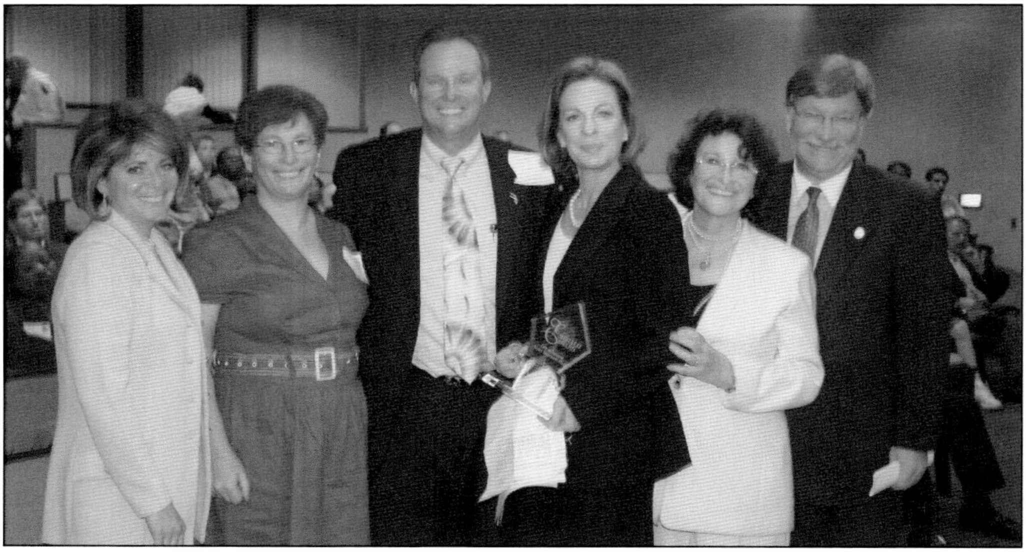

The Emerald Award. The Broward County Environmental Protection Department has twice awarded the Emerald Trophy (above) to Tamarac. In 2008, the city won the award in the category of Pollution Prevention, Hazardous Water Reduction. In 2011, the city won the award for its Climate Action Plan. The goal of the plan is to reduce governmental-operation greenhouse gas emission by at least seven percent by 2015. To achieve this goal, some of the city's initiatives include the use of solar panels at city facilities and the installation of induction bulbs in street lighting. (Courtesy of the City of Tamarac.)

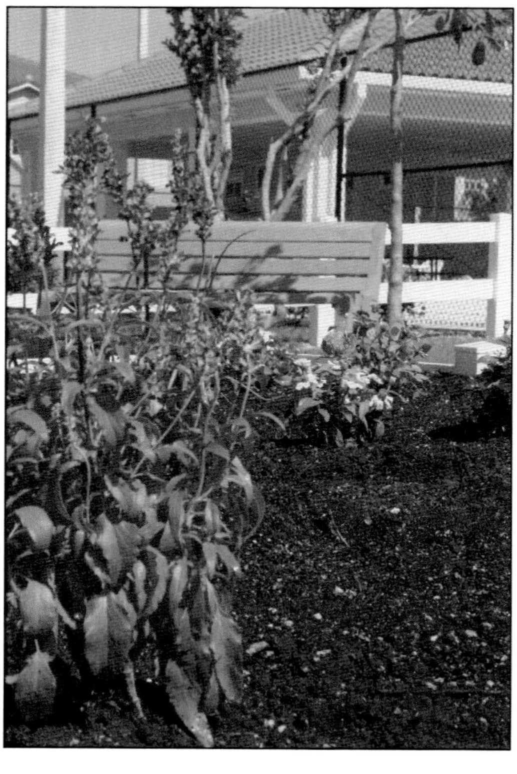

Environmental Stewardship Award. In August 2009, Tamarac was awarded the Environmental Stewardship Award at the Florida League of Cities annual conference in Orlando, Florida. The city won the award based on its affording residents to act as environmental stewards in proactive conservation efforts by its hazardous waste reduction program at the city's water-treatment plant and recycling measures in reducing solid and hazardous waste, and by planting a community garden adjacent to the Caporella Aquatic and Fitness Center. (Courtesy of the City of Tamarac.)

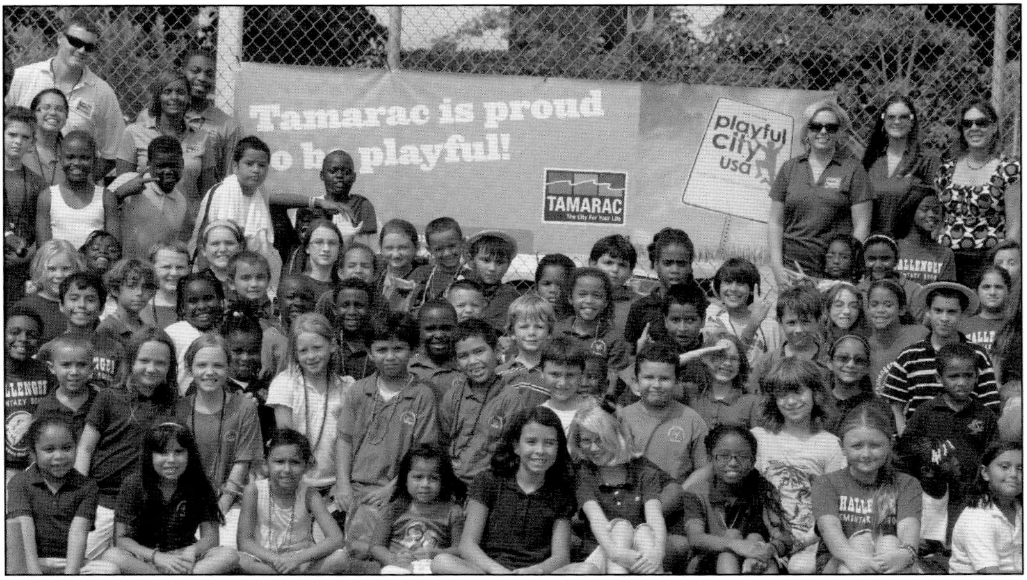

PLAYFUL CITY. Recognized in 2010 by the Playful City USA Program, Tamarac was named a "Playful City" and has held for three consecutive years an annual Day of Play, featuring fun and healthy activities for children and adults. The city's community agenda is to produce happier, smarter, and healthier children as well as a stronger community. (Courtesy of the City of Tamarac.)

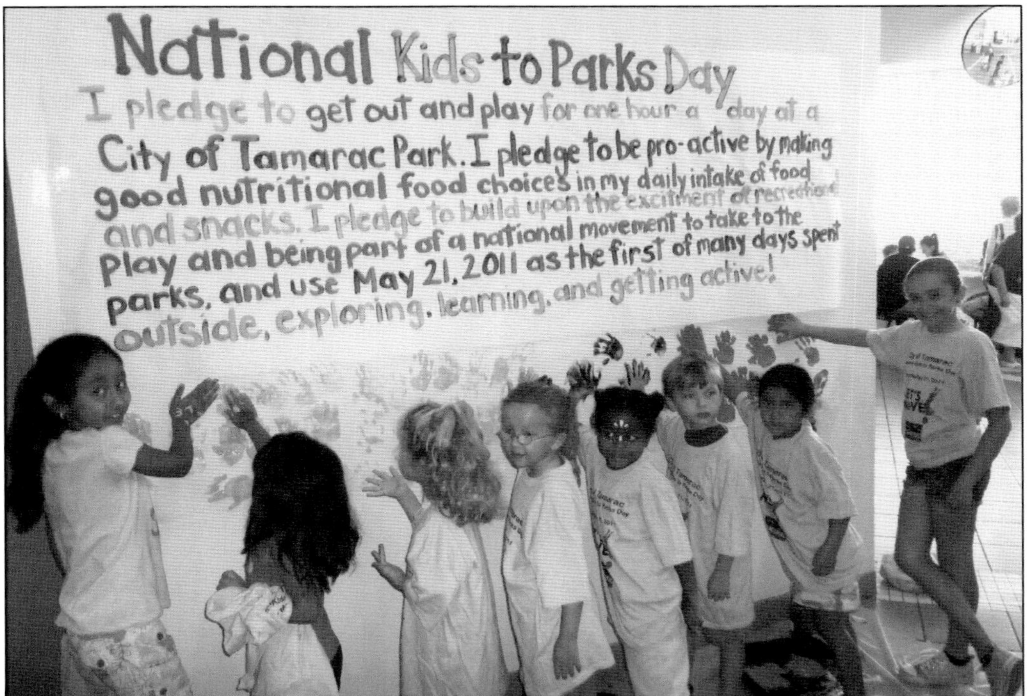

PLAYFUL CITY KIDS. At the city's Get Healthy, Go Green Expo held on May 21, 2011, at the community center, children signed their painted handprints as a pledge to get out and play in a city park, where a hometown with a sense of community starts. (Courtesy of the City of Tamarac.)

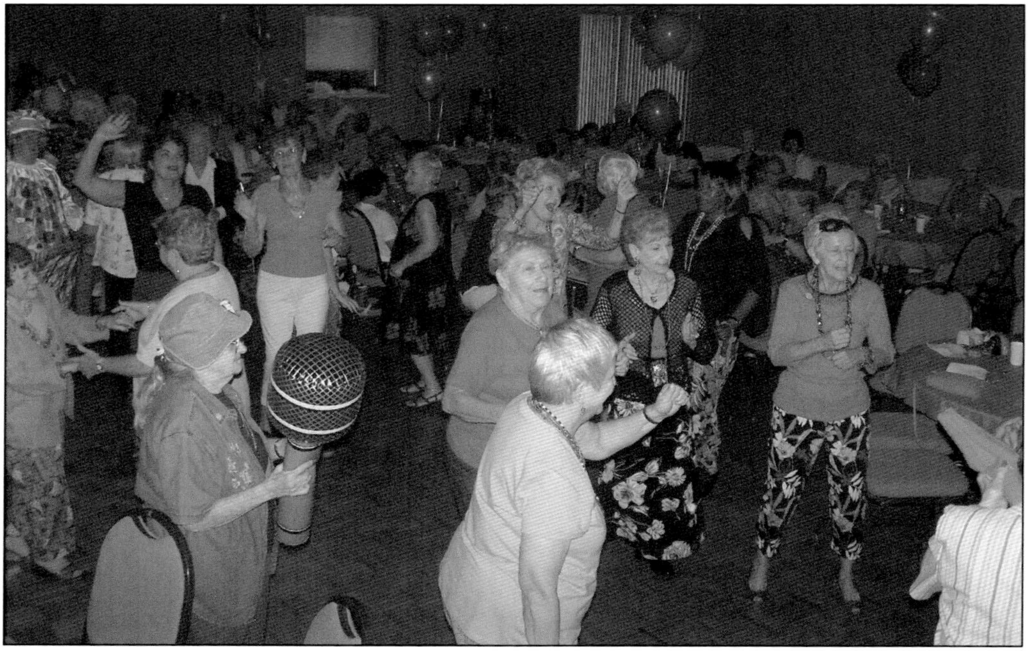

Forbes Declares. In 2011, *Forbes Magazine* recognized Tamarac as one of the "25 Top Suburbs for Retirement." The selection was based on the city's weather, average housing prices below $200,000, access to mass transit, a hospital within the city limits, and no state income tax. The city's community and recreation centers offer seniors a variety of social, fitness, and arts programs as well as senior service groups. (Courtesy of the City of Tamarac.)

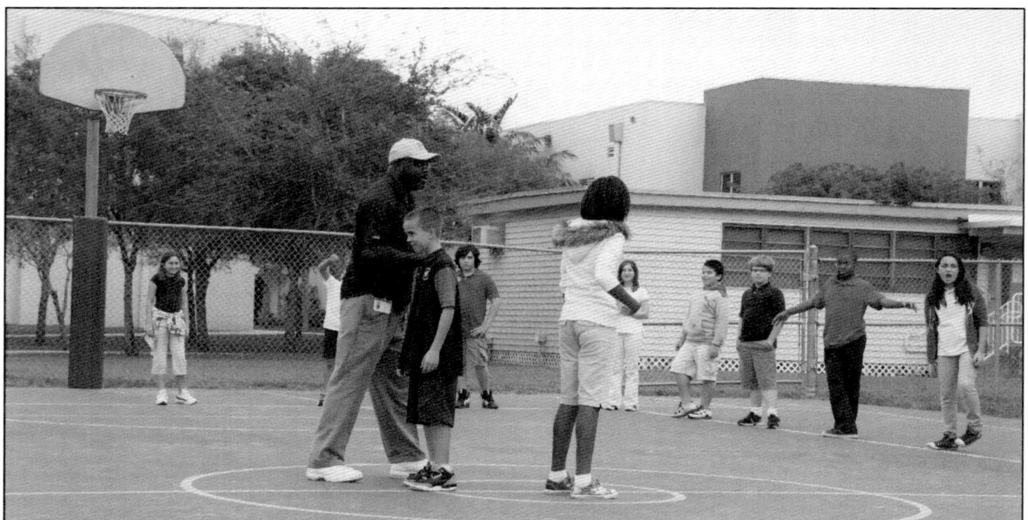

Livability Award. In June 2012, Tamarac received the 2012 City Livability Award from the US Conference of Mayors held in Orlando, Florida. The award honors mayors and city governments for developing programs that enhance the quality of life in urban areas. Tamarac was recognized for its CATCH (Coordinated Approach to Child Health) Program. Challenger Elementary School and the city's parks and recreation staff facilitated the program, which promotes physical activity and learning healthy eating habits. (Courtesy of the City of Tamarac.)

Tamarac University. Residents can attend a six- to eight-week course to learn about how the city works at Tamarac University each year. Members of the city staff present the inner workings of their departments. Students learn about the city budget, visit the police and fire departments for firsthand knowledge, and gain insight from the mayor, commissioners, and the city manager. (Courtesy of the City of Tamarac.)

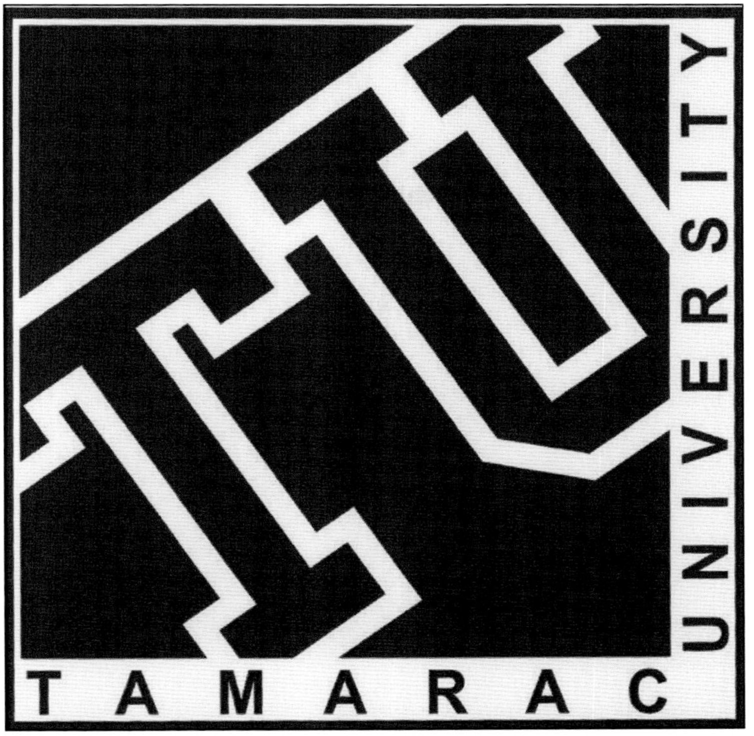

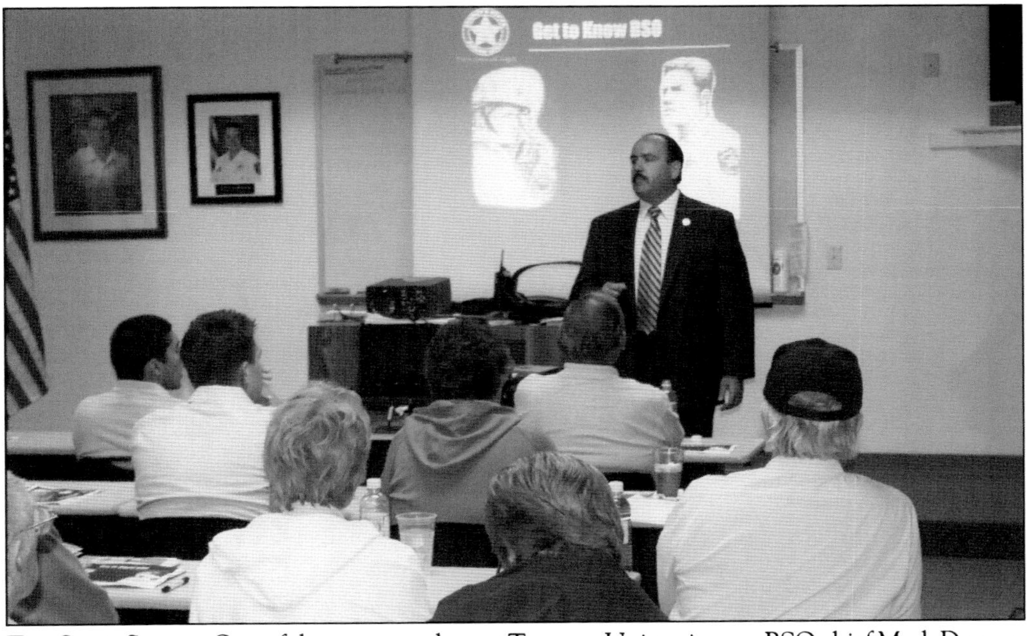

The Chief Speaks. One of the guest speakers at Tamarac University was BSO chief Mark Duguay. Through a PowerPoint presentation, the chief urged the members of the Tamarac University class to get to know BSO. A history of BSO was presented along with a tour of their building, including a chance to sit in a holding cell. Each speaker gave information about his or her department and was available for questions. (Courtesy of the City of Tamarac.)

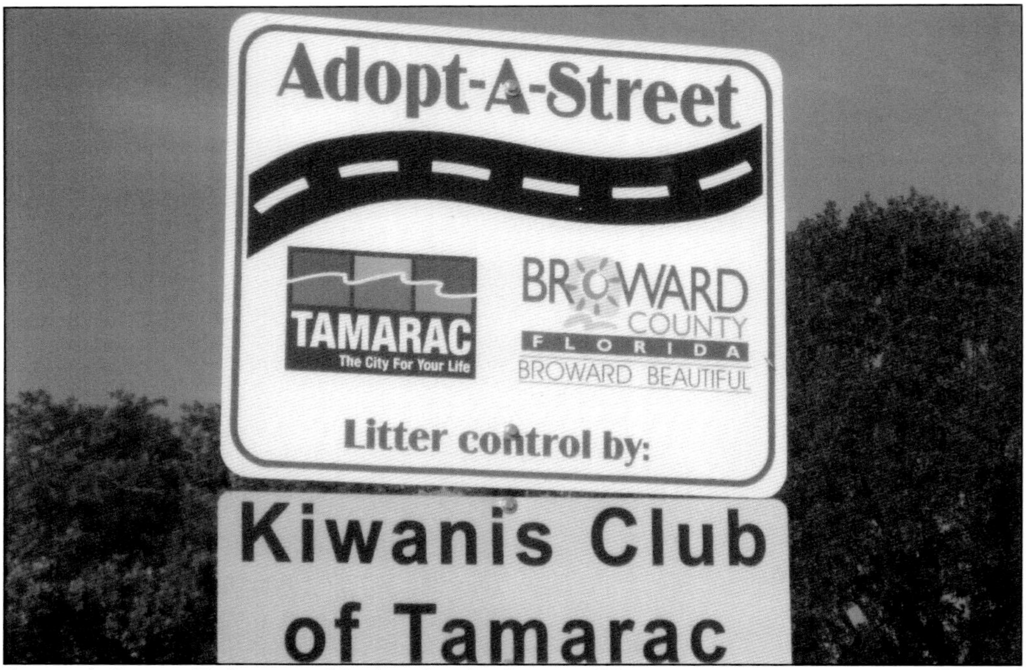

ADOPT-A-STREET. To foster neighborhood pride, the city of Tamarac is a participating city in Broward County's Adopt-A-Street Program. The program encourages residents and organizations to volunteer to adopt a street, half a mile long or more, to remove litter. (Courtesy of Joel Davidson.)

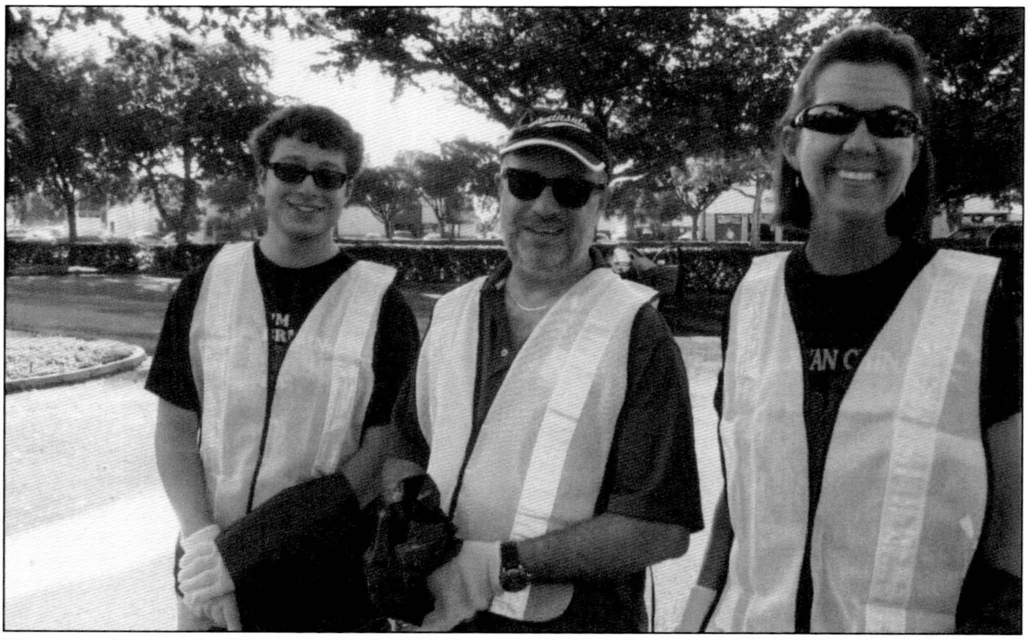

KIWANIS CLUB. The Kiwanis Club of Tamarac has joined the Adopt-A-Street Program. Four times a year, its members collect trash from University Drive and McNab Road east to Seventieth Avenue. Volunteers from the club keep their street clean and neat. This is only one of the many great programs at the Kiwanis Club. (Courtesy of Joel Davidson.)

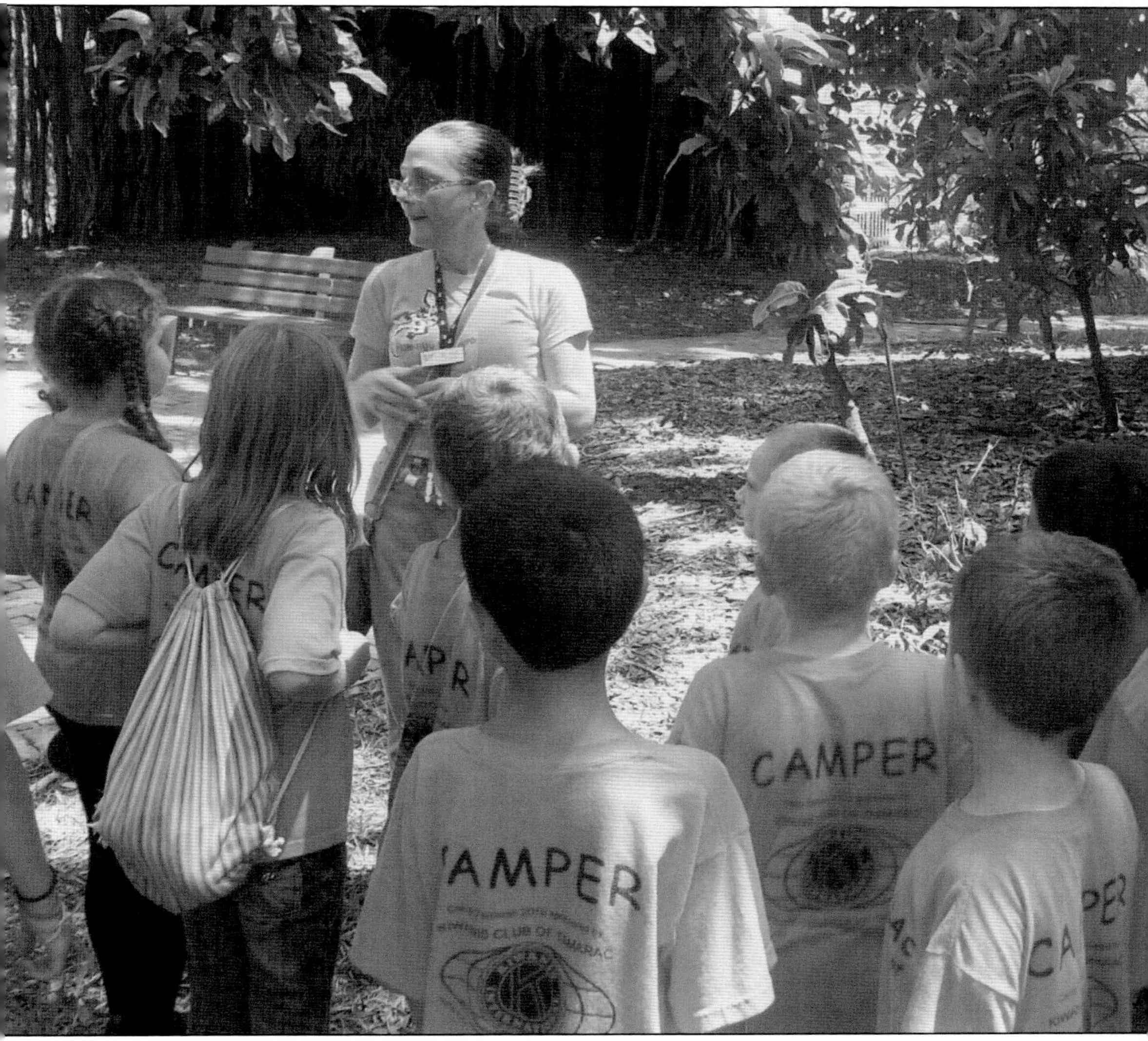

THANK YOU FOR SUMMER CAMP. The Tamarac Kiwanis Club has a long history of helping others. It has donated money and school supplies as well as sponsored children for summer camp. (Courtesy of the City of Tamarac.)

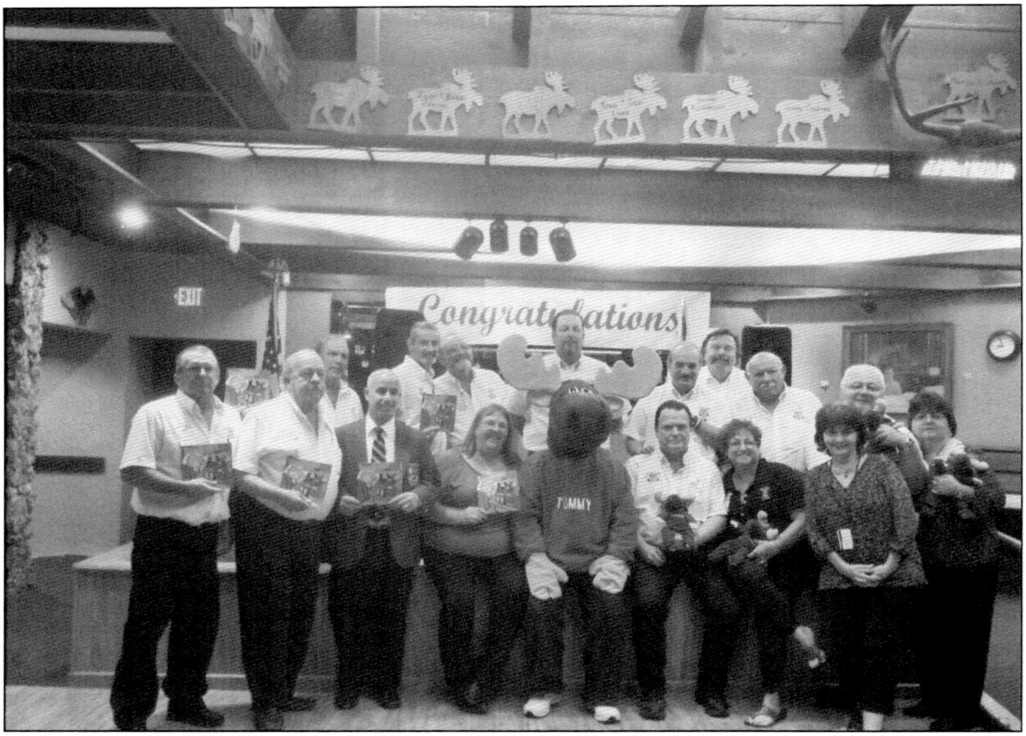

Moose Club. Tommy Moose is a part of Tamarac's history. He is a stuffed moose who cares about children and wants to bring comfort to those whose lives have been altered by a tragic event. Tommy Moose rides along with first responders and comforts children. Tommy Moose dolls and coloring books are distributed to bring some relief and a distraction from the trauma unfolding. (Courtesy of Emma DeFelice.)

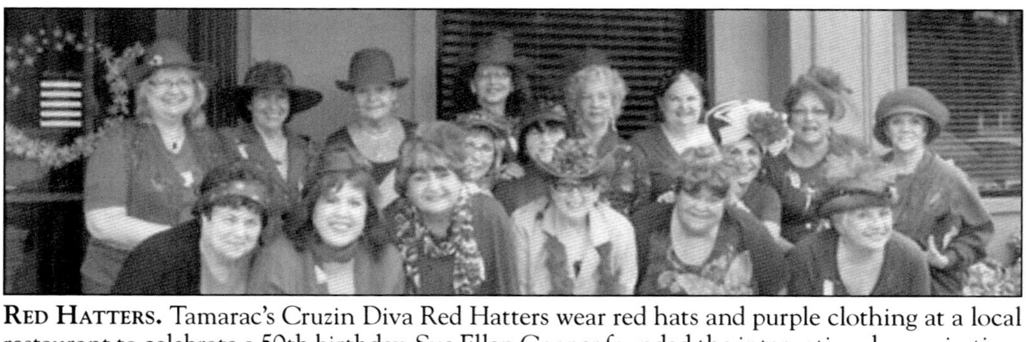

Red Hatters. Tamarac's Cruzin Diva Red Hatters wear red hats and purple clothing at a local restaurant to celebrate a 50th birthday. Sue Ellen Cooper founded the international organization; the first red hat is on display at the Smithsonian Museum. (Courtesy of Rudy Hoffmann.)

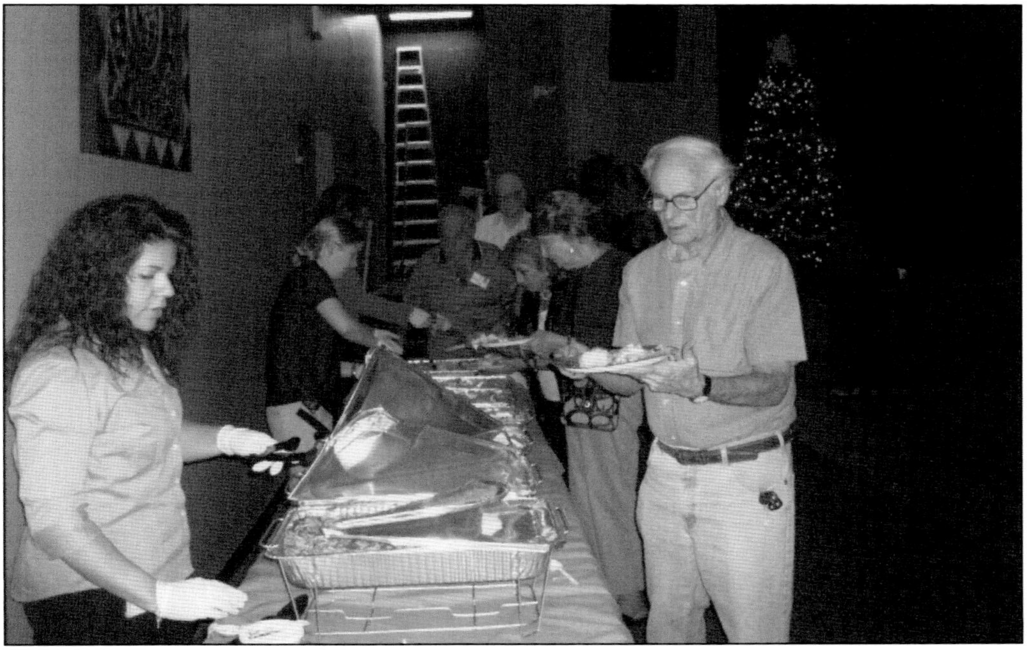

VOLUNTEER LUNCH. The city presents awards to its volunteers at the parks and recreation department's annual volunteer luncheon. Volunteers from all age groups contribute their time, services, and expertise at city-sponsored events and at city facilities. (Courtesy of the City of Tamarac.)

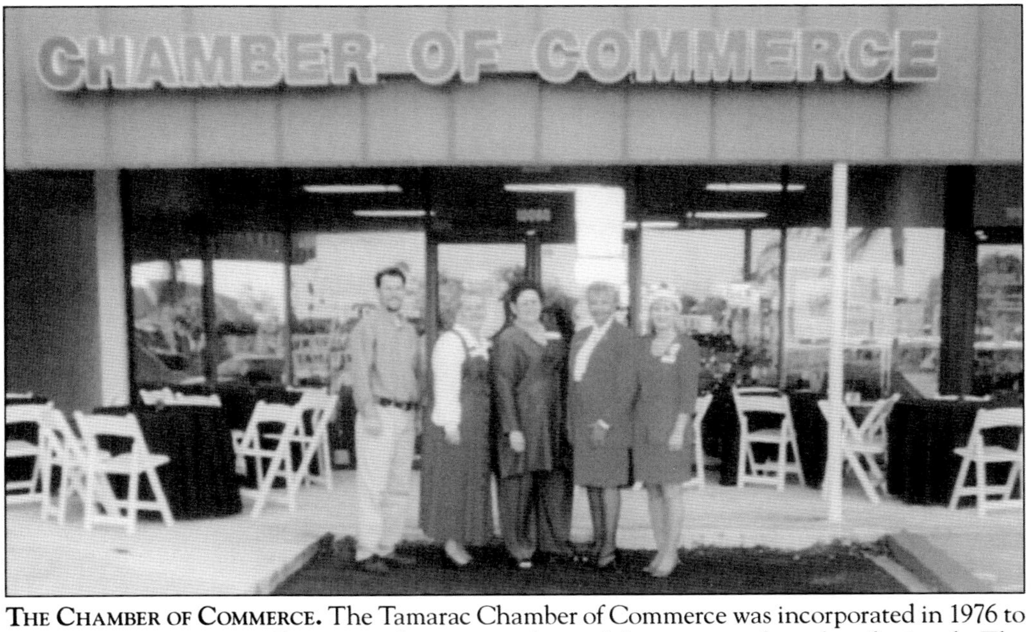

THE CHAMBER OF COMMERCE. The Tamarac Chamber of Commerce was incorporated in 1976 to promote cooperation in all matters of interest to the city's businesspeople and professionals. The purpose is to unite the business community, local government, community organizations, and residents for the benefit of everyone. Benefits of membership are business networking, advertising, business development, special events, and a voice with city government. (Courtesy of the Tamarac Chamber of Commerce.)

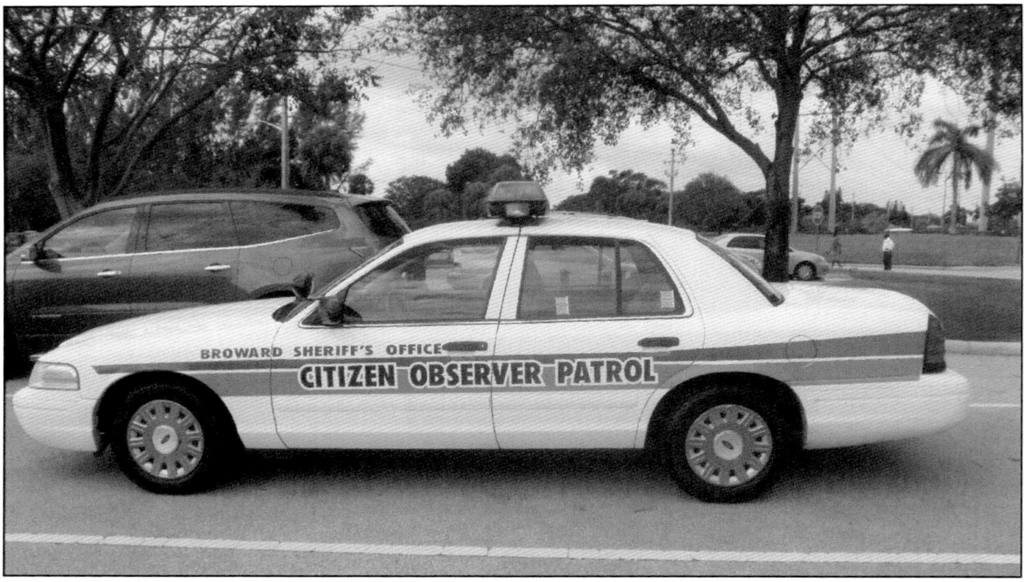

Citizen Observer Patrol. Better known as BSO's COP program, volunteers of the Citizen Observer Patrol are given four hours of training to help fight crime. They can then patrol the city's neighborhoods in uniform and with a marked vehicle. They assist the BSO by looking for suspicious activity, checking on the elderly or unoccupied homes, and reporting potential problems or hazards. (Courtesy of the Tamarac Historical Society.)

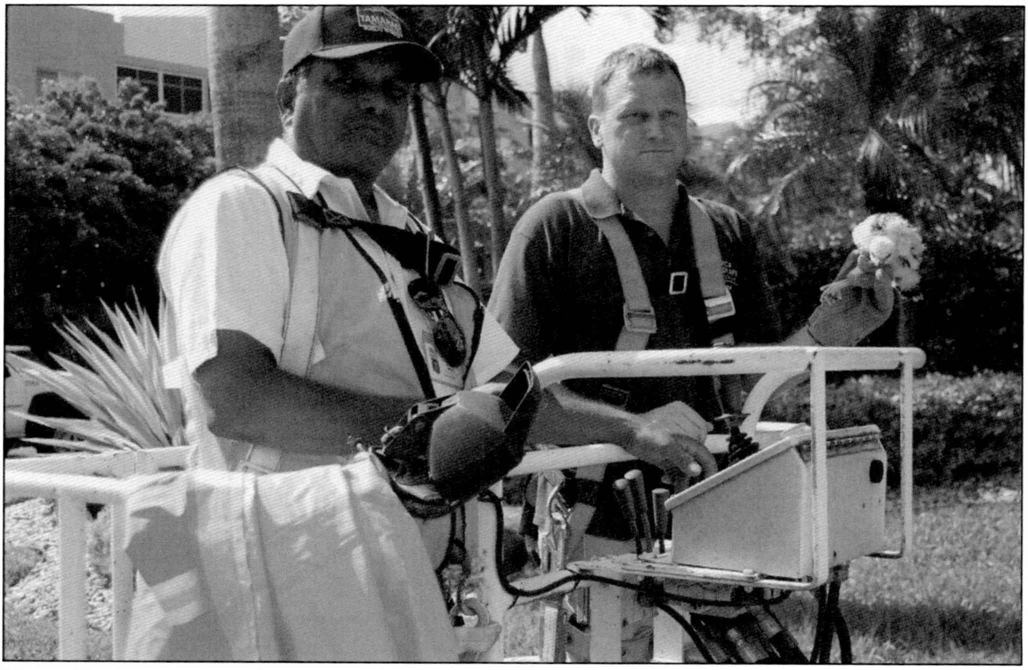

Hawk Rescue. An employee of the City of Tamarac's public works department assists the South Florida Wildlife Center in the safe rescue of a baby Cooper's hawk, which had fallen 40 feet from its nest at the Weldon Community of Kings Point. The mother hawk circled above the nest as the rescue took place. (Courtesy of the City of Tamarac.)

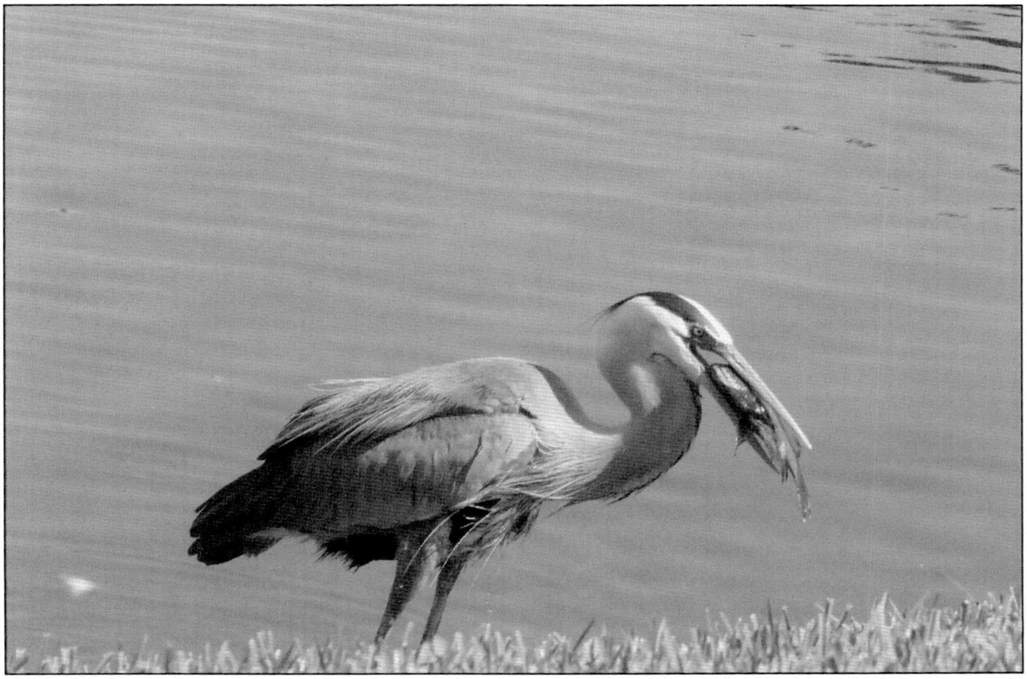

Do Not Feed the Wildlife. A blue heron fishes at an Isles of Tamarac community lake. Tamarac is home to a variety of indigenous species including raccoons, opossums, ducks, and water birds. The city encourages residents not to feed wildlife. (Courtesy of Rudy Hoffmann.)

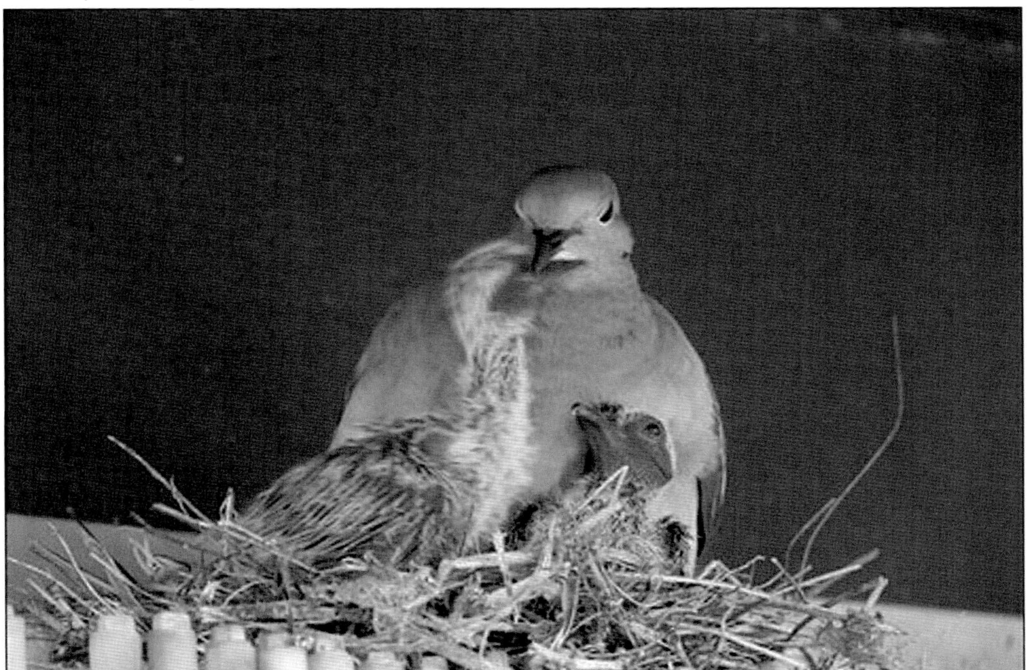

Mourning Doves. Some of Tamarac's most frequent yard birds are mourning doves. Here, a mother nestles with her babies in a gutter at an Isles of Tamarac home. (Courtesy of Rudy Hoffmann.)

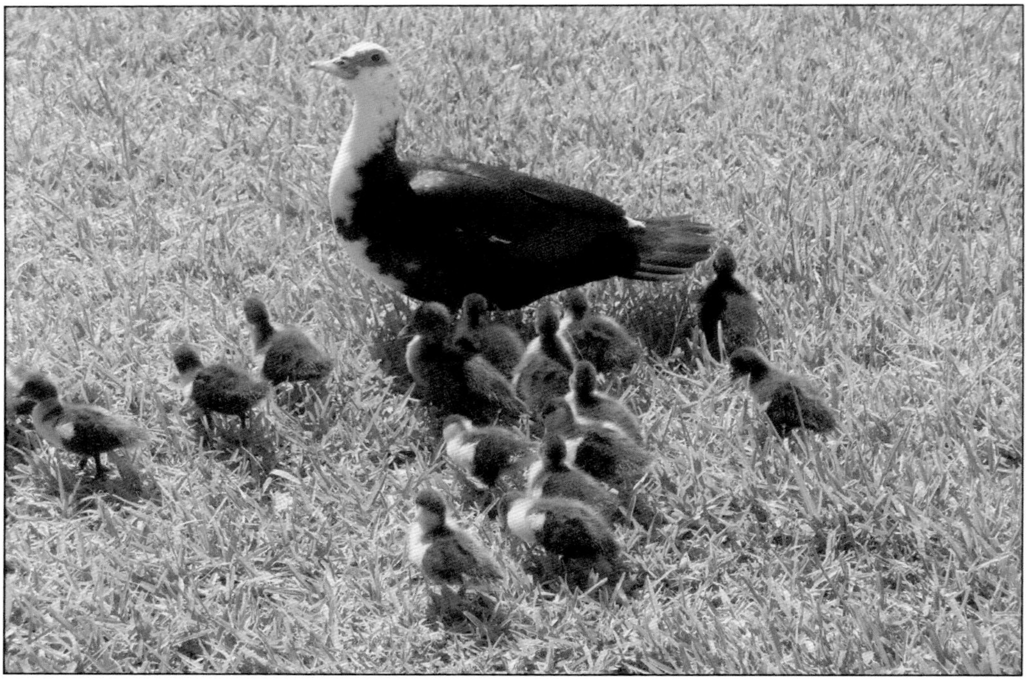

Muscovy Ducks. Widely populating Tamarac neighborhoods are Muscovy ducks. Many residents enjoy the ducks while others consider them a nuisance. Muscovies came to Florida as domestic stock; they are multicolored with red growths on their faces. (Courtesy of Marian Daly.)

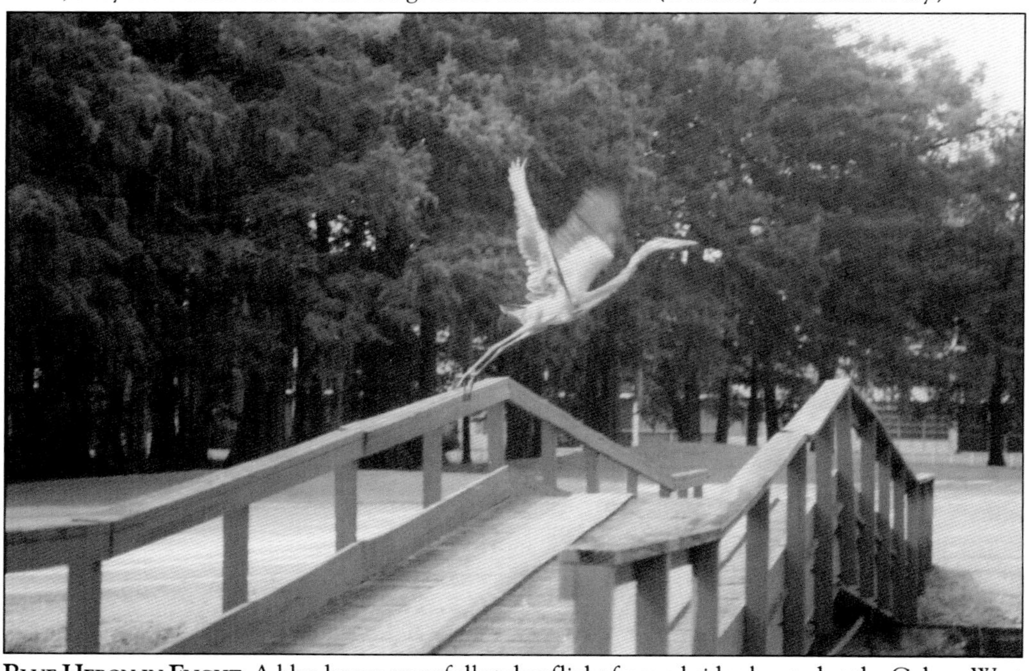

Blue Heron in Flight. A blue heron gracefully takes flight from a bridge located at the Colony West Country Club. Golfers on the course not only enjoyed a top-rated public golf course but also many of Tamarac's water birds such as herons, egrets, and ibises. (Courtesy of the City of Tamarac.)

Five

City For Your Life

IT STARTS IN PARKS

Coaching. Connecting. Community

Tamarac's Parks. Tamarac has pocket-sized and multipurpose parks that include playgrounds for children, activities and sports, happy hours for residents and their dogs, and plenty of walking paths for peaceful early morning and evening strolls. (Courtesy of the City of Tamarac.)

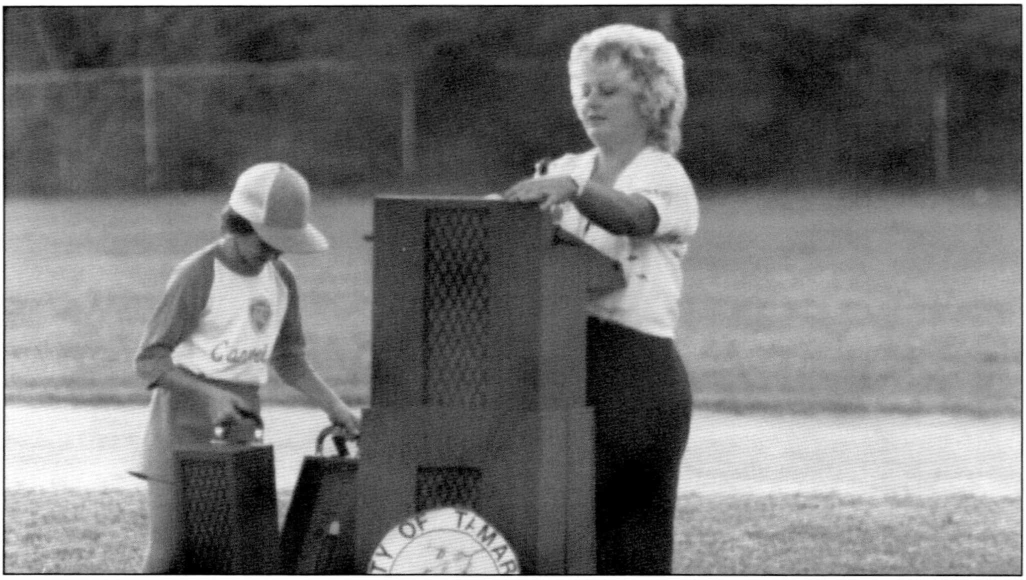

Sharon Ellis. On April 3, 1978, the city named Sharon Ellis the director of its newly formed parks and recreation department. A former Washington Redskins cheerleader for 12 years, Sharon earned a bachelor's of science degree in parks and recreation administration from the University of Maryland and came to the city with more than 13 years of work-related experience. With the city's first park, Tamarac Park, dedicated on the same day she took office and the city's population reaching over 30,000 residents, Sharon's innovative programs included holiday special events, fields for baseball, soccer, and football, courts for basketball and handball, and youth and senior recreational activities. (Courtesy of the City of Tamarac.)

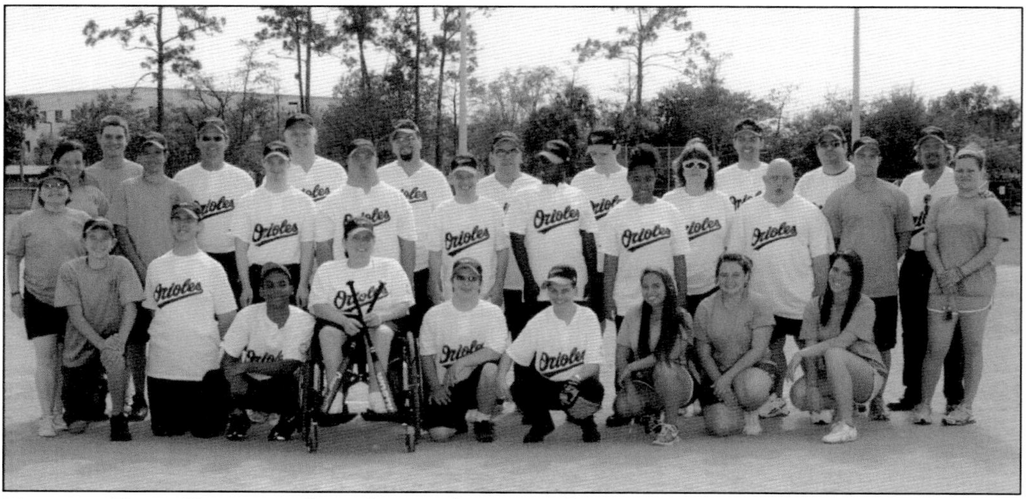

Tamarac Park. Youngsters from the Heathgate-Sunflower communities were among the first to play ball at Tamarac Park's baseball fields. In February 1974, the first Little League was organized in the city. Many teams have enjoyed playing on these fields over the years as well as the Challenger Baseball having been part of Tamarac Little League since 1990. Challenger offers disabled children the opportunity to play baseball. Thanks to their "buddies," the Challenger kids all hit and field. Uniforms, equipment, pictures, trophies, and more are all provided at no charge to the Challenger families thanks to private sponsors like the City of Tamarac. (Courtesy of Randy Hibshman.)

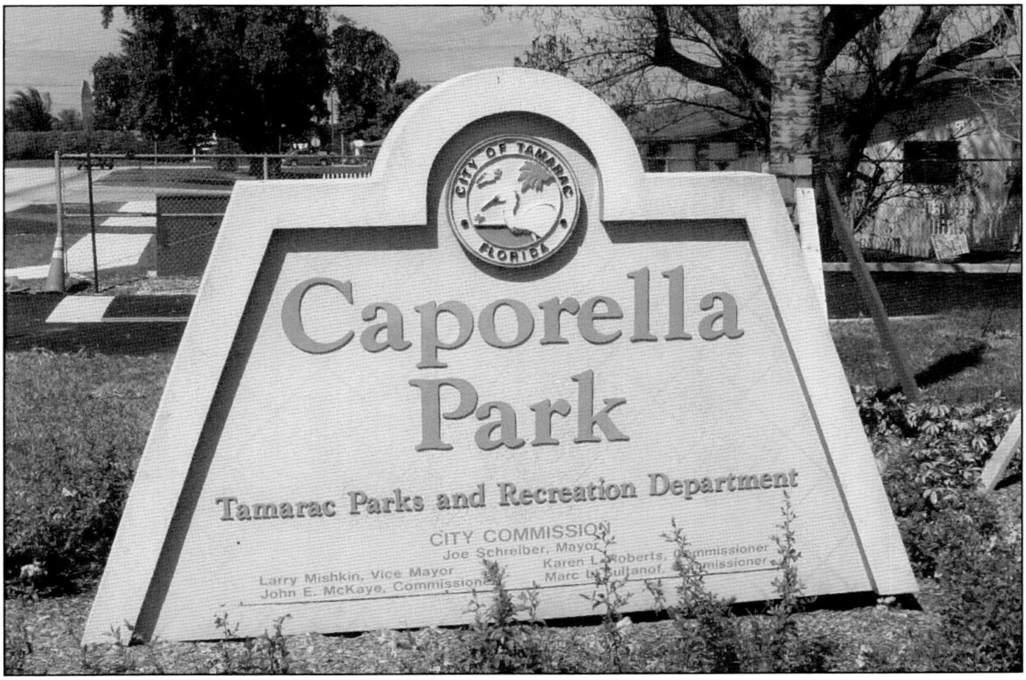

CAPORELLA PARK. Caporella Park's nine acres were deeded to the city in 1979 by the Caporella family and was improved in 2004. With an entrance off Prospect Road, the area is great for picnics near the lake, fishing off the pier, or strolling the walkways. And there are grills and rest rooms to maximize visitors' comfort. (Courtesy of the City of Tamarac.)

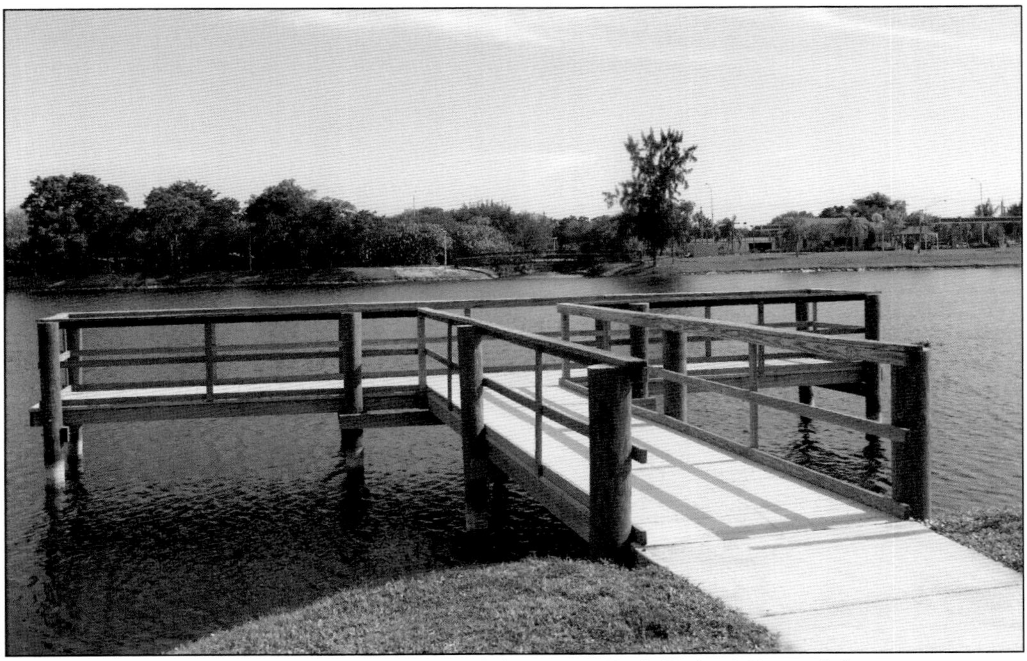

THE PIER. This eastside park is unique for its fishing pier. Each Father's Day, a fishing tournament is held here for city anglers. (Courtesy of the City of Tamarac.)

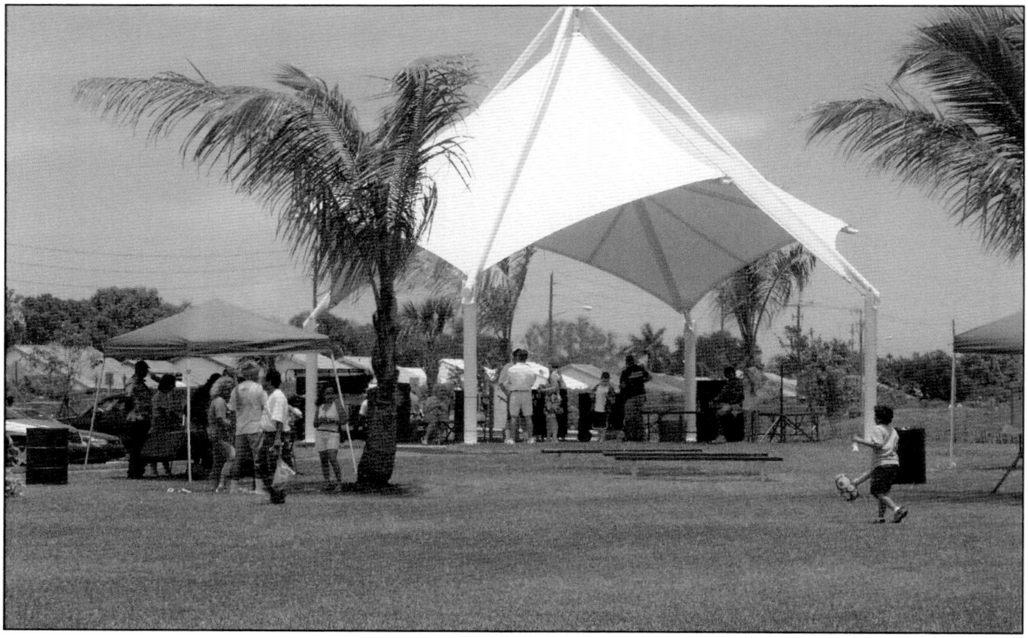

Sunset Point. Sunset Point, located at the western end of McNab Road, was opened to the public in 2004. Wetlands and a canal fringe its 8.5 acres. This facility features a nature-study kiosk, a small band shell, a Universal/ADA (Americans with Disabilities Act) playground, and rest rooms. It also has a fitness path and covered playground area. (Courtesy of the City of Tamarac.)

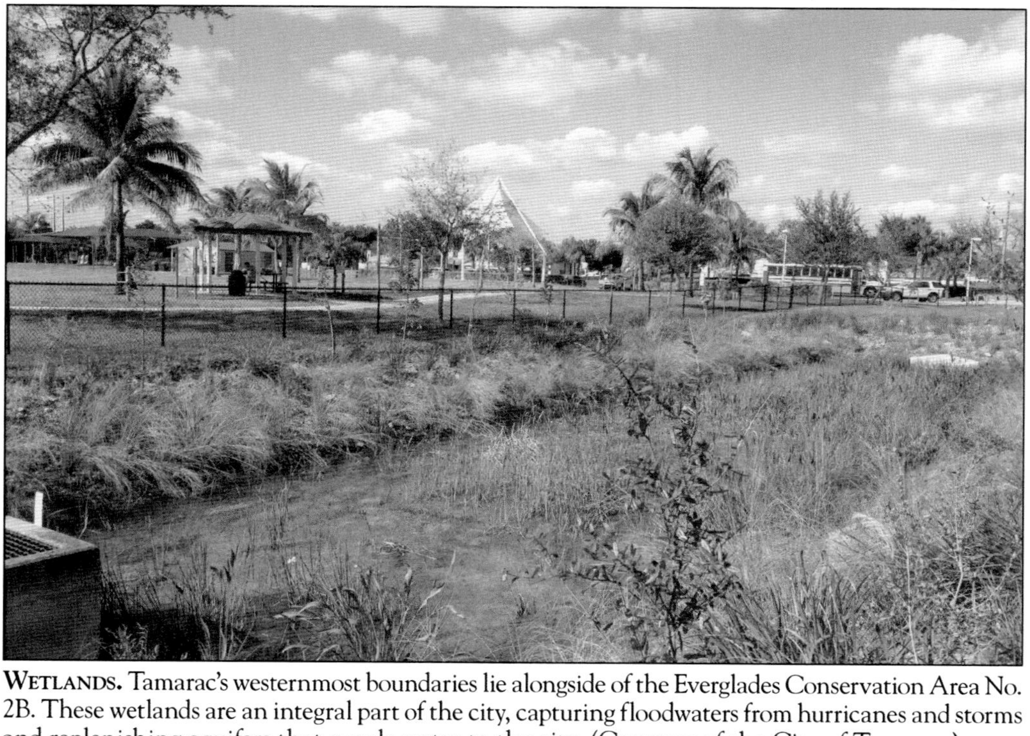

Wetlands. Tamarac's westernmost boundaries lie alongside of the Everglades Conservation Area No. 2B. These wetlands are an integral part of the city, capturing floodwaters from hurricanes and storms and replenishing aquifers that supply water to the city. (Courtesy of the City of Tamarac.)

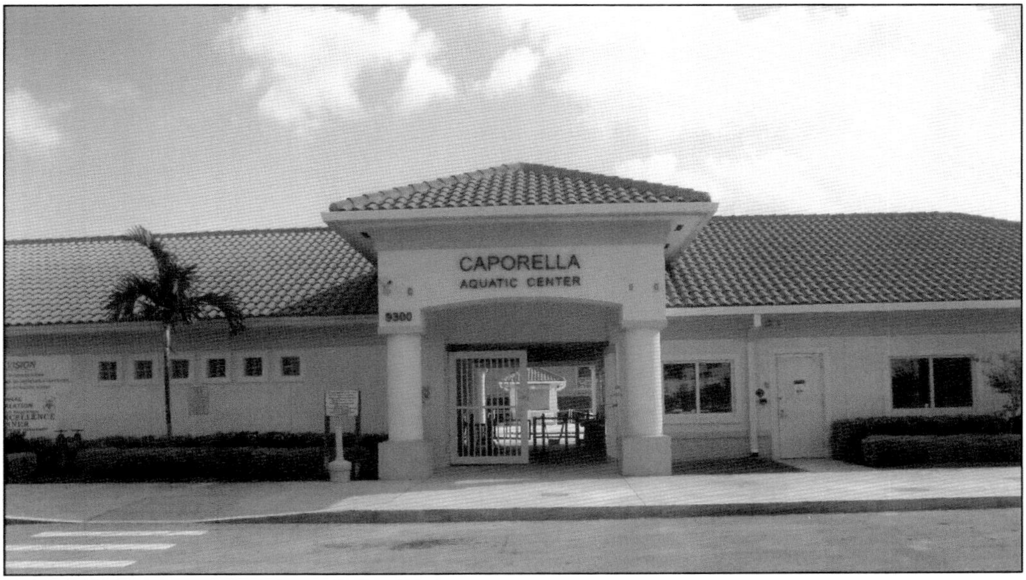

Caporella Aquatic Center. The Caporella Aquatic Center is located at 9300 Northwest Fifty-eighth Street on land donated by the Caporella family. Here, children have the opportunity to learn to swim, practice their water skills, and become lifesavers. The ground-breaking ceremony took place in 2005. The completion was celebrated in 2007. (Courtesy of the City of Tamarac.)

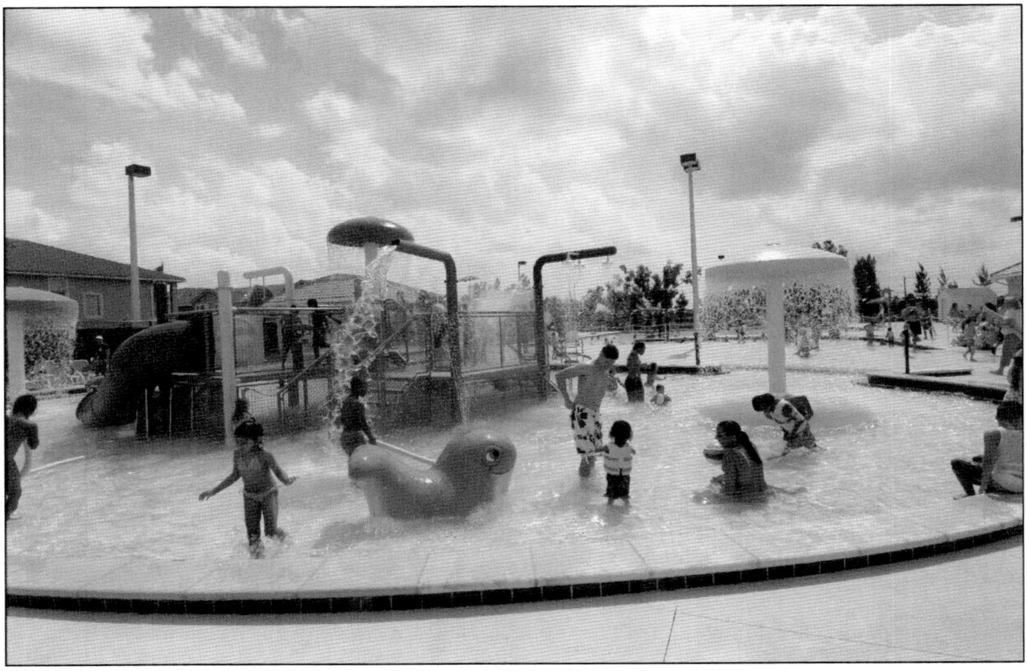

Kiddie Pool. The aquatic center includes pool areas for everyone. Nonswimming tots have their own area playing among the water fountains, slides, and water animals. (Courtesy of the City of Tamarac.)

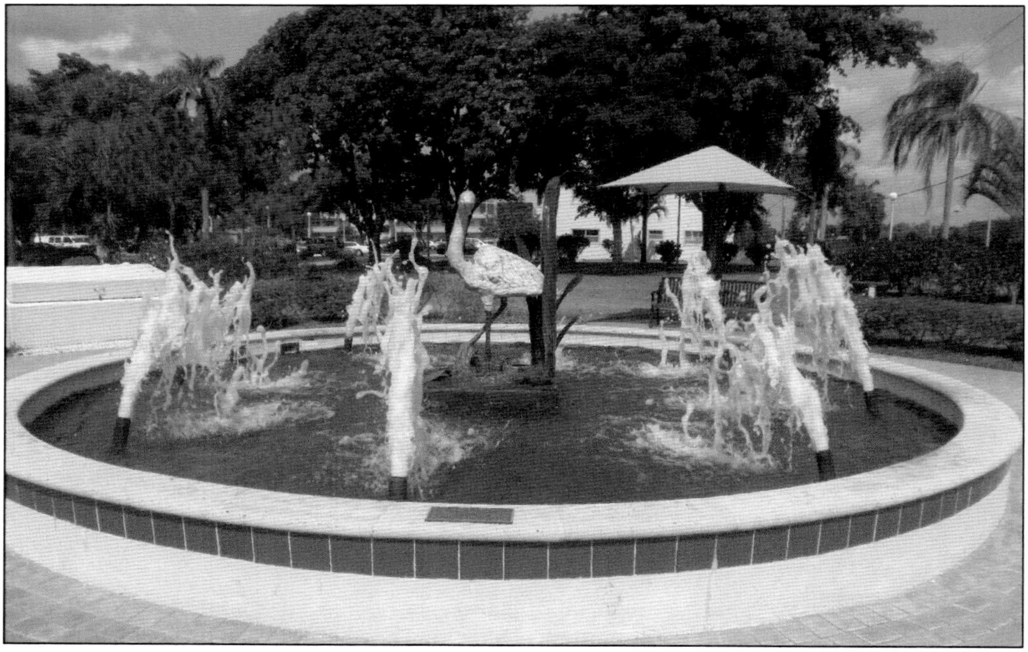

TAMARAC COMMONS PARK. Tamarac Commons Park was welcomed to the parks system in 2005. Located in a formerly unsightly, neglected corner lot, it was transformed into a pocket of beauty and serenity. Tamarac resident and artist George Gadson created the sculpture of the life-sized snowy egret, a concept chosen by members of the community. (Courtesy of the City of Tamarac.)

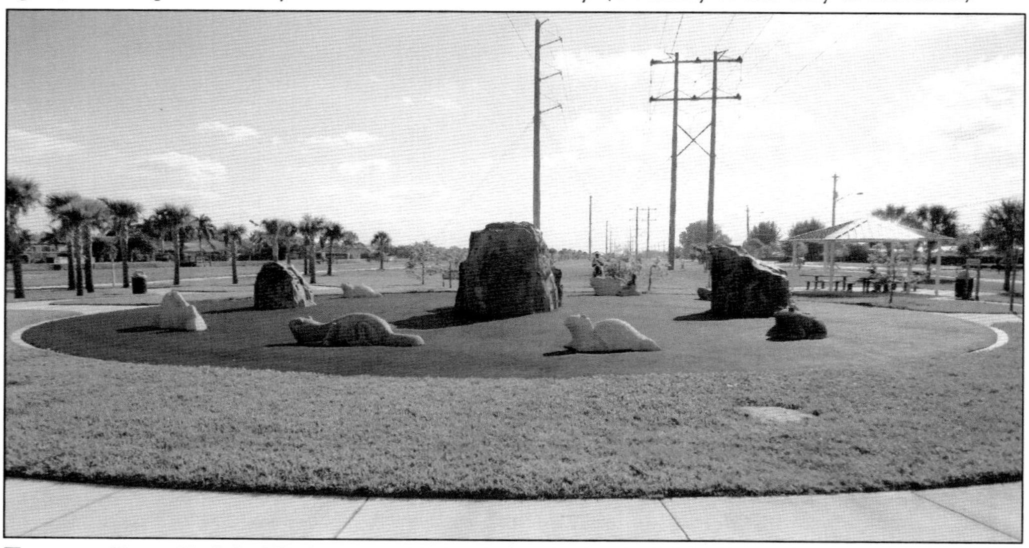

TEPHFORD PARK. Tephford Park was commissioned after receiving input from residents of surrounding communities. It serves as a trailhead for the Broward County Greenway system. Three public workshops resulted in a showcase facility. This linear strip of land between the C-14 Canal and Southgate Boulevard was transformed into a multipurpose playground for those who enjoy walking, picnicking, playing on the playground, fishing off the pier. Named after Broward Sheriff's Office deputy Brian Tephford, a father of three who lost his life while on duty in Tamarac, this park opened in 2008. (Courtesy of the City of Tamarac.)

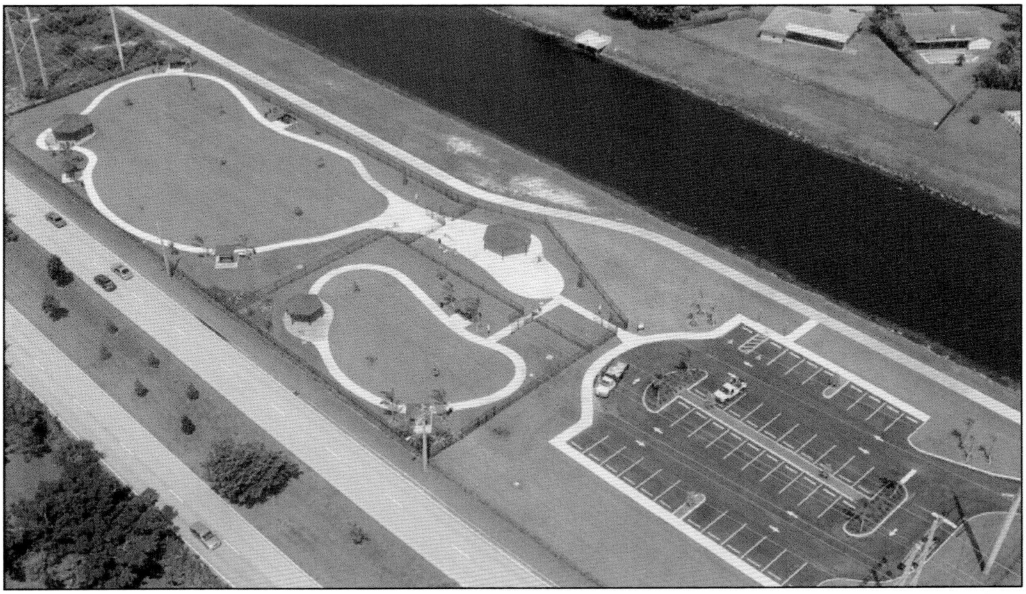

Gary B. Jones Park for People and Pups. The Gary B. Jones Park for People and Pups offers canine companions the opportunity to run off-leash. Considering the fact that there are more than 6,500 dogs registered in Tamarac, it was time (September 27, 2008, to be exact) to accommodate the beloved four-footed comrades with an array of facilities: separate areas for large and small animals, benches, shelters, drinking fountains, and even a washing facility. The park was named after Gary B. Jones, the late director of the building department and chief building official. (Courtesy of the City of Tamarac.)

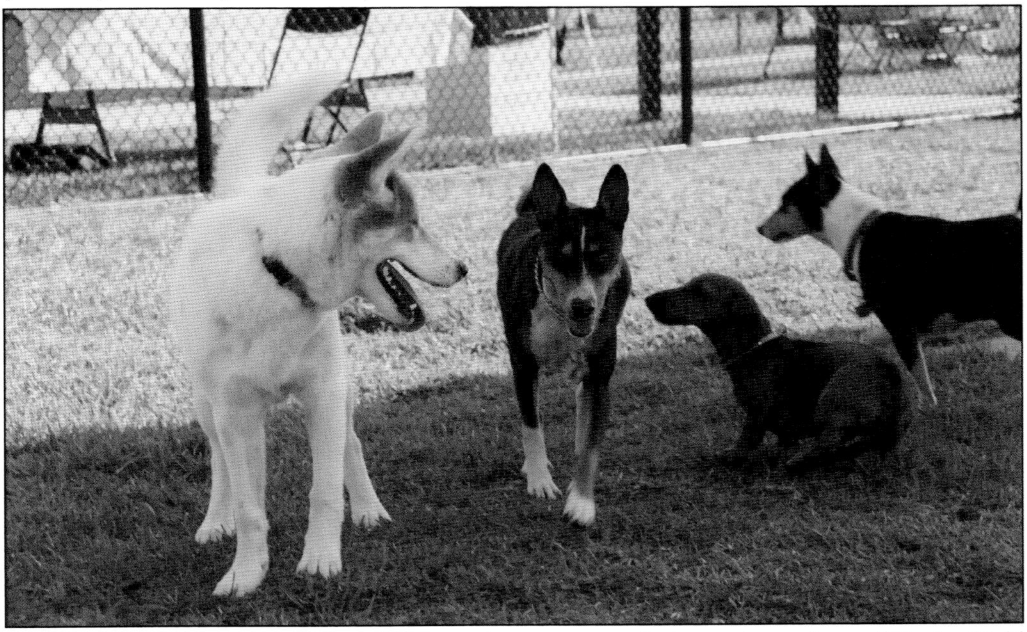

Playful Dogs. Representatives of Tamarac's canine population enjoy a day at Wiggley Field and Tam-A-Bark Run at the Gary B. Jones Park for People and Pups. (Courtesy of the City of Tamarac.)

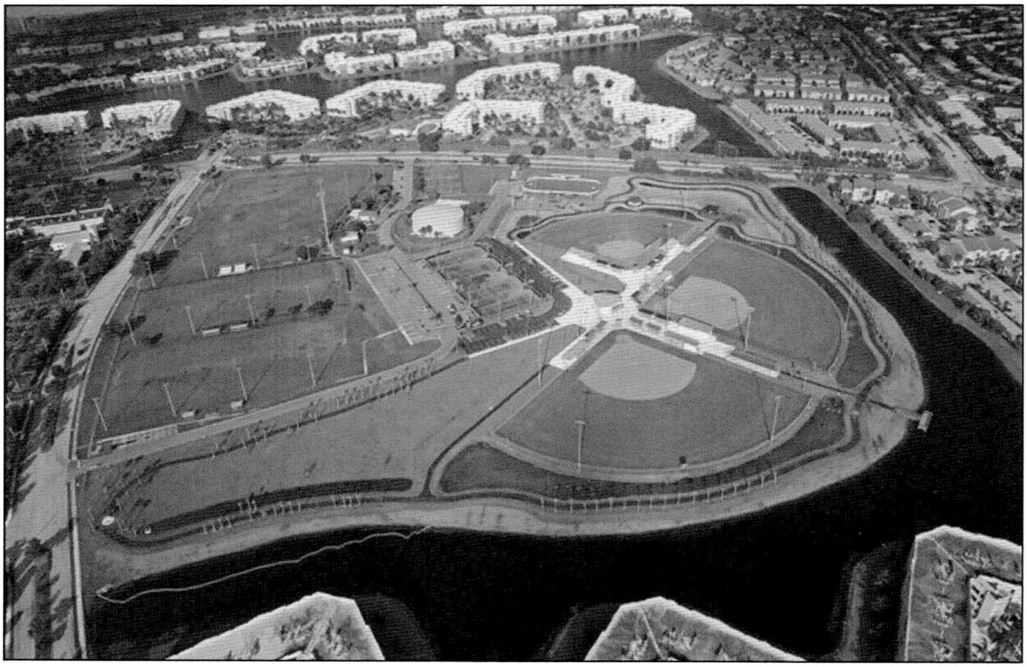

Tamarac Sports Complex. The Tamarac Sports Complex expansion was completed in 2009. It serves people of all ages who love baseball, soccer, and other sports. (Courtesy of the City of Tamarac.)

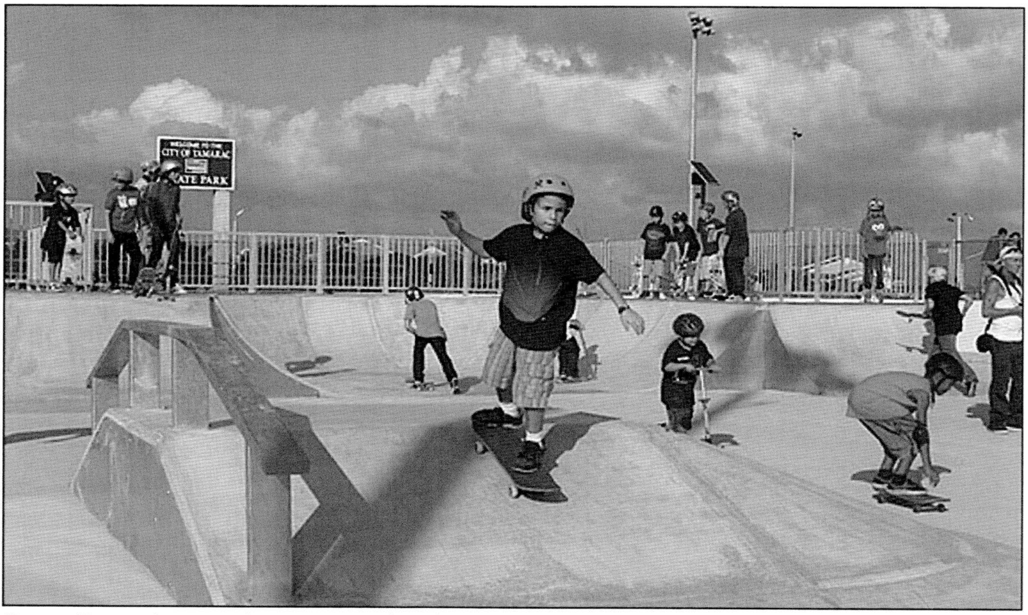

Skate Park. A young boy practices his skateboarding tricks and jumps at Tamarac's Skate Park. The park opened in the fall of 2010 and is located within the sports complex. Many skateboarders from surrounding cities enjoy this facility. The park does not charge an entrance fee and provides a safe environment for skateboarders of all ages. (Courtesy of the City of Tamarac.)

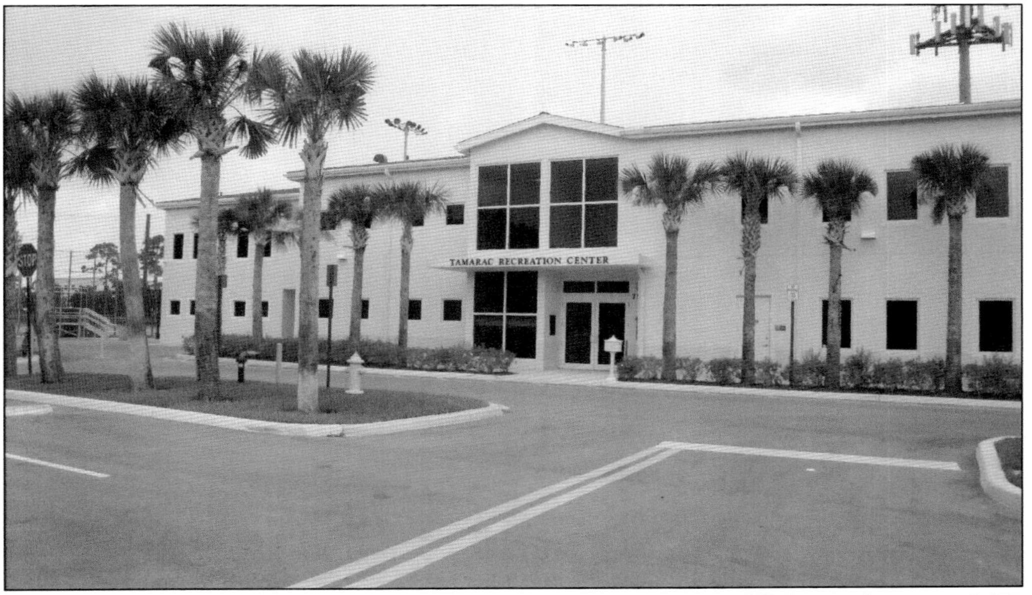

RECREATION CENTER. The population of Tamarac is getting younger. With a median age of 47.1 years (according to the US Census Bureau, 2010), the Tamarac Recreation Center meets the needs of an increasingly diverse community. The center provides a wide range of activities, programs, events, and services to ensure the city is meeting the cultural, social, physical, and wellness needs of its 60,427 residents. (Courtesy of the City of Tamarac.)

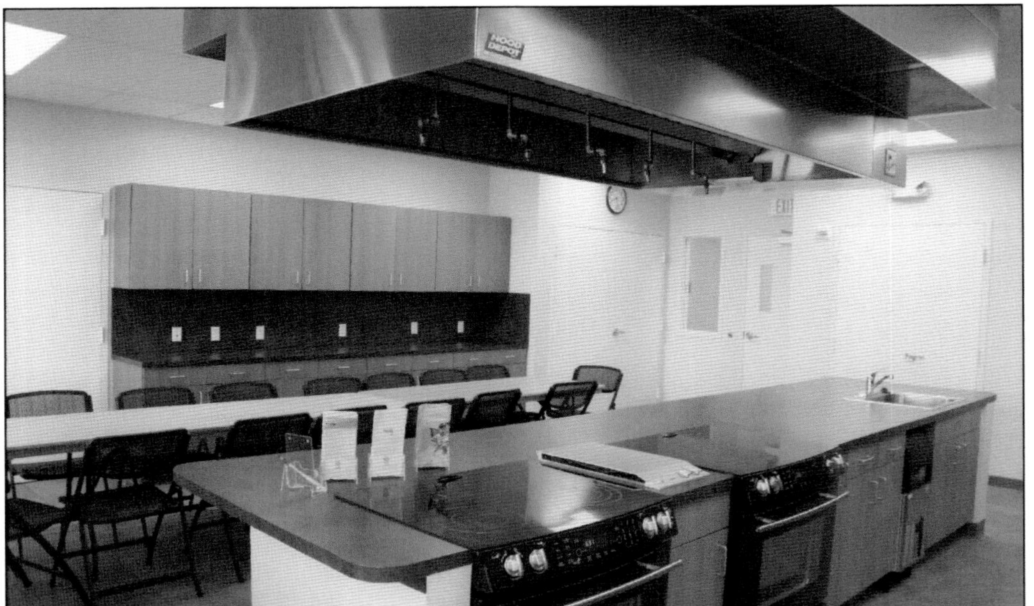

WHAT'S COOKING? Each recreational area in the city has a unique feature. The fully equipped kitchen, suitable for cooking classes, belongs to the Tamarac Recreation Center. The kitchen is also the site of the Tamarac University Alumni Annual Potluck Dinner held at the beginning of each year. (Courtesy of the City of Tamarac.)

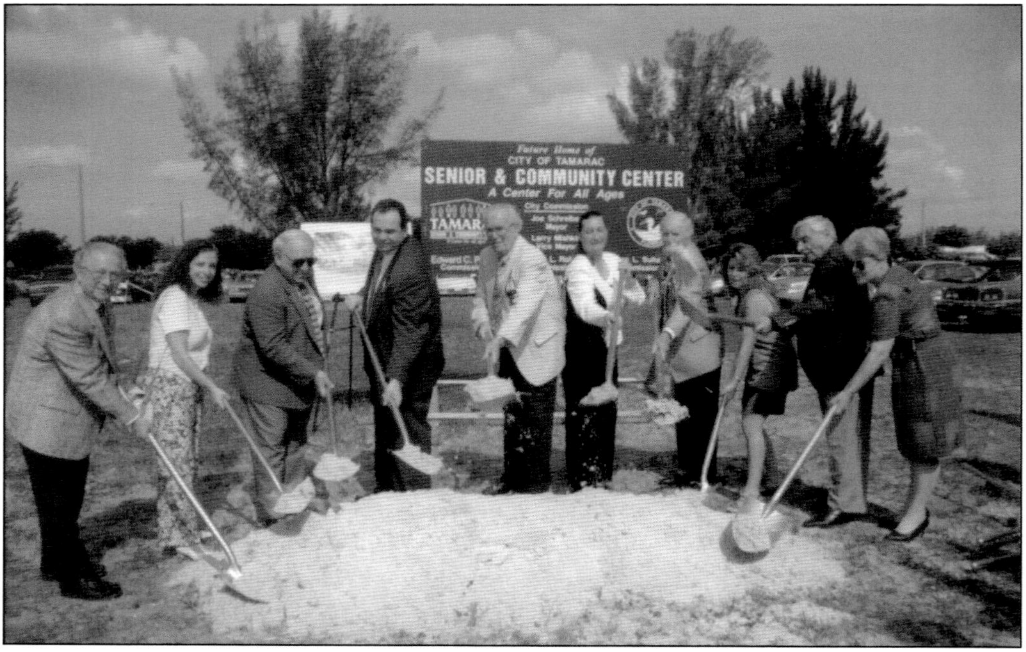

GROUND-BREAKING CEREMONY. In July 1999, the City of Tamarac broke ground for the long-awaited senior and community center on Commercial Boulevard. The motto, "A Center for All Ages," aptly describes this all-purpose center. (Courtesy of the City of Tamarac.)

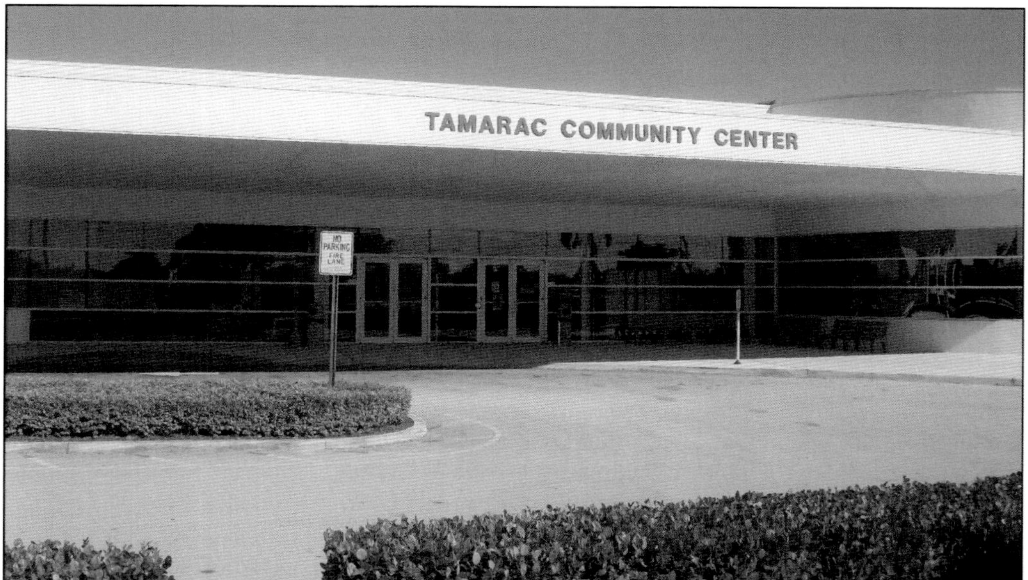

TAMARAC COMMUNITY CENTER. A hub of activity for all ages, the Tamarac Community Center (TCC) hosts senior programs including Meals on Wheels, adult trips, special events, special services, exercise programs (including chair aerobics, spinning, and Jazzercise), and even indoor sports. The West Commercial Boulevard building plays host to the Holiday Lighting Ceremony, Taste of Tamarac, health expositions, and the community garage sales. (Courtesy of the City of Tamarac.)

Six

City Landscapes

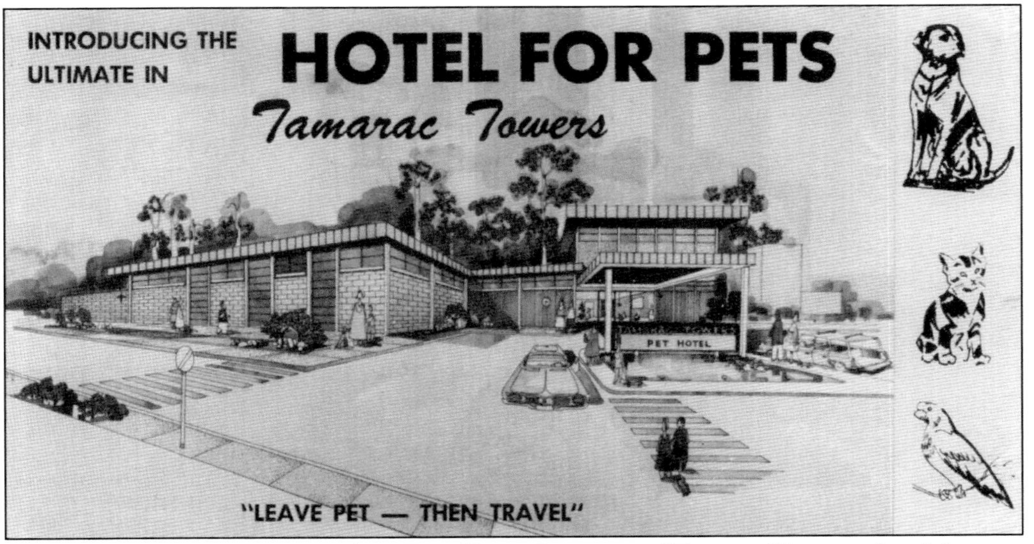

Hotel for Pets. "Leave Pet—Then Travel" was the motto of Tamarac Towers, a hotel for pets. The business began in 1968 and is located at 3910 Northwest Forty-ninth Avenue in a building that has been a pet resort for more than four decades. Each pet has its own private accommodations; special diets are prepared in an ultra-modern kitchen; there are 24-hour attendants; FM music plays throughout; and canines, felines, and birds are equally catered to. Today, the Arfington's Pet Resort carries on the Tamarac Towers tradition and even includes aromatherapy, pet grooming, dog training, a pet boutique, and a pool for swimming. And cats get to watch fish in a "virtual aquarium." (Courtesy of Marti Metzger.)

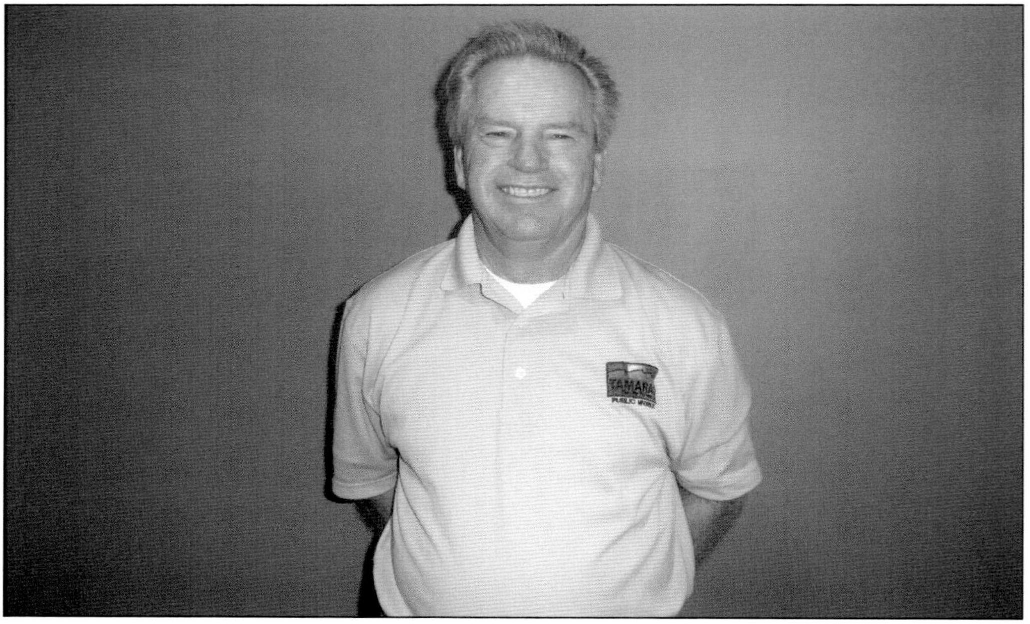

Supt. Bill Lewis. Along with being the city's public works superintendent, he is also a paleontology enthusiast. In 2002, city workers broke ground for a pump station. During the excavation for the foundation of the building, Lewis and others began to notice shells in the dirt. (Courtesy of Bill Lewis.)

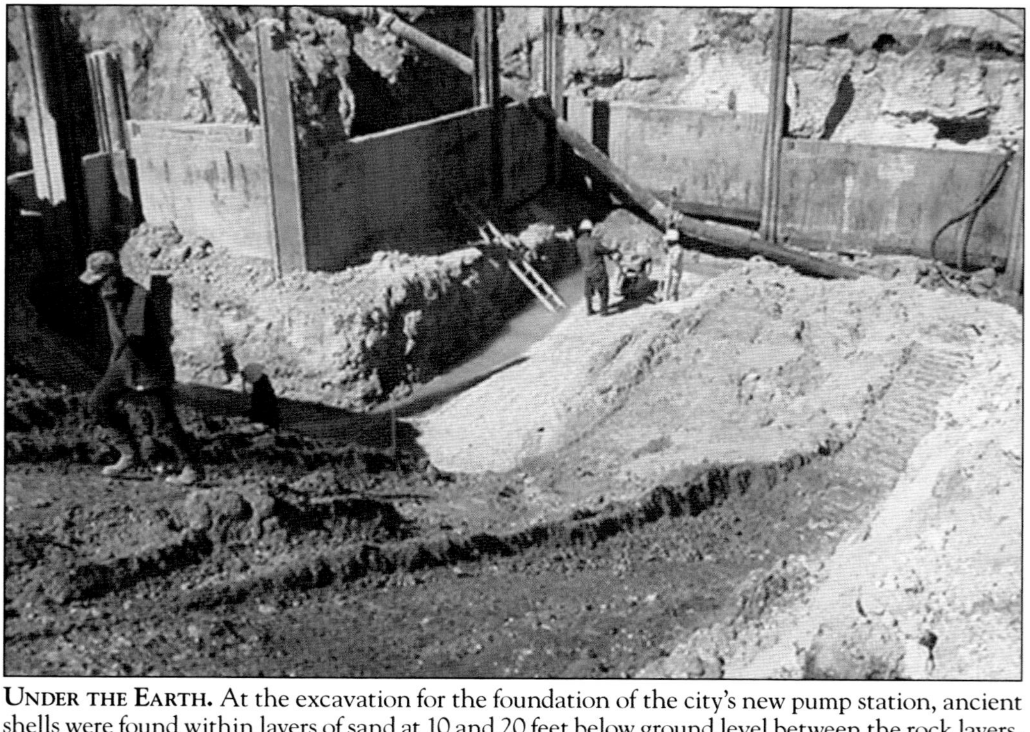

Under the Earth. At the excavation for the foundation of the city's new pump station, ancient shells were found within layers of sand at 10 and 20 feet below ground level between the rock layers. Many workers helped save the shells at the request of Bill Lewis. (Courtesy of Bill Lewis.)

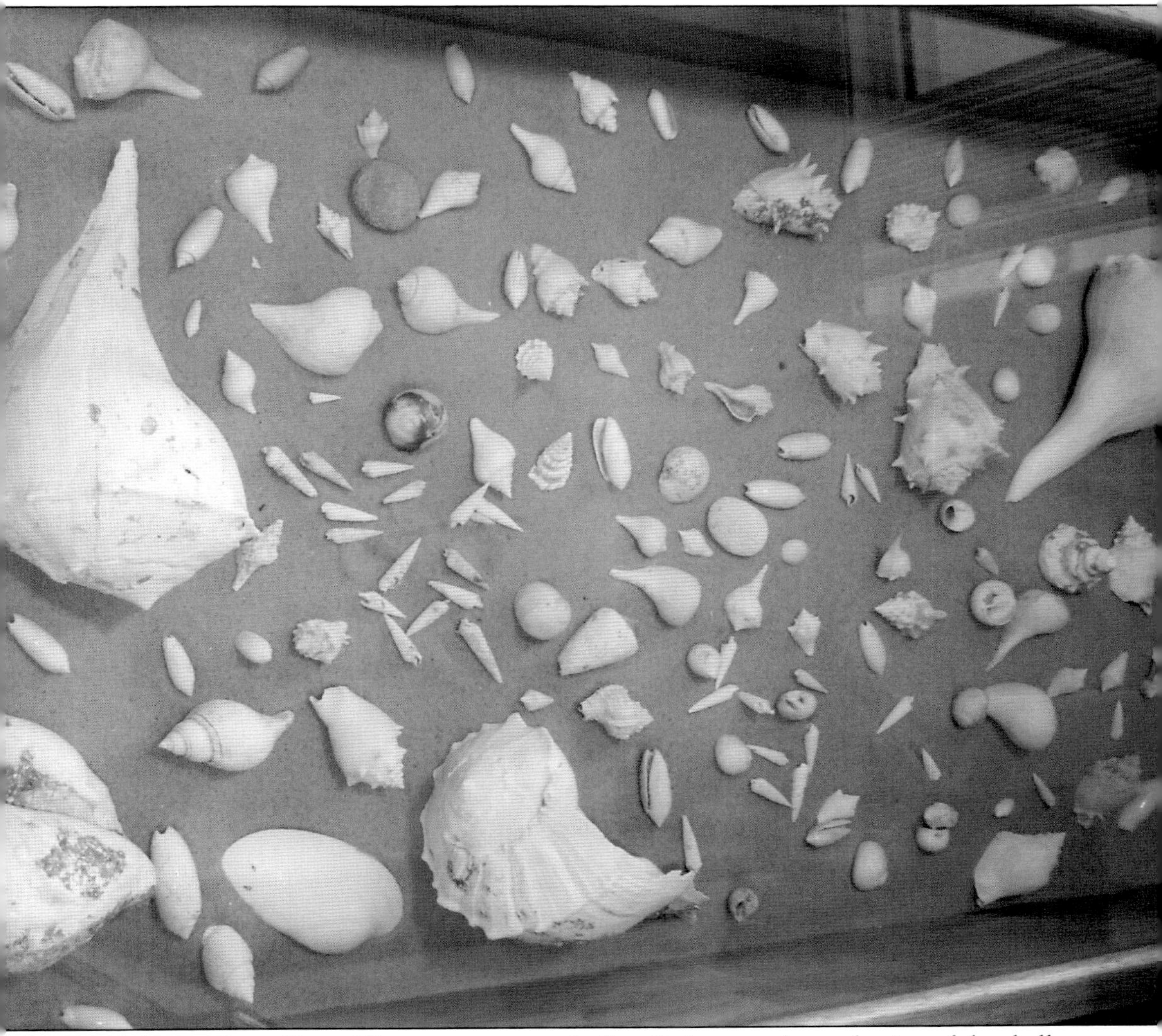

Fossil Shell Case. Kevin Ellis, city carpenter, built a display case for a selection of the shells, which can be seen at the City of Tamarac Public Works Building. These fossils shells are gastropods known more commonly as snails and slugs. This type of shell was salvaged for practical reasons, though many shell types were present. Research, along with advice provided by expert Alex Kittle of the Florida Museum of Natural History, suggests that they are between one and three million years old. (Courtesy of Bill Lewis and the Florida Museum of Natural History.)

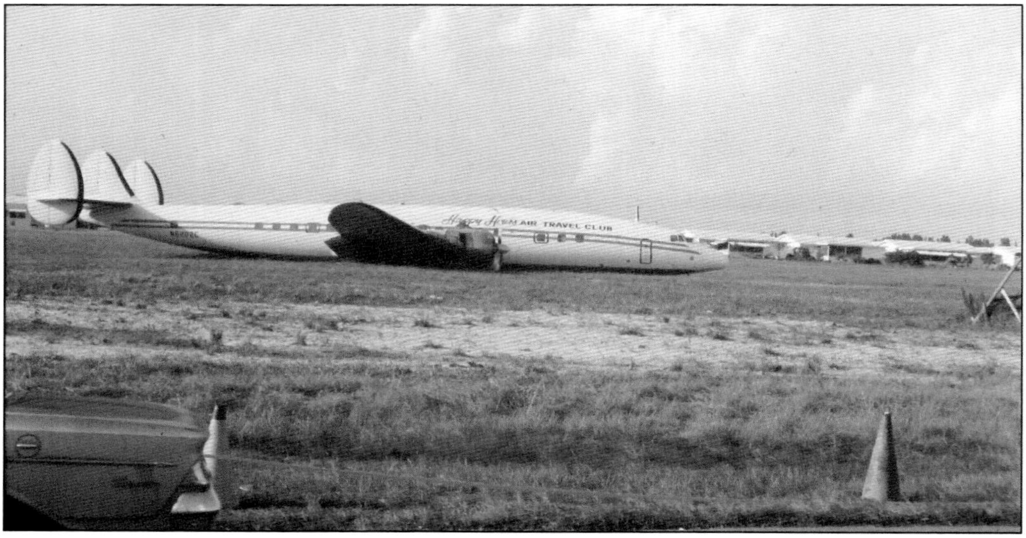

Emergency Landing. On Sunday evening, August 5, 1973, a plane made an emergency landing into an empty field off University Drive and Commercial Boulevard (at the present location of the Denny's on Fifty-seventh Street and University Drive). Happy Hours Air Travel Club owned and operated the 22-year-old Lockheed Constellation that flew a route between the Bahamas and Fort Lauderdale. Towards the end of the trip, all four engines lost power due to a fuel shortage. The pilot chose to glide the plane in for a wheels-up landing on the empty field. (Courtesy of John Brown.)

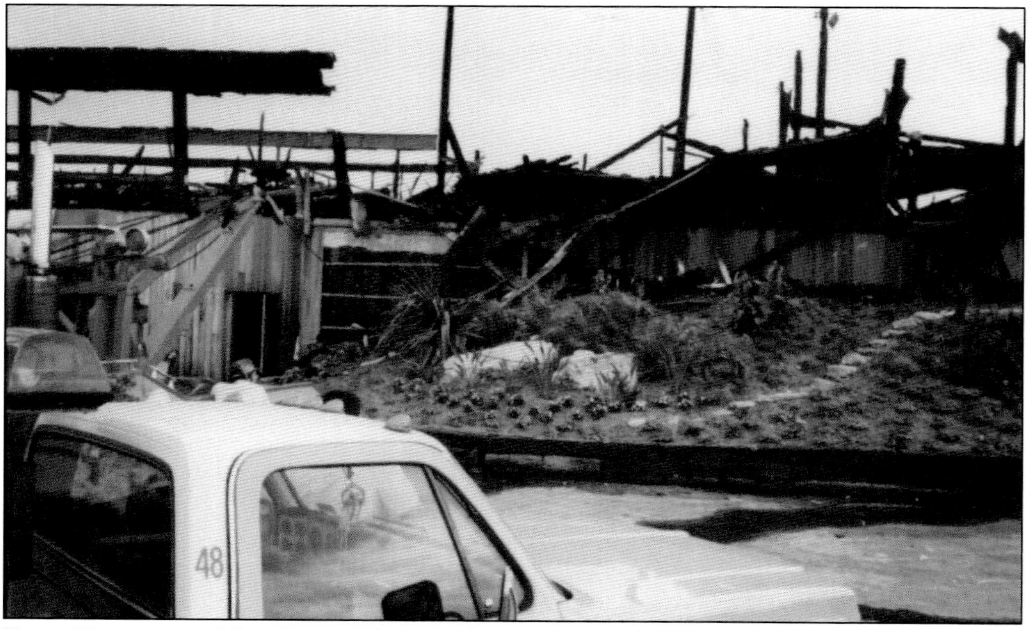

Fired Up for the New Year. The Woodmont Country Club, originally known as Timber Run, promised a night to remember on December 31,1977. The club was celebrating its first New Year's Eve: great food, lively music, and members dressed to the nines. After the last guests had departed, a fire started that demolished the clubhouse with the wooden exterior in a very short time. (Courtesy of the City of Tamarac.)

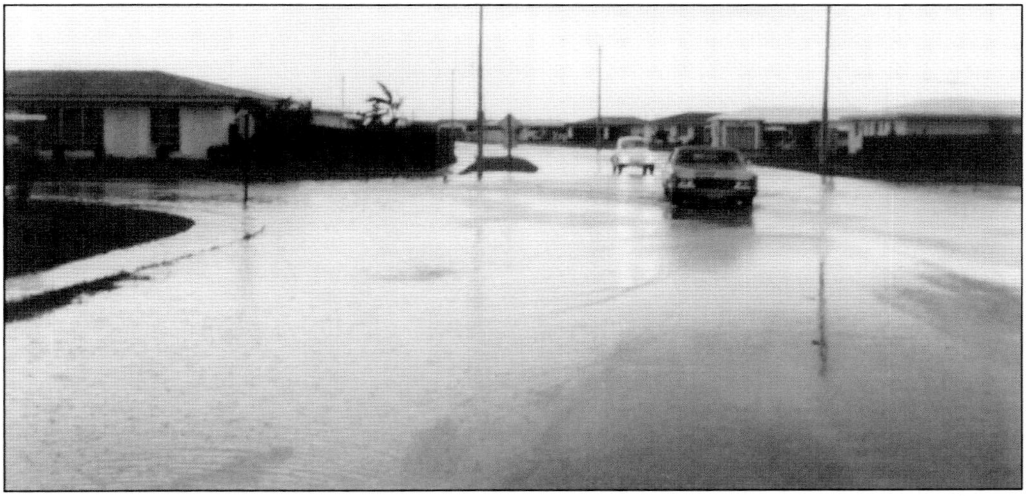

NEIGHBORHOOD FLOOD. No one would have expected a flood this far from open water, but in 1978, such was the case. A new homeowner recounted: "A week into my new home we awoke to a rainstorm. Little did we know that we had received upwards to 18 inches of rain in just a few hours. The first evidence was a soggy carpet, then floating tiles in the kitchen and finally the children rowing in a canoe past the front door. Water was everywhere and it was days until we dried out." (Courtesy of the City of Tamarac.)

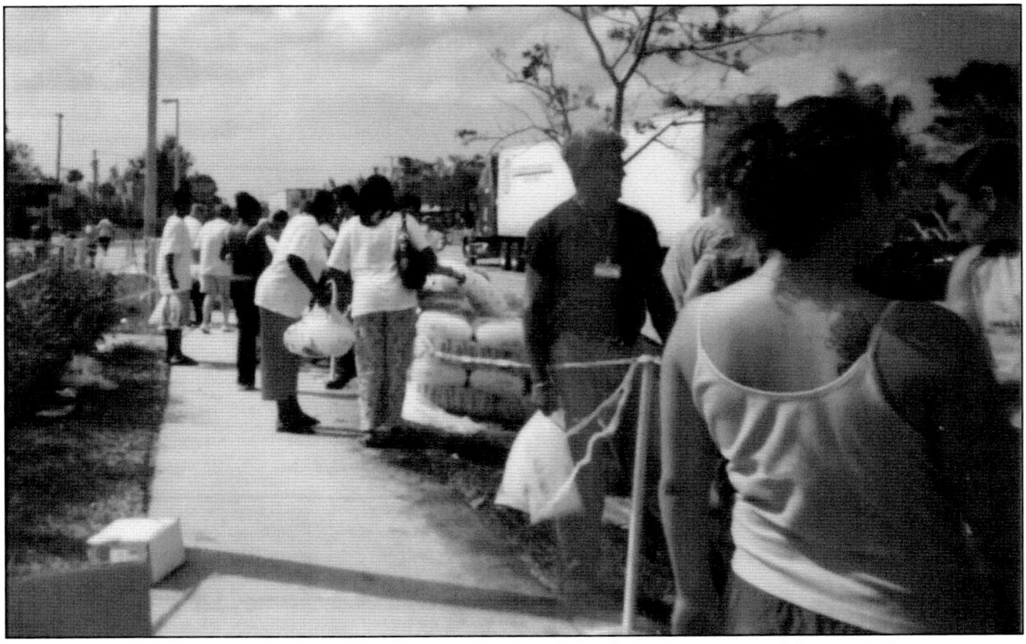

THE WATER LINE. Hurricane Wilma hit South Florida with a vengeance. Often, residents prepare the windows with tape, stock the fridge with water, and buy extra nonperishable food just to have much of it go unused. Not so this time. On October 24, 2005, the hurricane made landfall as a Category 2 storm, knocking out power in Tamarac for days and leaving enormous tree and roof damage. Long lines emerged at the word of free ice being at certain locations, helping people survive until power was restored. (Courtesy of Lee Kamerling.)

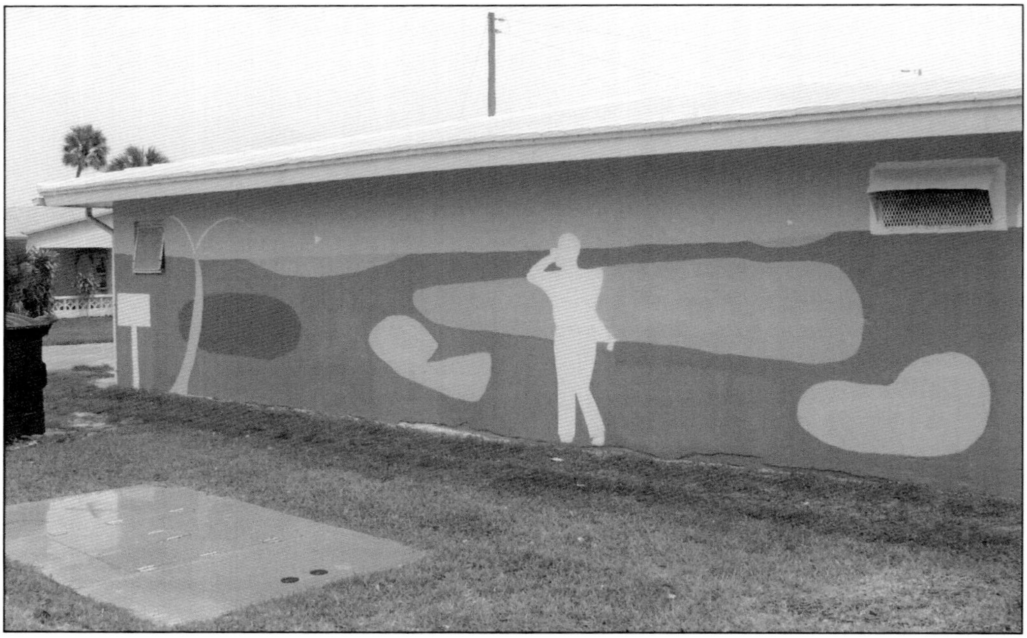

Sabal Palms. Open to the public and sporting dual greens as part of it signature, Sabal Palms opened in 1965 on the corner of Rock Island Road and Commercial Boulevard, then the western end of the city. At 6,165 yards, the course was built on flat ground and was well bunkered with five ponds and six canals. Greens fees were $3 with an electric golf cart fee of $4. This painted mural was an iconic part of the course landscape. (Courtesy of the Tamarac Historical Society.)

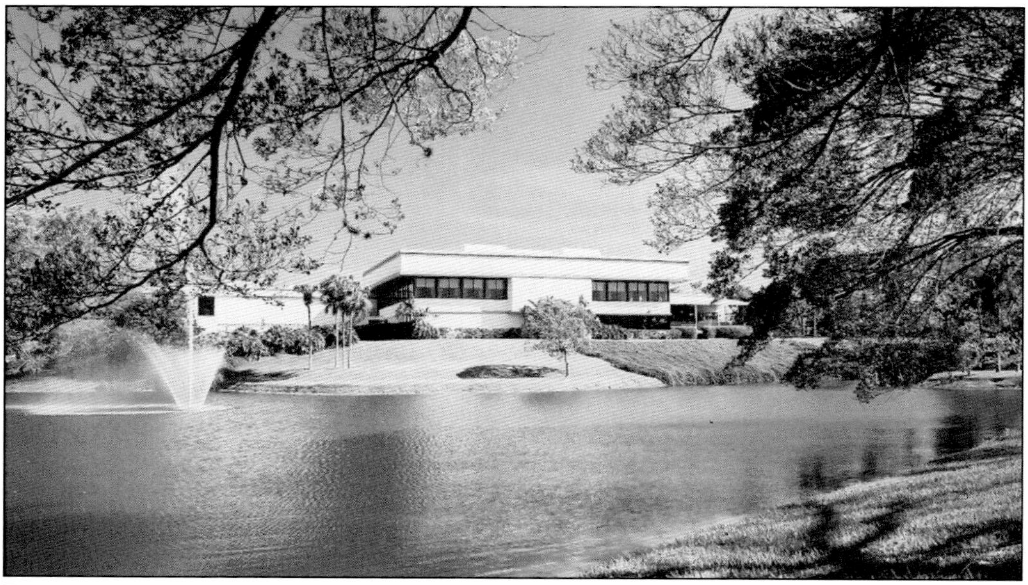

The Woodlands Country Club. As an avid golfer himself, Behring wanted only the best amenities for the private country club community he was building in his westward expansion. The well-known golf course designer, Robert Von Hagge, designed two courses originally limited to 600 members. The course sported 40 to 50 bunkers, well-maintained fairways, long and narrow greens, and accommodated golfers of all skill levels. (Courtesy of the Woodlands Country Club.)

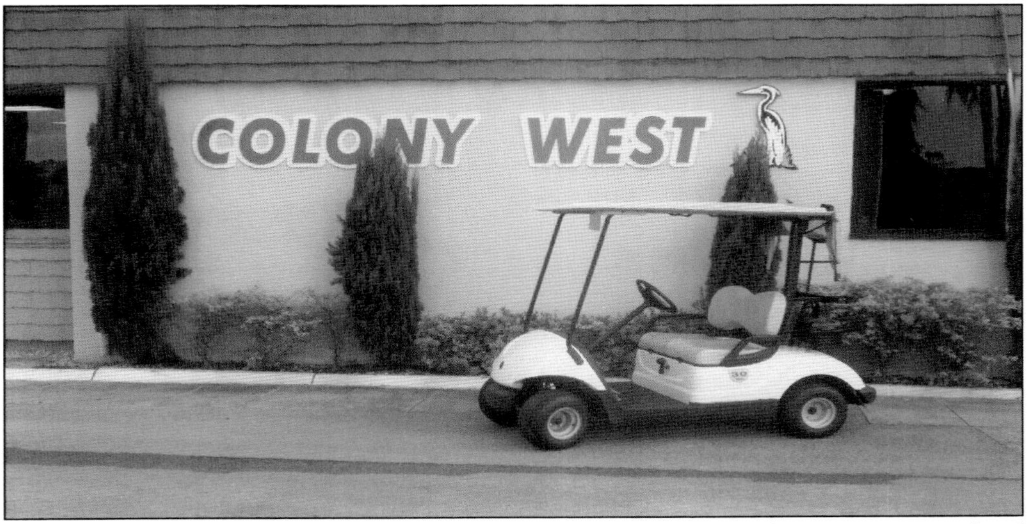

COLONY WEST COUNTRY CLUB. In 1971, the design team of Devlin and Von Hagge completed two courses—one considered to be a championship course and another for those golfers who wish to walk the course. With 15 water holes and voted one of South Florida's toughest courses, it is certainly a challenge. In December 1985, the championship course was renovated, and Colony West Country Club was rated by *Golf Digest* as one of the top 50 public courses in the United States. (Courtesy of Colony West.)

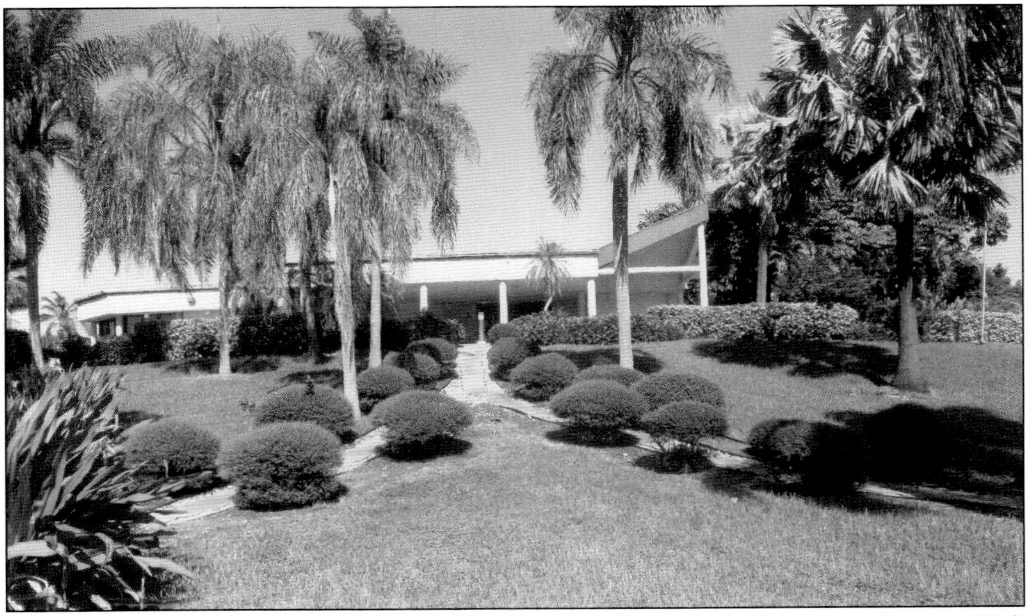

WOODMONT COUNTRY CLUB. The last club built in Tamarac in 1974, Woodmont Country Club was originally called Timber Run. By then, designer Bruce Devlin was very successful in the Tamarac golfing world and was commissioned to design one more patch of green heaven. Two courses were built among the pine trees with plenty of strategically placed water hazards. The Cypress Course had narrow fairways, while the Pines Course had a more generous, wide-open layout. Several par-threes are over water, which is a beautiful but intimidating sight for some. (Courtesy of the Tamarac Historical Society.)

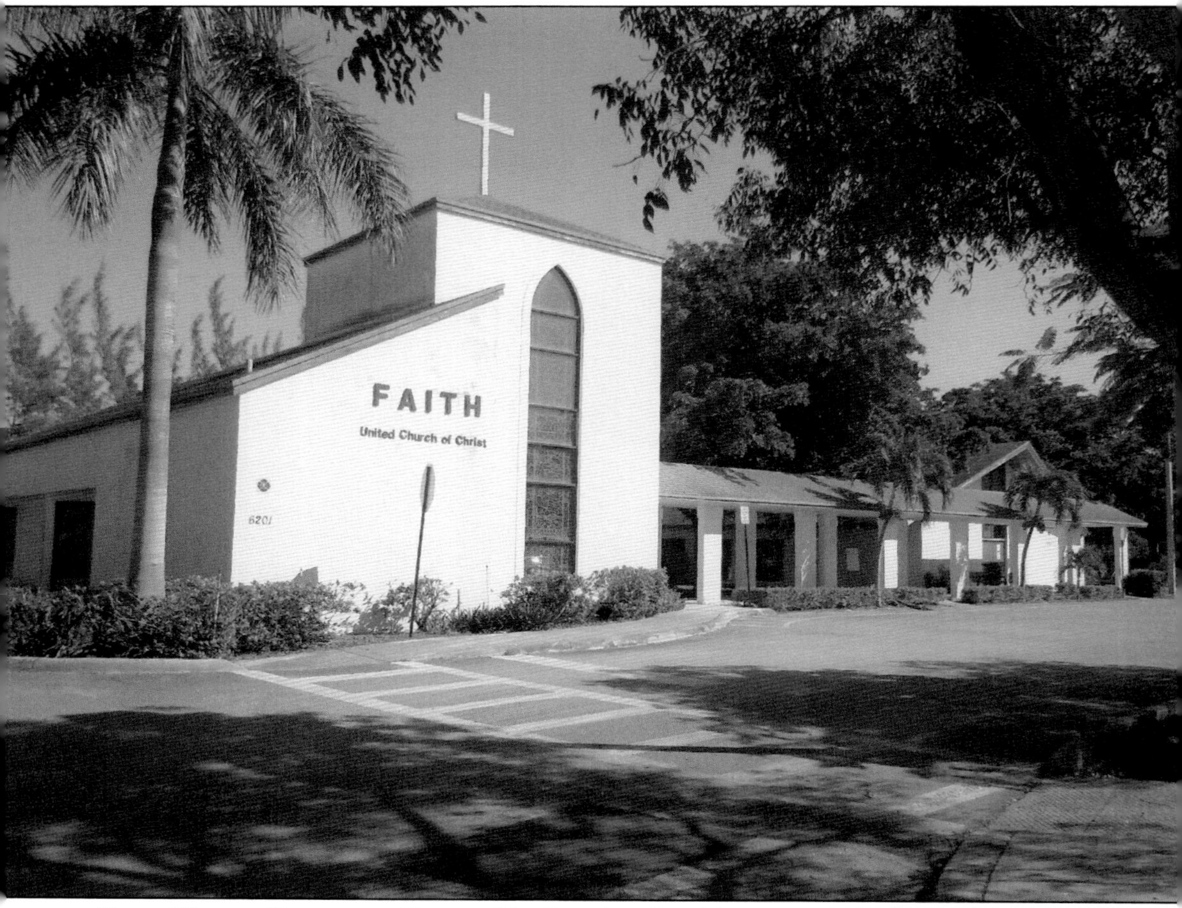

FAITH UNITED CHURCH OF CHRIST. The first church in Tamarac was the Faith United Church of Christ, which began in April 1971. The Behring Corporation had a master plan for the city, which included churches of all faiths. Rev. Frank Nagy was the organizing pastor. The church would eventually consist of a sanctuary, a cluster of classrooms, and a manse. (Courtesy of Marian Daly.)

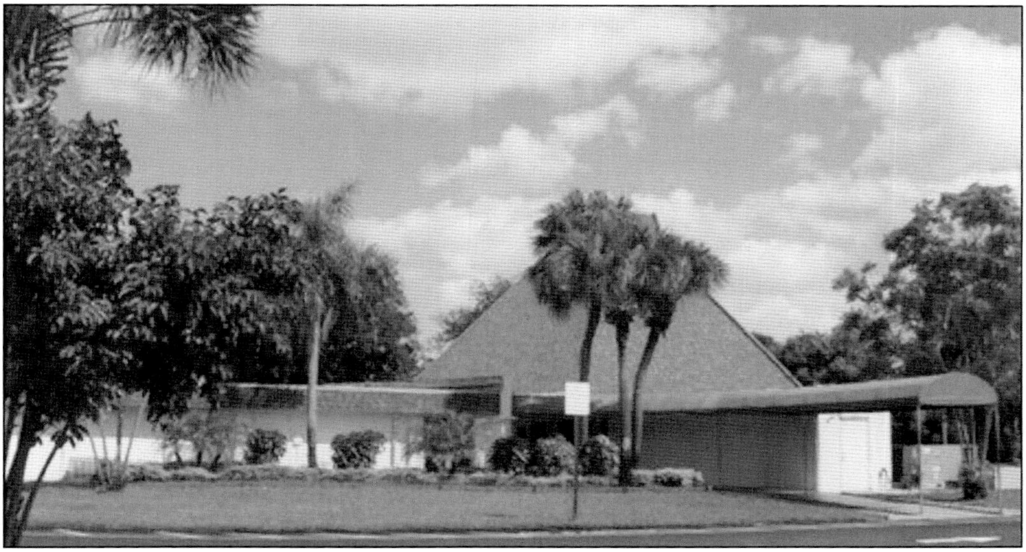

ALL SAINTS LUTHERAN CHURCH. On Sunday November 5, 1972, a formal, organizational service was held at the Faith United Church of Christ. The Lutheran congregation's church was under construction at the corner of University Drive and Northwest Seventy-sixth Street. Until the completion, Faith United Church of Christ shared its facility to allow All Saints Lutheran Church to hold its services. (Courtesy of Rudy Hoffmann.)

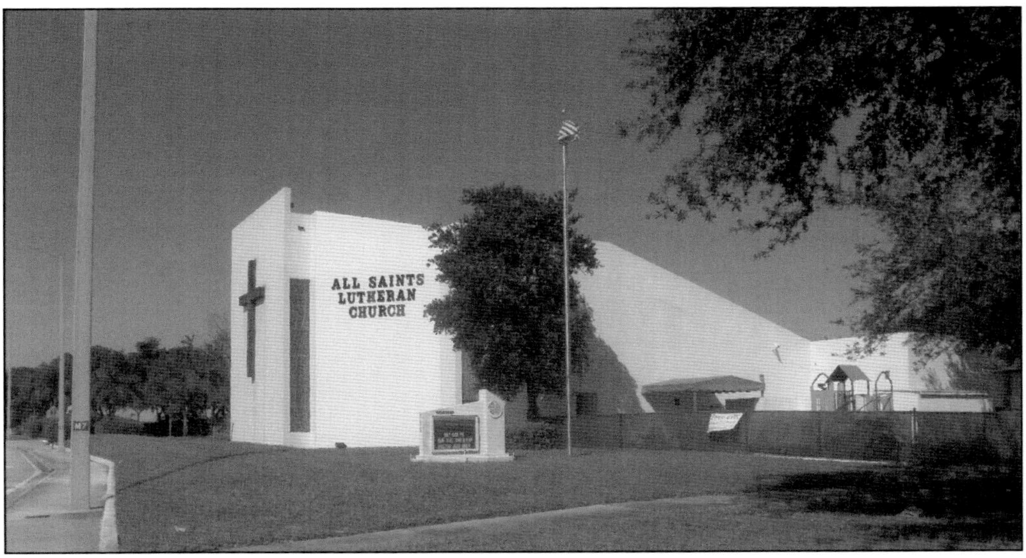

TODAY'S ALL SAINTS LUTHERAN CHURCH. When the Lutheran Church moved into its new home on McNab Road, the original building continued to serve the community. The building is now the Eliathah Seventh-day Adventist Church. The All Saints Lutheran Church's new, larger building promoted expanded offerings for the congregation. (Courtesy of the Tamarac Historical Society.)

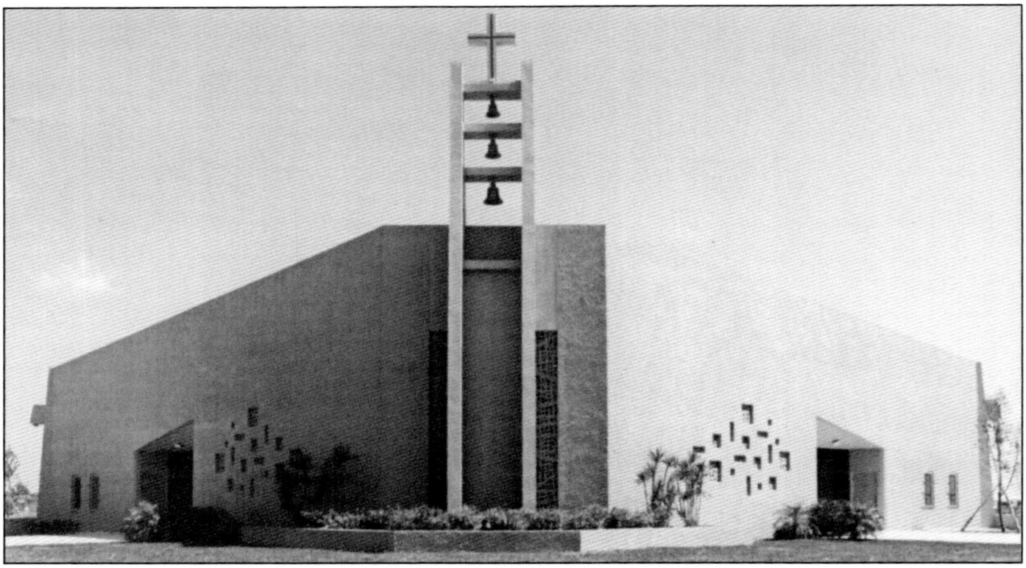

Saint Malachy Church. Behring properties determined a Catholic church would be erected at the intersection of University Drive and Sixty-first Street. The plot of some 10 acres had been purchased by the archdiocese on the advice of the Most Reverend Archbishop Coleman F. Carroll, who had the wisdom and foresight to plan a parish in Tamarac to take care of the growth explosion to the west of Fort Lauderdale. Prior to this structure, newly appointed pastor Fr. Timothy G. Hannon held Saturday evening and Sunday masses in several rented locations. One such site was the cafeteria at the Behring Plant on the west end of Fifty-seventh Street. In 1972, a group of parishioners conducted a building fund campaign, raising $225,000 in pledges in just five weeks. On Sunday July 2, 1972, the first shovel went into the weed-covered patch of land that soon would become the St. Malachy Church. The dedication of the church was in March 1973. (Both, courtesy of Saint Malachy Church.)

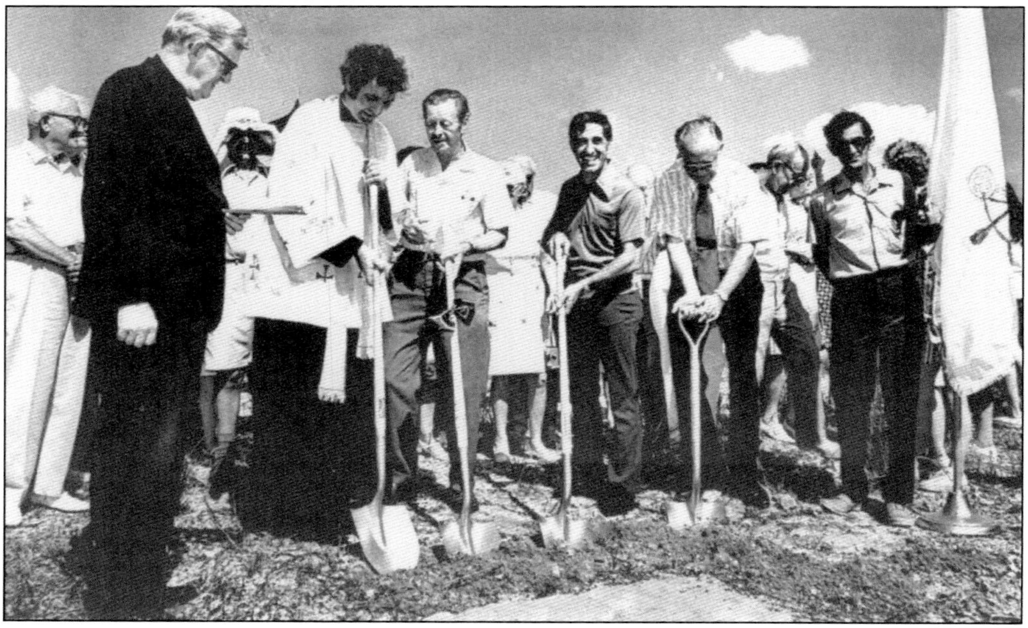

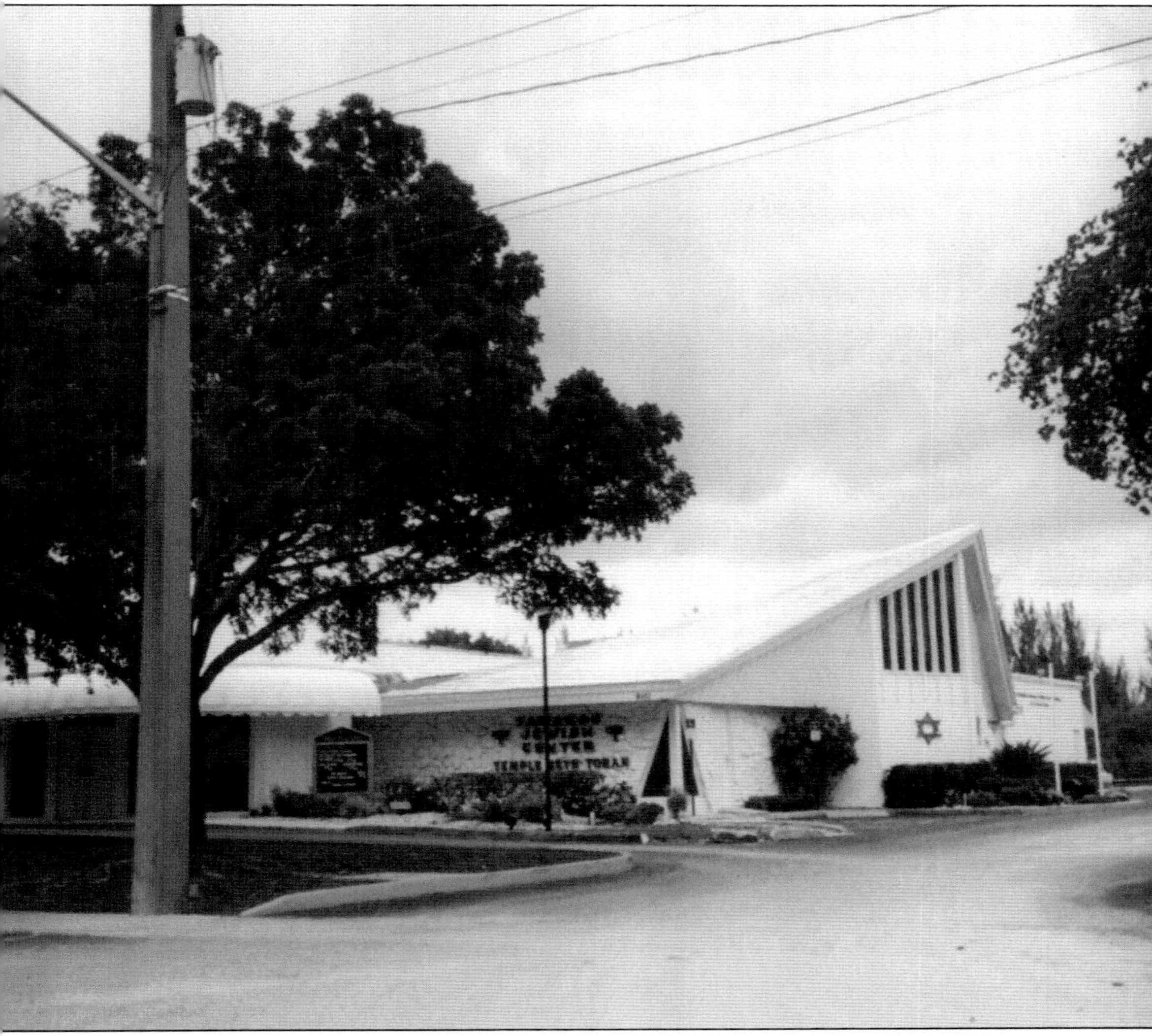

TAMARAC JEWISH CENTER. Started in February 1972, eight residents got together and began a synagogue in a borrowed storefront. In just seven short months, they had their first celebration, Rosh Hashanah, the Jewish New Year of 5723. The synagogue has thrived in the city ever since. (Courtesy of the City of Tamarac.)

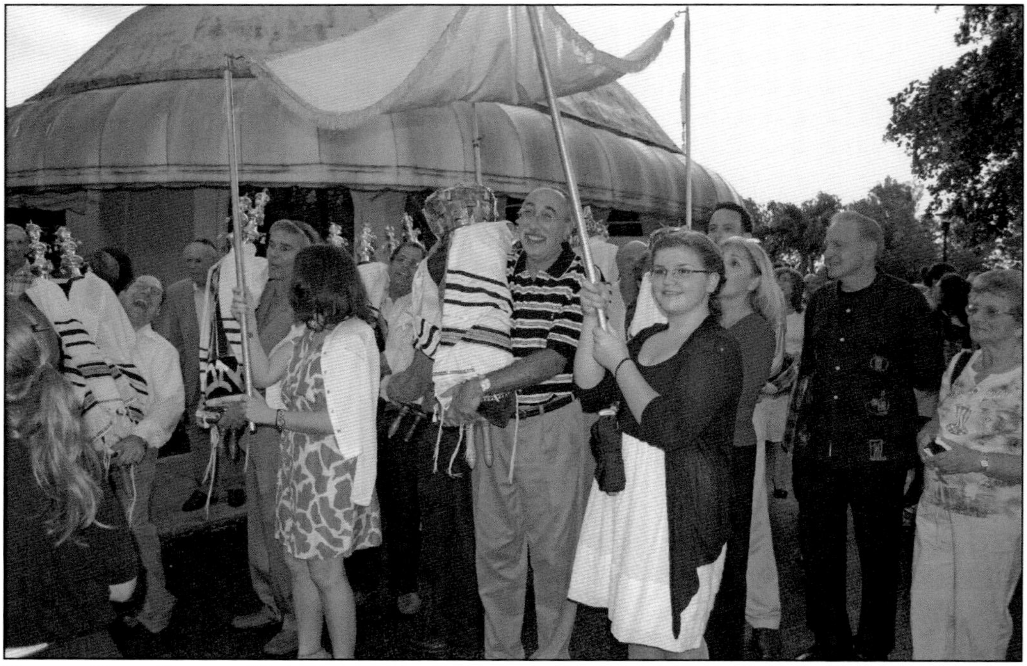

Temple Beth Torah. With the opening of the new building, the sacred Torahs must be moved from one home to another. This is a cause for great celebration. The members came to help move the Torahs with song, dance, and great joy. (Courtesy of Caryn DuBrow.)

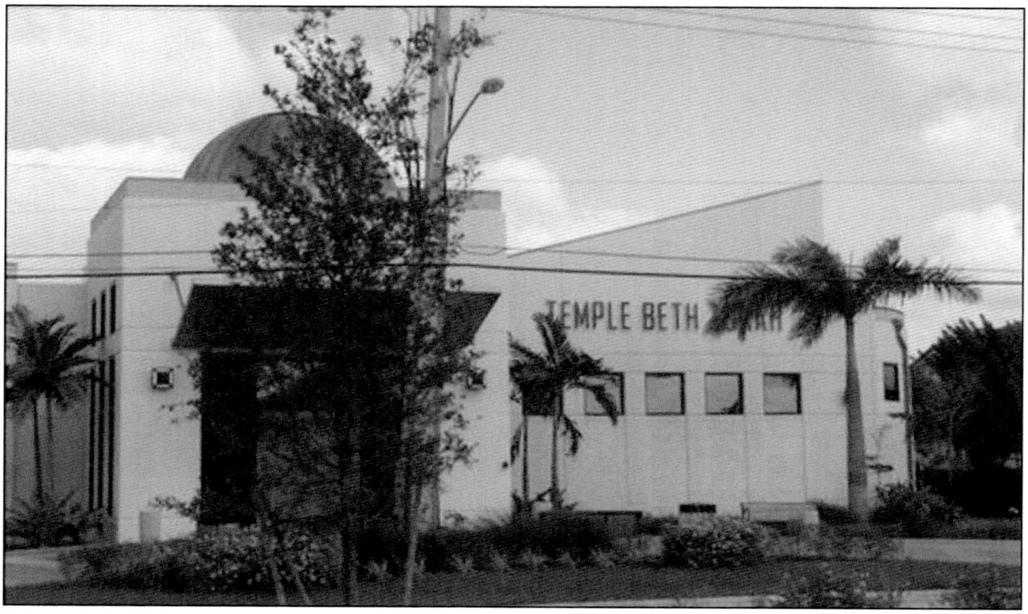

New Temple Building. The Conservative Synagogue, serving the community since 1972, moved into its new building on August 26, 2010. The building was erected just a short way from the original building, which has since been demolished. The temple's sanctuary was expanded, and programs—including a preschool, religious school, a Judaica Shop, library, and activities—make this an all-inclusive house of worship. (Courtesy of Rudy Hoffman.)

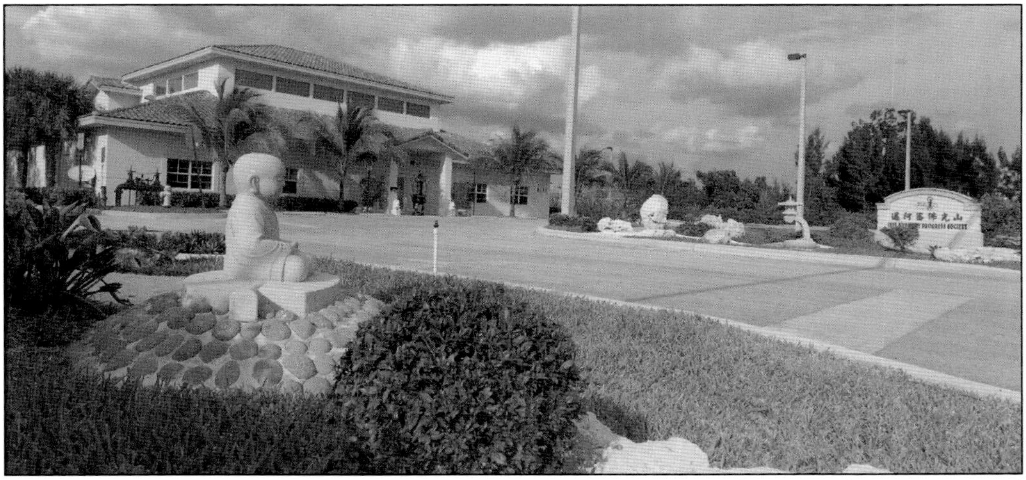

INTERNATIONAL BUDDHIST PROGRESS SOCIETY. After five years of planning, the International Buddhist Progress Society built a modern and multifunctional Temple in the City of Tamarac in 2003. Venerable Master Hsing Yun, the founder of Fo Guang Shan, presided over the grand opening ceremony. The Temple is located on 1.24 acres of land, with a main shrine, dining hall, multipurpose classrooms, a gift shop, and an outdoor Chan Garden. The temple serves as a place of worship and a full-service educational facility for the community. (Courtesy of the International Buddhist Progress Society Miami.)

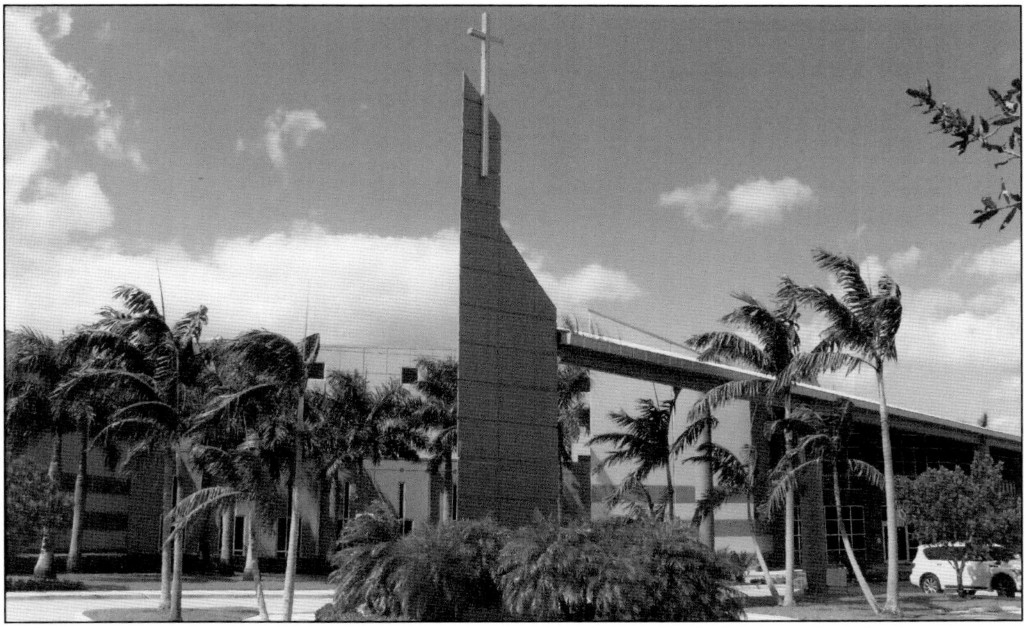

COMMUNITY CHRISTIAN CHURCH. A nondenominational Bible-believing church, Community Christian Church (CCC) serves and represents the diverse city of Tamarac. The growing church has enjoyed a positive relationship with residents and city leaders since even before opening its new building at Commercial Boulevard and Nob Hill Road in December 2007. The CCC places a premium on caring for people through Sunday services, almost daily programming (including a Spanish and deaf ministry), and events such as Community Impact. (Courtesy of John Chace, chairman of the elders, Community Christian Church.)

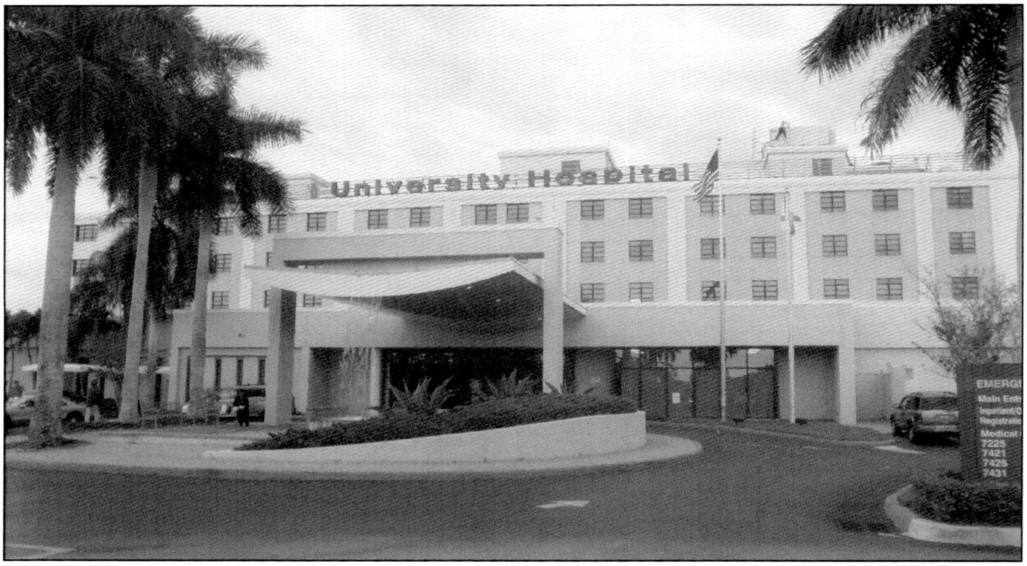

University Hospital. Under the guidance of Dr. Thomas Frist, Founder of HCA, University Hospital opened its doors on August 4, 1974, with 130 employees. Since then, the hospital has grown to include medical offices and a pavilion for behavioral health services. In 2012, it was staffed by approximately 411 physicians and more than 700 employees. (Courtesy of Marian Daly.)

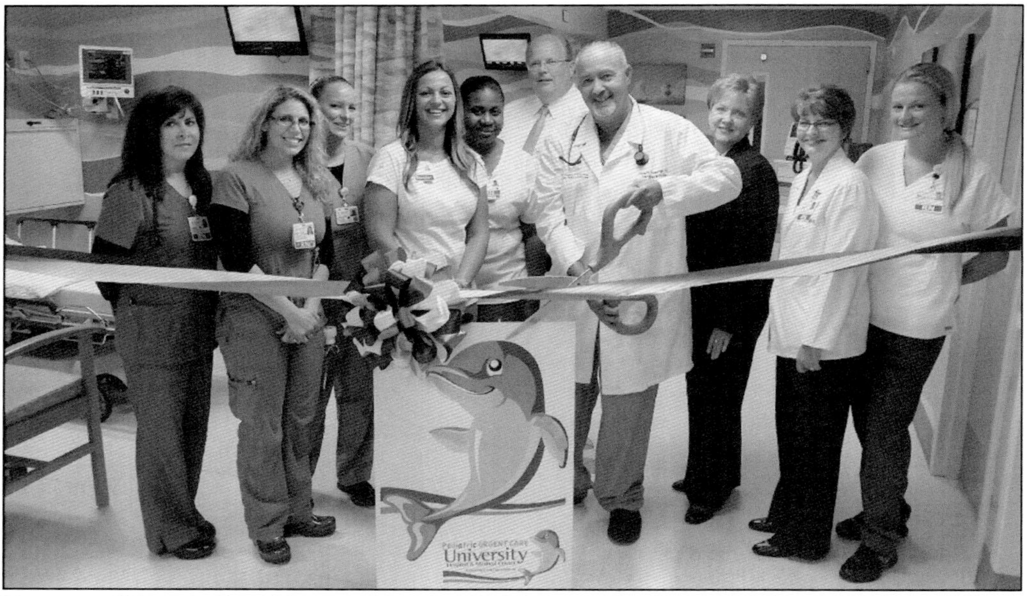

Pediatric Urgent Care Ribbon Cutting. Celebrating the opening of the new Pediatric Urgent Care area in August 2012 at University Hospital and Medical Center are, from left to right, Leslie Bates, RN; Heather Epstein, RN; Melanie Evans, paramedic; Simone Jordan, RN; Floda Louisdor, RN; Mark Rader, chief executive officer; Marianne Schram, University Hospital and Medical Center board trustee and member of Tamarac Chamber of Commerce; Sandra Emeott, chief nursing officer, and Nicole Miller, clinical coordinator. Cutting the ribbon is Dr. Kenneth Greenberg, MD. (Courtesy of University Hospital.)

Seven

City Celebrations

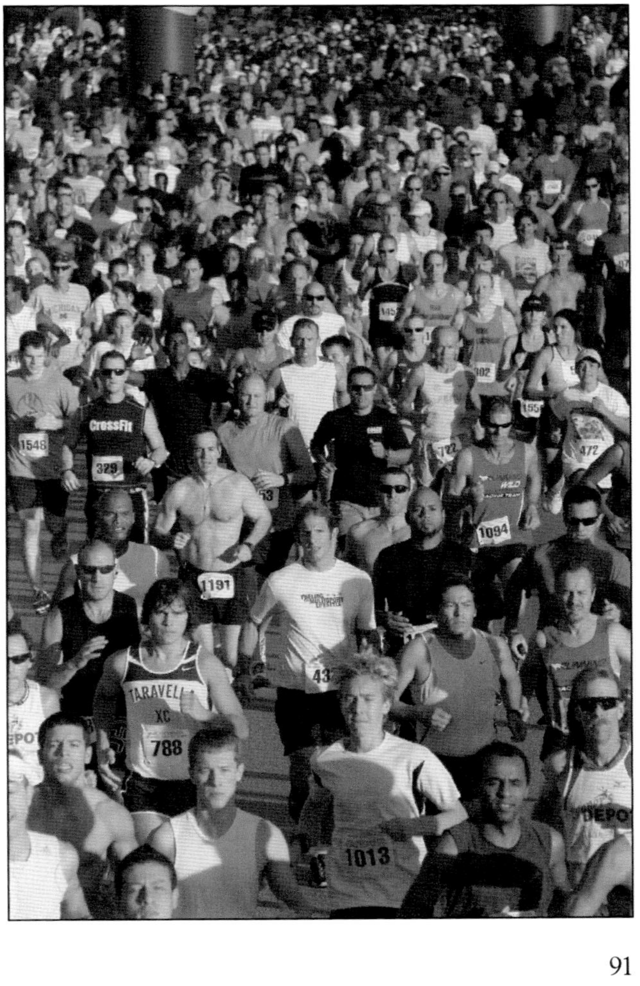

Tamarac Turkey Trot. Tamarac celebrates the start of the holiday season with its annual signature event, the Turkey Trot 5K Run. The race attracts runners of all skill levels, ranging in age from 12 and under to over 80 years old, all from across South Florida. The event features music, complimentary food and refreshments for the participants, and the race awards ceremony. The 2012 race held on Thanksgiving Day marked the city's 32nd annual 5K run. The event has grown from approximately 400 racers in 1982 to approximately 1,600 runners in 2011. The city provides fluid stations, which are in contact with a medical team on call should runners need assistance. (Courtesy of the City of Tamarac.)

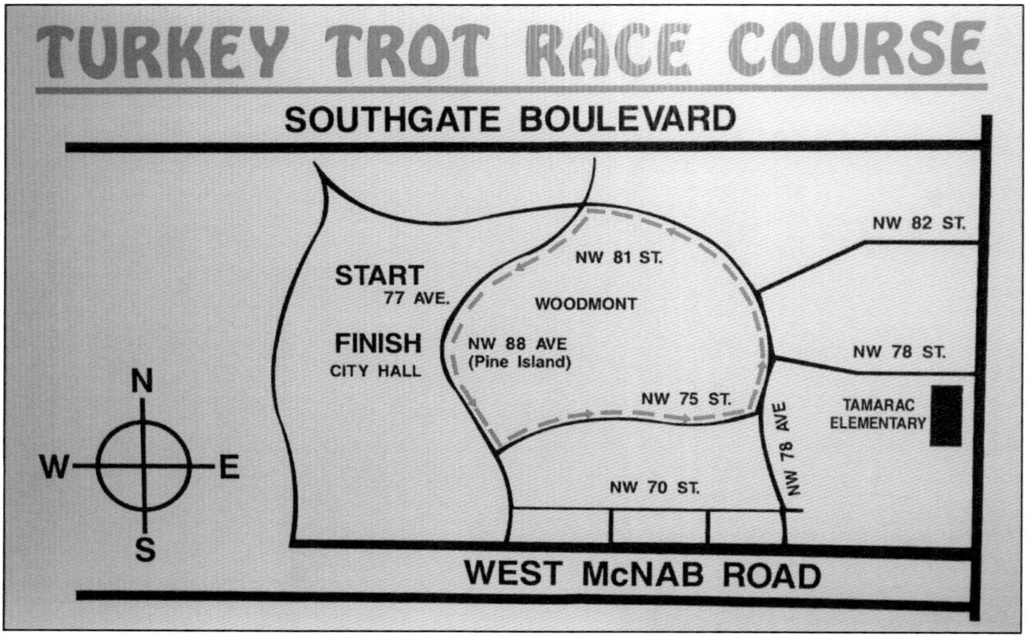

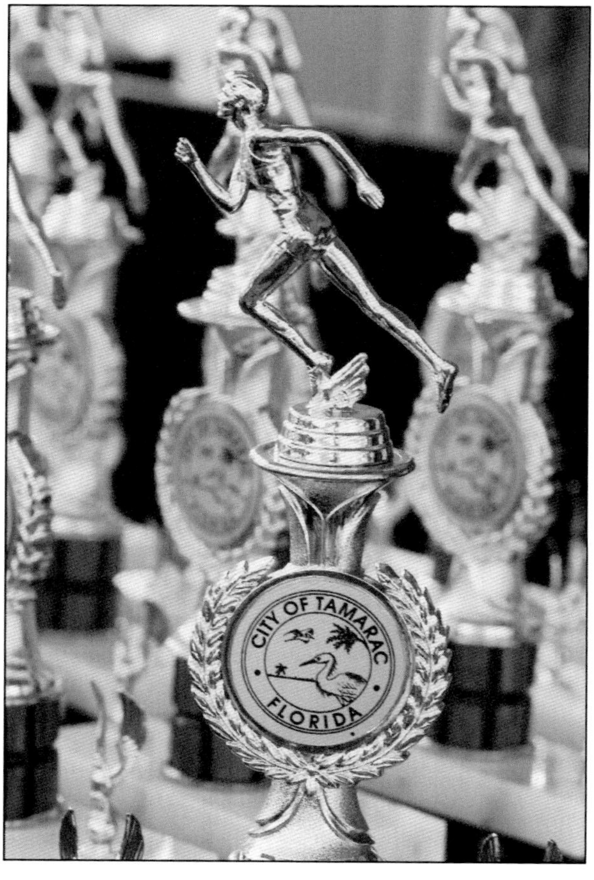

The Course. The Turkey Trot Race is a USA Track & Field (USATF)–certified, 5K (3.1-mile) course that is flat and fast with many corners through the Woodmont neighborhood of Tamarac. The race starts at city hall on Pine Island Road, continues east on Seventy-fifth Street, then north on Eightieth Street, loops back to Pine Island Road, then heads south to the finish line. (Courtesy of the City of Tamarac.)

Turkey Trot Awards. Tamarac's Turkey Trot awards are given to the first three overall finishers based on gun time, with trophies presented to first-place age group winners and medals to second- and third-place age group winners based on net time. The race is on a ChronoTrack timing system. (Courtesy of the City of Tamarac.)

Patriotism. Two children wave the American flag while watching the Veterans Day parade. (Courtesy of the City of Tamarac.)

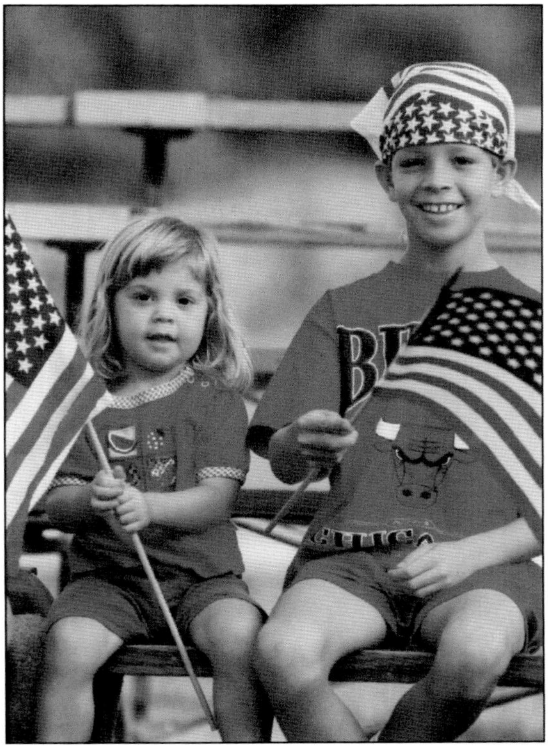

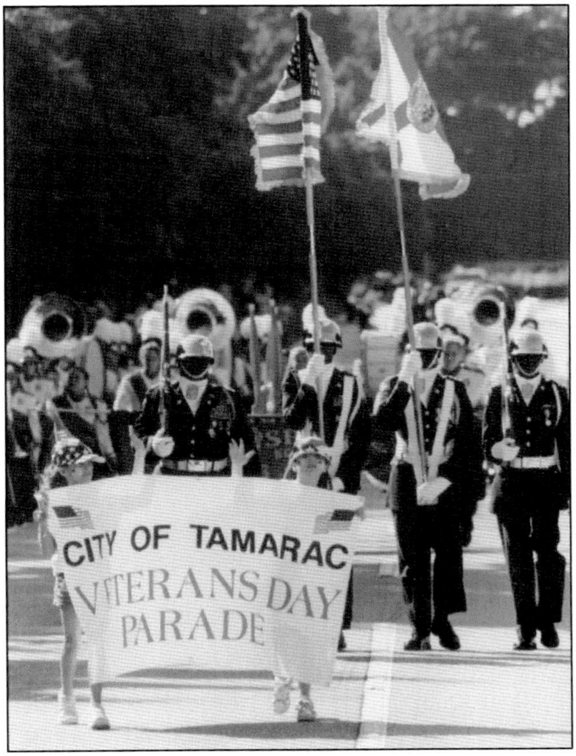

Veterans Day Parade. The city of Tamarac honors its veterans with an annual Veterans Day ceremony held at Veterans' Memorial Park. Celebratory parades ran between 1999 and 2008. The ceremony features the presentation of colors, music by local schools, and guest speakers. (Courtesy of the City of Tamarac.)

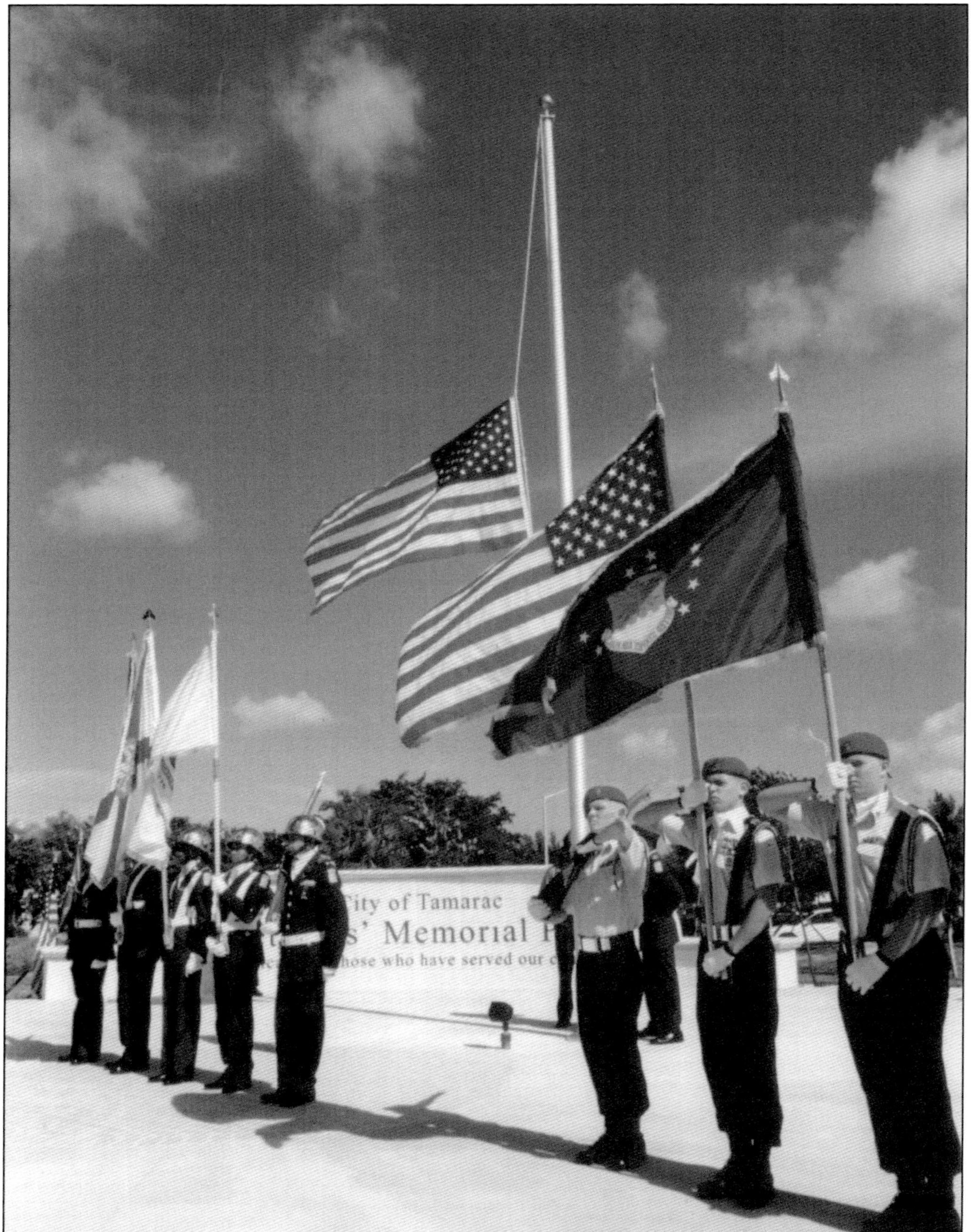

Color Guard Salutes Veterans. To promote public awareness and patriotism, the city code provides a Veterans Affairs Committee. The committee consists of at least one member from the Disabled American Veterans (DAV), American Legion, Jewish War Veterans of the USA, AM Vets, Military Order of the Purple Heart, American Ex-Prisoners of War, and Marine Corps League. The committee helps veterans understand their rights, benefits, and any other special needs. (Courtesy of the City of Tamarac.)

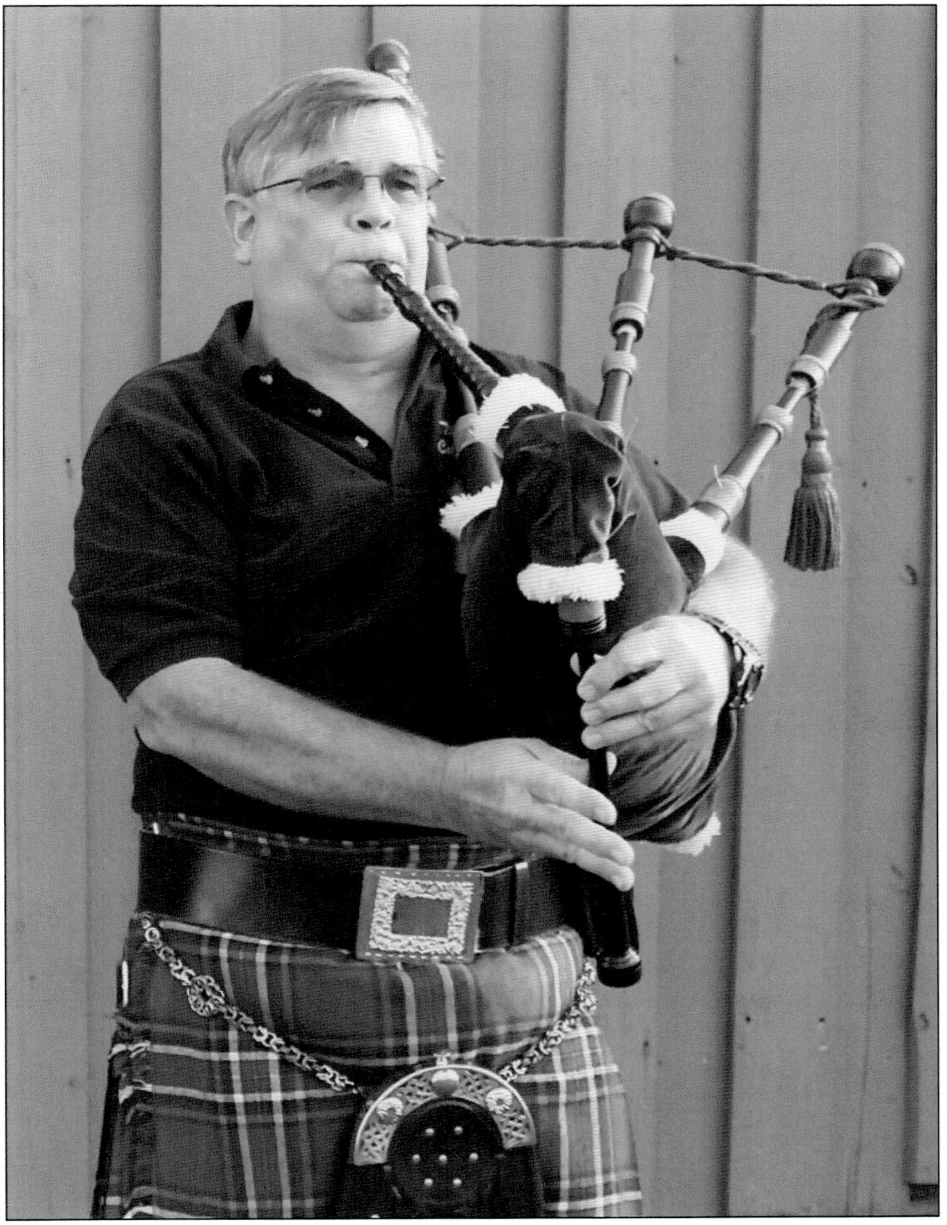

Paul Kinney. A 30-year-long career as a firefighter at Tamarac Fire Department, Kinney's duties included EMT and driver engineer and performing maintenance of fire and rescue trucks. When retirement came, he decided to invest in a hobby that would allow him to continue serving the community. Finding the bagpipe, he has played in numerous bands, traveled far and near, and met some pretty amazing people along his journey. He has actively served the Tamarac community after retirement, seeking opportunities to play the bagpipe for his fellow civil workers. He was humbled and honored the first time he was asked to play for the Memorial and Veterans Services at Tamarac Veterans' Memorial Park. Since then, they always have an accompaniment of a bagpipe to honor those fallen and serving. Quoting Paul Kinney, "Serving other people is very important, and giving back to your community through your passion is one way to do just that." (Courtesy of Paul Kinney.)

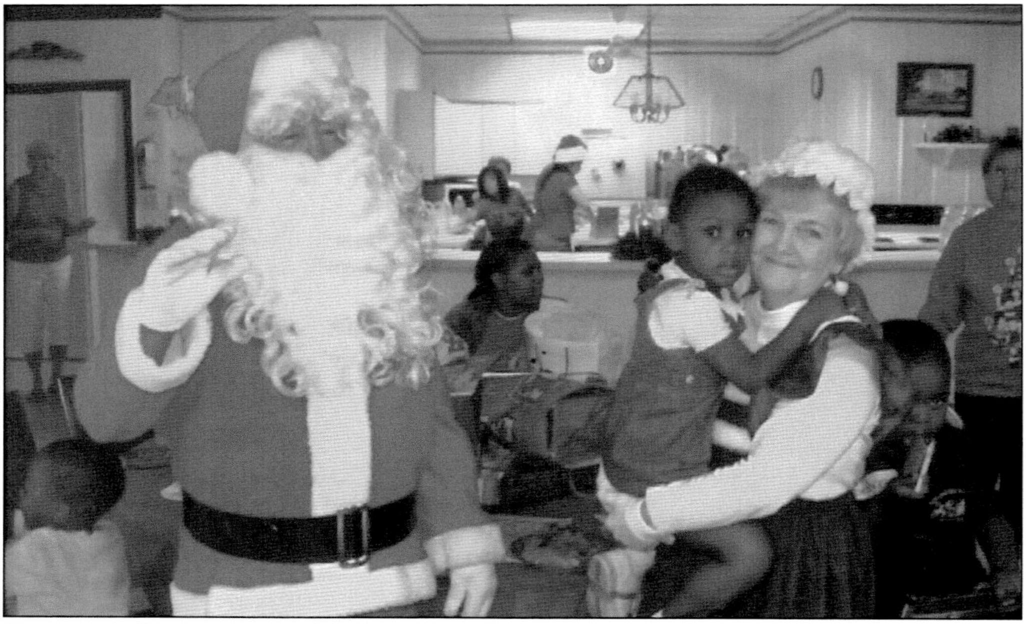

Children's Christmas Party. The Mainlands 3 Women's Auxiliary gave a Christmas party for 52 children from day care centers affiliated with Family Central. Residents picked a child's name and purchased a gift for that child. At the party, Santa (Neil Flynn) and Mrs. Claus (Anne Flynn) called children's names to come and get their gifts. (Courtesy of Rea Mills.)

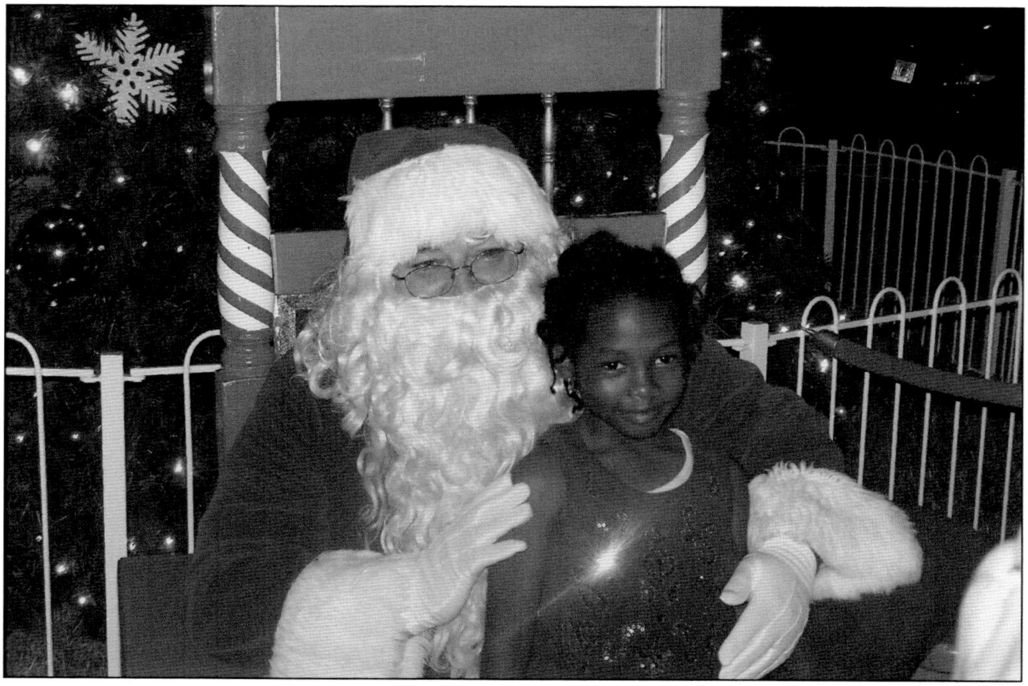

Lighting Ceremony. Every year, at the lighting ceremony held at the community center, children anxiously await their turn to meet with Santa and to tell him their hopes and dreams for holiday gifts. (Courtesy of the City of Tamarac.)

SEASON'S GREETINGS. Each year, the city of Tamarac erects a Christmas tree and Chanukah Menorah to brighten up the evenings with their colorful bright lights. (Courtesy of the City of Tamarac.)

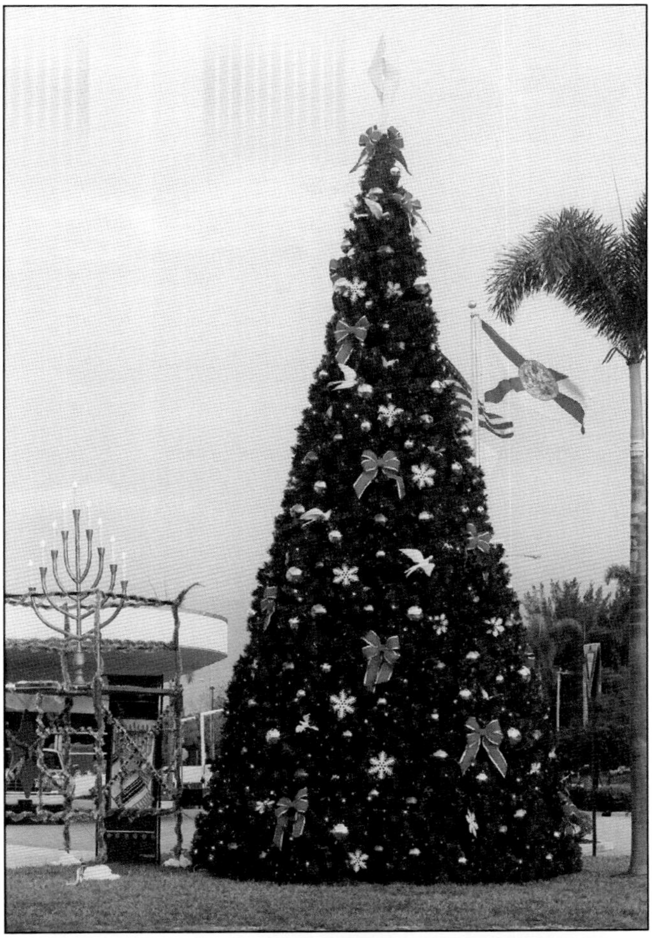

BEAUTIFUL VOICES. To make the season complete, children sing holiday songs during the seasonal celebration each year as the holiday lights are illuminated. Many children sing and sign their songs. (Courtesy of the City of Tamarac.)

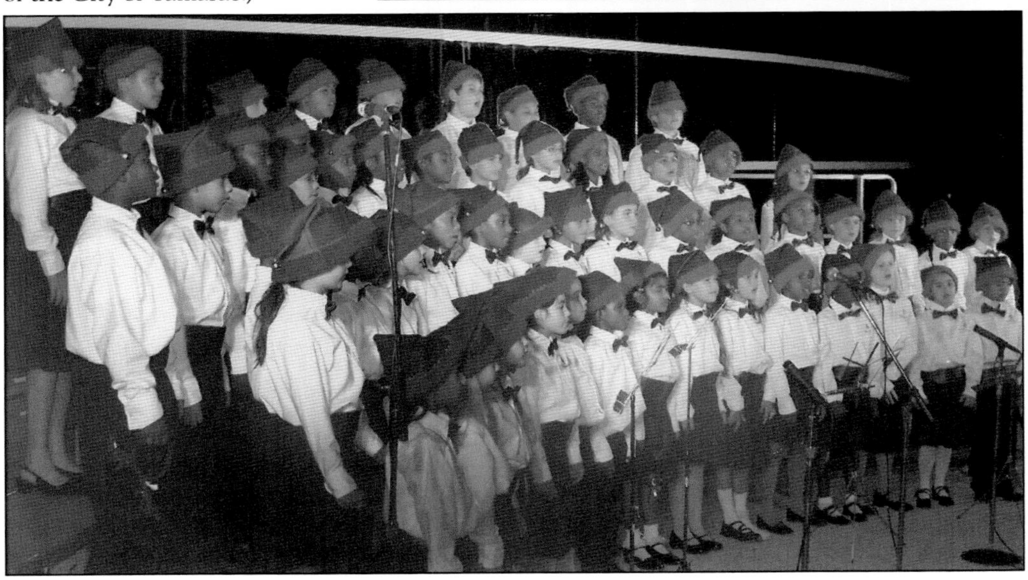

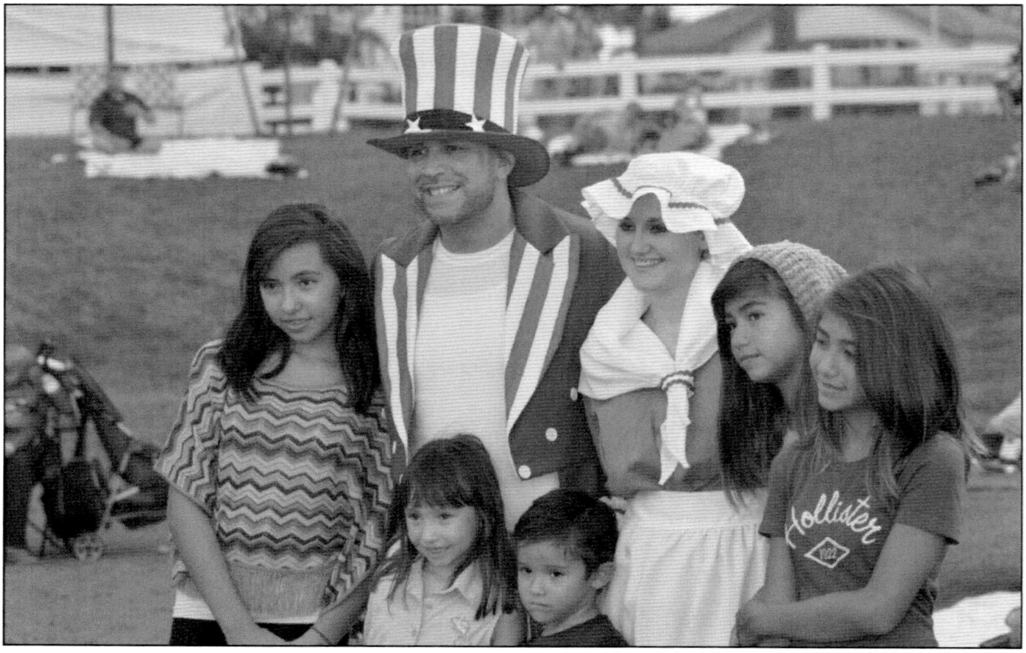

All-American Celebration. Tamarac's annual Fourth of July All-American Celebration is held at the sports complex. The day's festivities include an outdoor concert, arts and crafts booths, rides, games, and dancing, and it ends with a spectacular pyrotechnical fireworks display. (Both, courtesy of the City of Tamarac.)

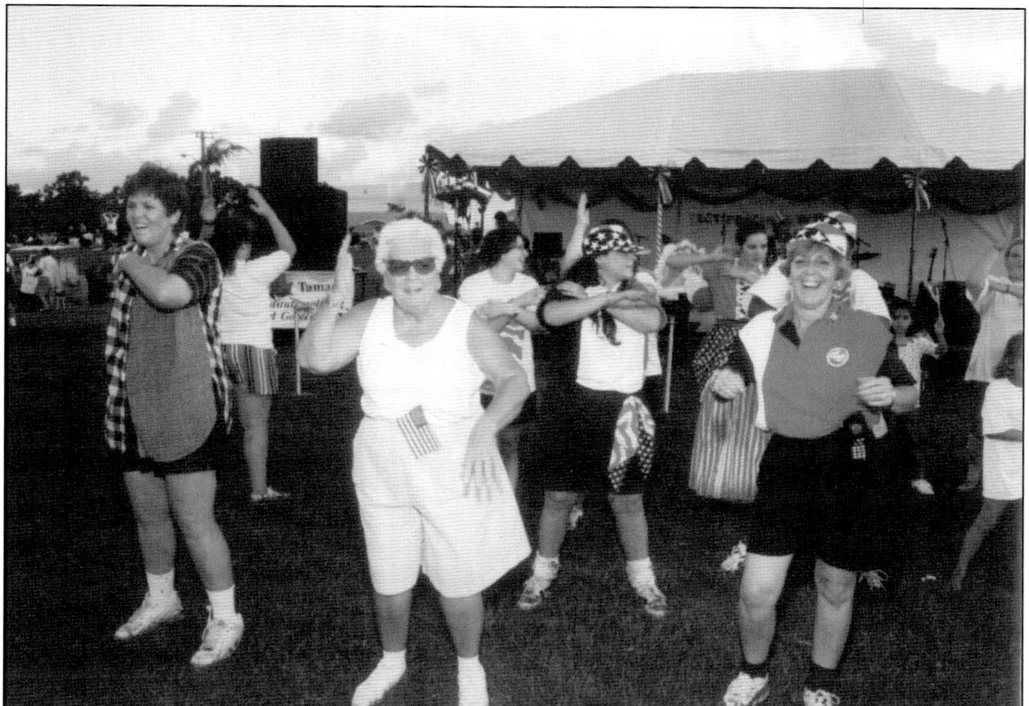

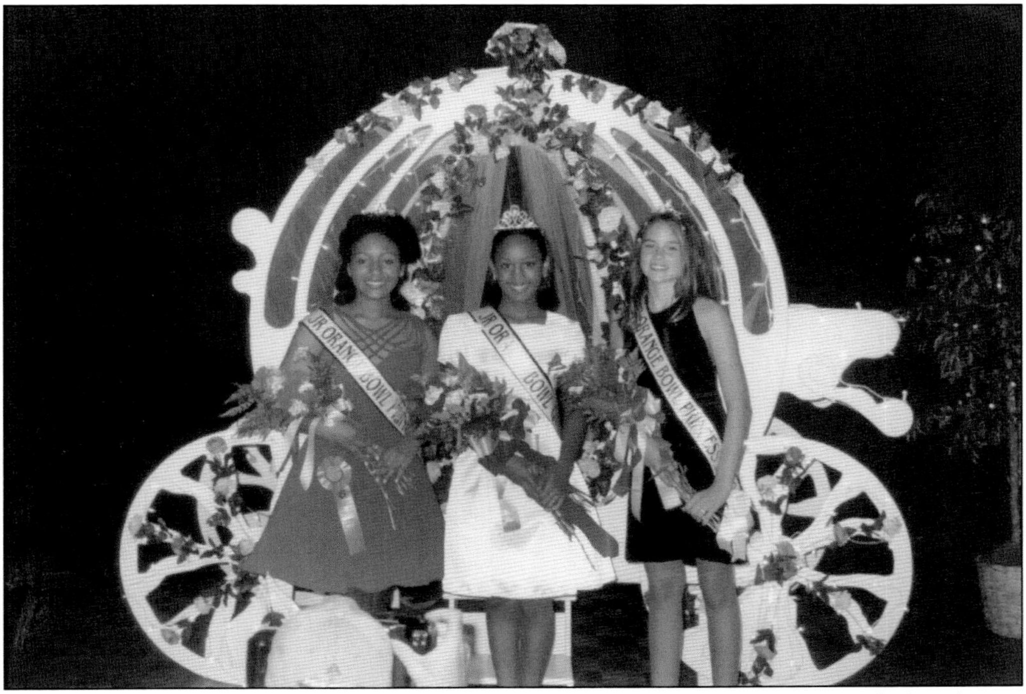

TAMARAC JUNIOR ORANGE BOWL COURT. College football's Orange Bowl festivities include the selection of a Junior Orange Bowl Queen and her princesses. The 2002 Tamarac Court is pictured here; they are chosen based on personality, poise, and community dedication. (Courtesy of the City of Tamarac.)

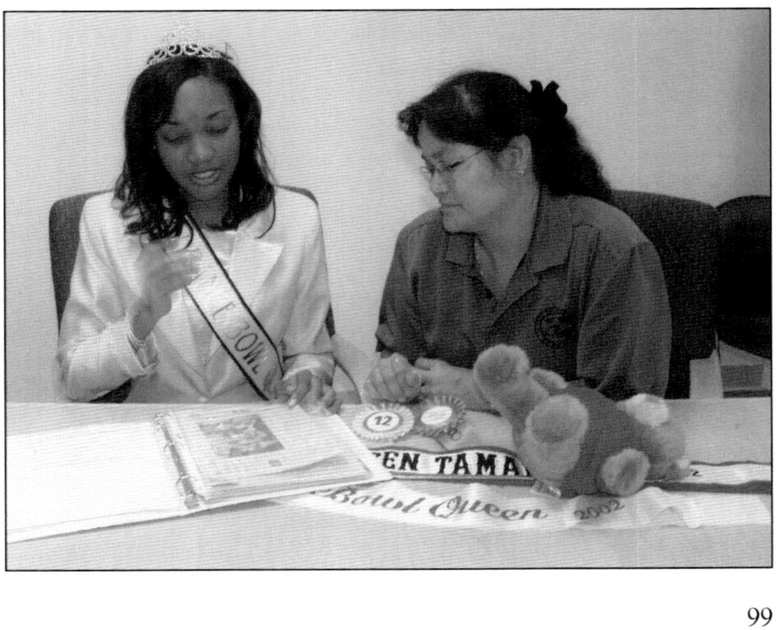

ORANGE BOWL CONTESTANT. Special Events manager Charlene Nevadomski gives tips and advise to an Orange Bowl Queen contestant in Tamarac. (Courtesy of the City of Tamarac.)

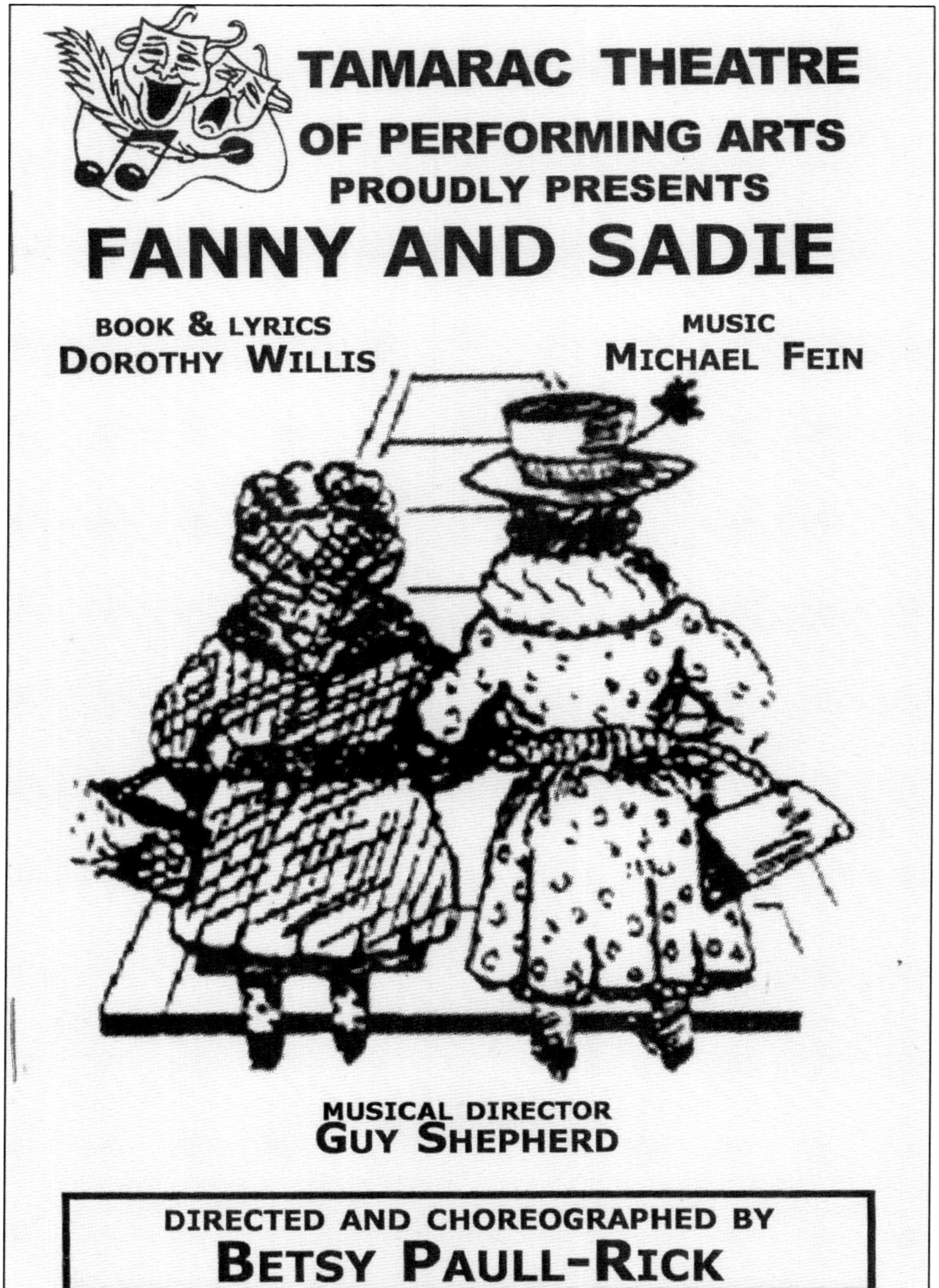

TAMARAC THEATRE OF THE PERFORMING ARTS. The production *Fanny and Sadie* was written by theater founder Dorothy Willis. The Tamarac Theatre of the Performing Arts has had a presence in Broward County for more than 32 years and is considered to be one of the foremost small theater companies in South Florida. Located at 7143 Pine Island Road, the theater provides an intimate setting to enjoy plays, musicals, concerts, and workshops. (Courtesy of the Tamarac Theatre of the Performing Arts.)

Eight

City Public Art

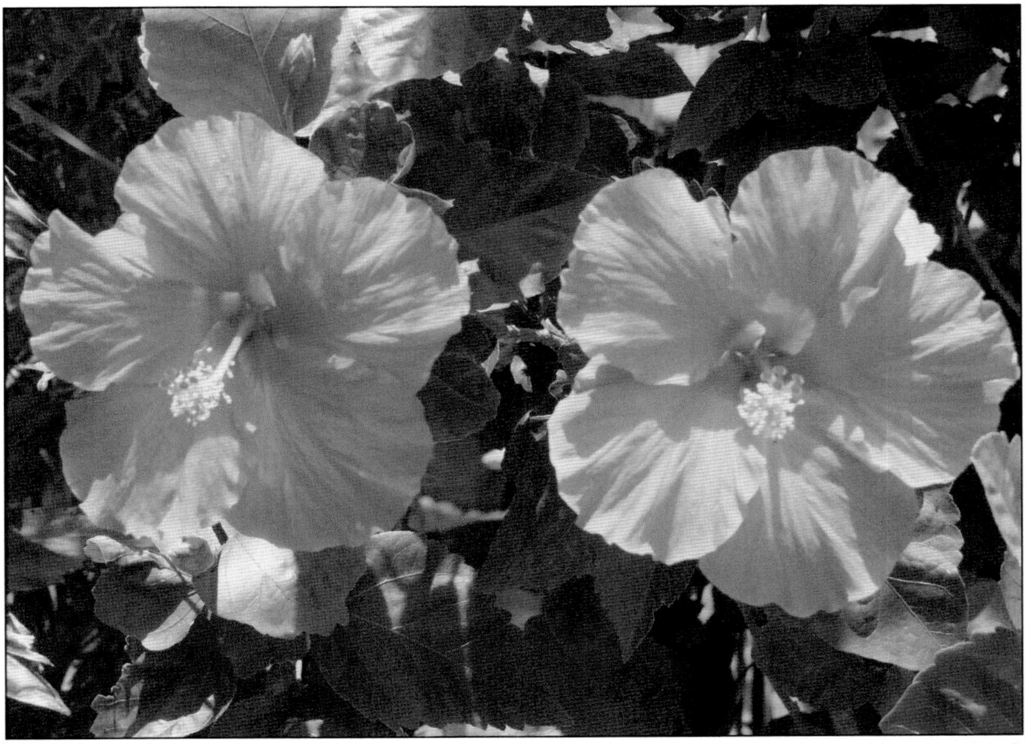

The City Beautiful. Tamarac's Public Art Program is funded through the Public Art Fund, which was established with the passage of the Public Art Ordinance. The ordinance requires that one percent of the construction value of new projects or improvements be set aside for public art. The program is committed to beautifying the city, commemorating city history, and enhancing cultural opportunities in the city through art. (Courtesy of Rudy Hoffmann.)

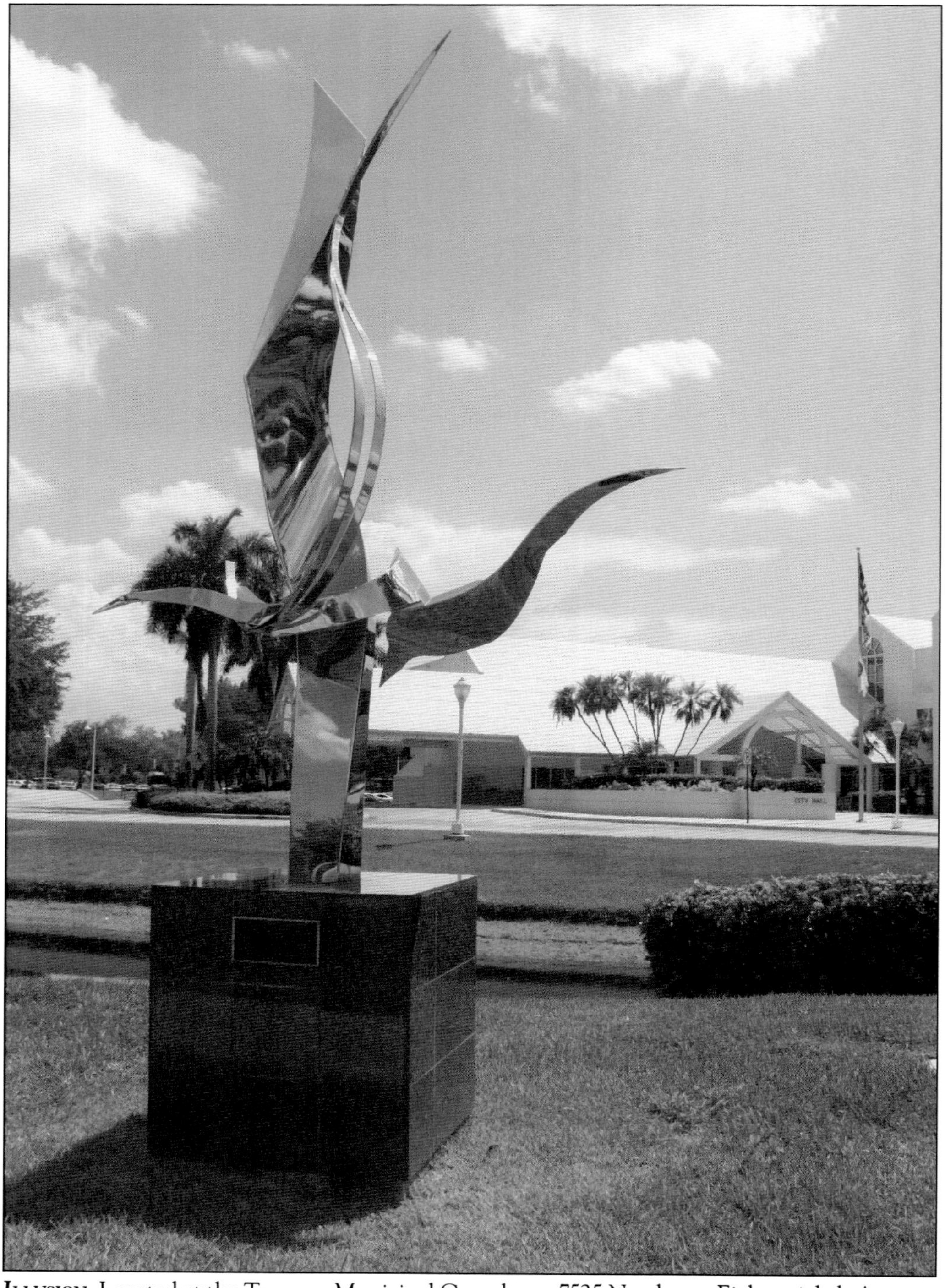

ILLUSION. Located at the Tamarac Municipal Complex at 7525 Northwest Eighty-eighth Avenue, *Illusion* by Leonardo Nierman is a modern, stainless-steel sculpture donated by Tamarac residents Paul Yelin and Sally Robbins to bring peace, beauty, and diversion to the city. (Courtesy of the City of Tamarac.)

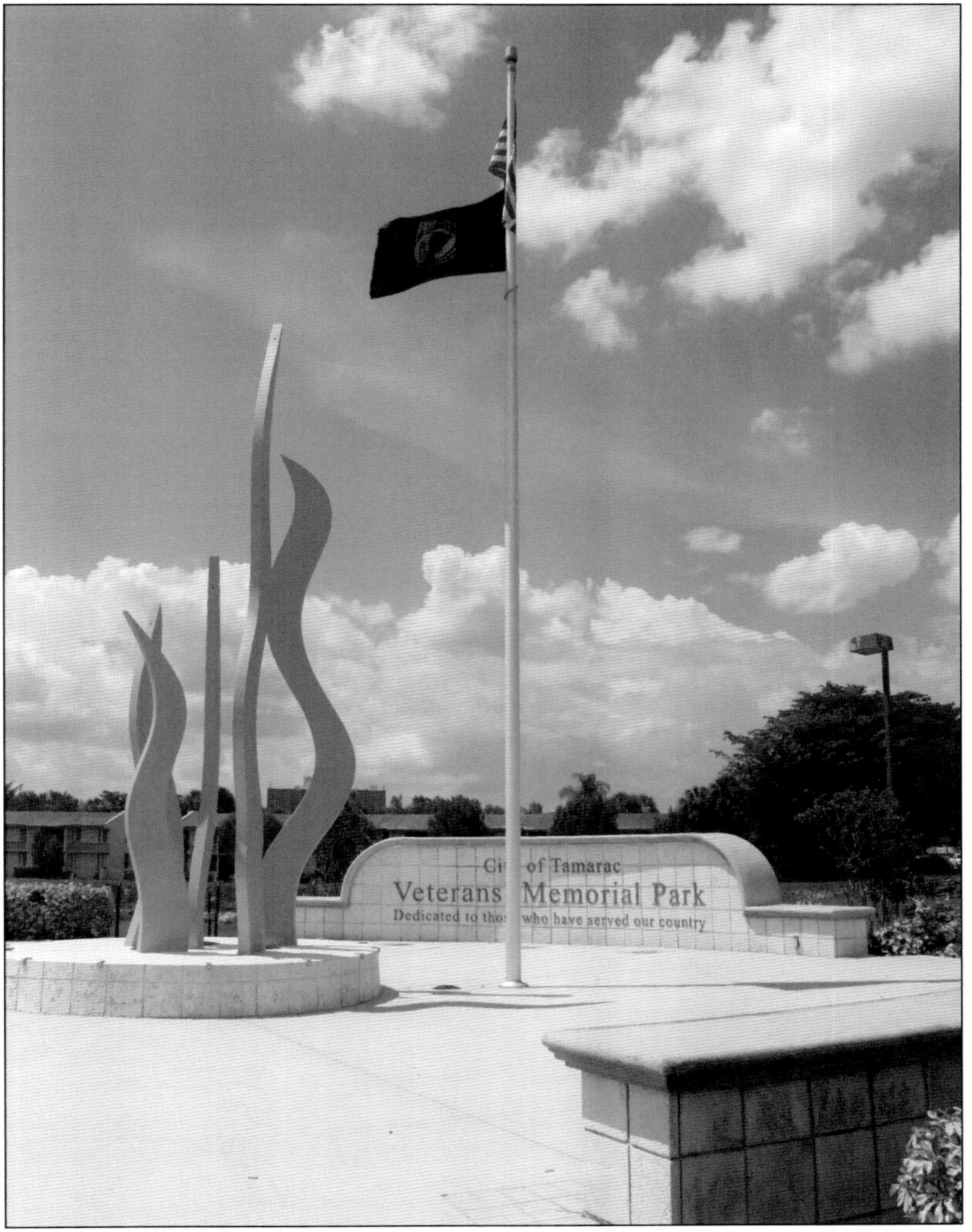

In the Spirit of Peace. Located at Veterans' Memorial Park (7825 Southgate Boulevard), *In the Spirit of Peace* by Beth Ravitz symbolizes an everlasting flame. Each of its five abstract branches represents a branch of the country's armed services. Ranging in height from 22 feet, 15 feet, 12 feet, and 11 feet, and 9 feet wide by 6 inches deep, the sculpture is silver during the day but transforms into a glowing flame by night. To achieve this effect, the sculpture has three lights embedded in its base with colored lenses and is fabricated from powder-coated aluminum. (Courtesy of the City of Tamarac.)

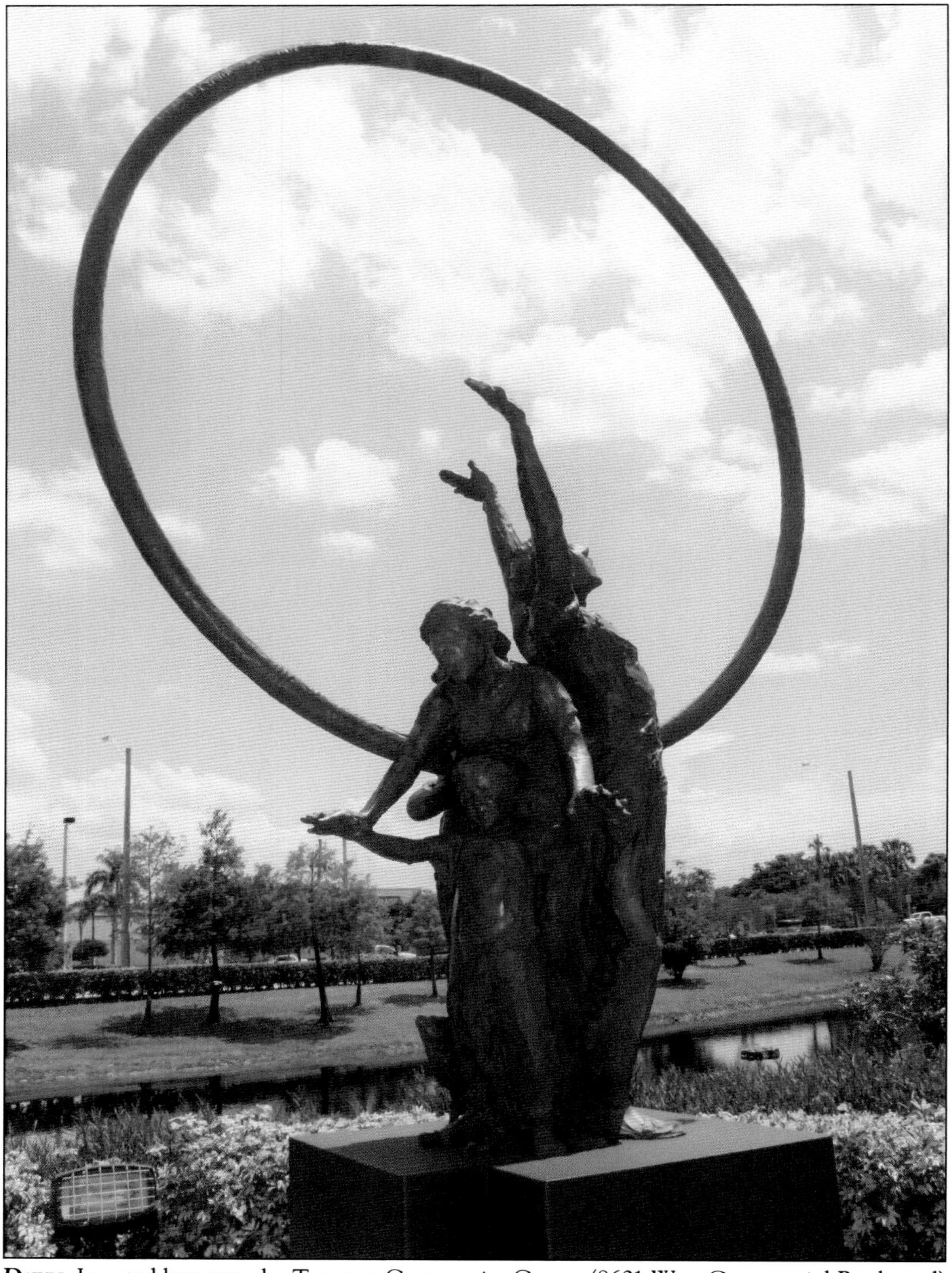

DAWN. Located between the Tamarac Community Center (8601 West Commercial Boulevard) and the Tamarac Public Library (8701 West Commercial Boulevard), *Dawn* by Jane DeDecker is designed to celebrate the community as it rises to greet the day. *Dawn* depicts four figures with arms stretched toward the sky. The silhouette of the figures represents reeds and cattails flowing in the breeze. (Courtesy of the City of Tamarac.)

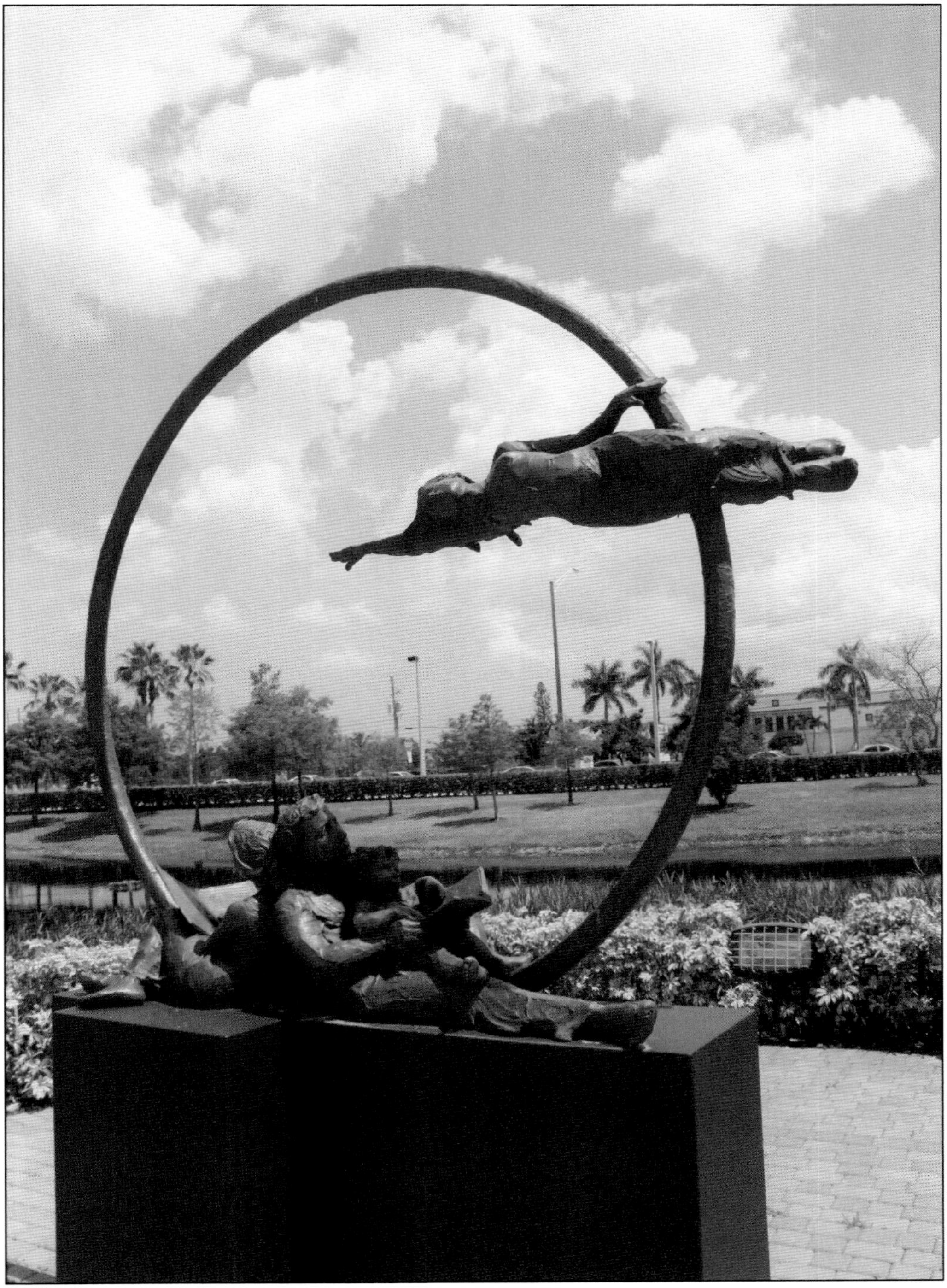

Dusk. Also located between the Tamarac Community Center and the Tamarac Public Library, *Dusk* by Jane DeDecker is designed to celebrate the community as it retires for the evening. *Dusk* shows four figures nestled together. The silhouette of the figures evokes a tree line at sunset. (Courtesy of the City of Tamarac.)

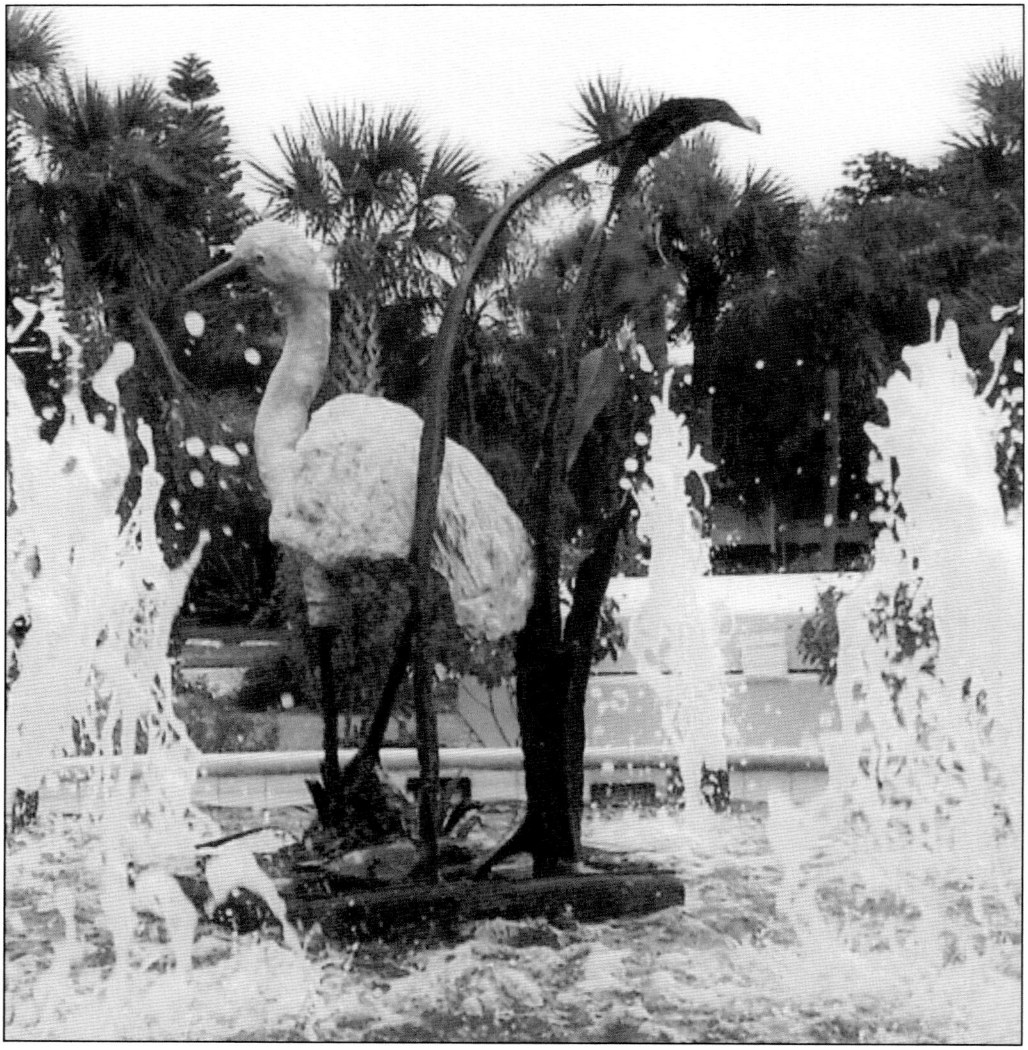

EGRETTA THULA (SNOWY EGRET). Located at Tamarac Commons Park (McNab and Pine Island Roads), *Egretta Thula* by George Gadson reminds the community of the importance of preserving wildlife and the natural environment. The idea for the design was developed through a community participation process that solicited feedback from members of the business community, residents, and children. The work was made through the lost-wax process for bronze casting. Color variation in the work was achieved by applying acid to the bronze surface at varying temperatures. The sculpture weighs approximately 600 pounds. (Courtesy of the City of Tamarac.)

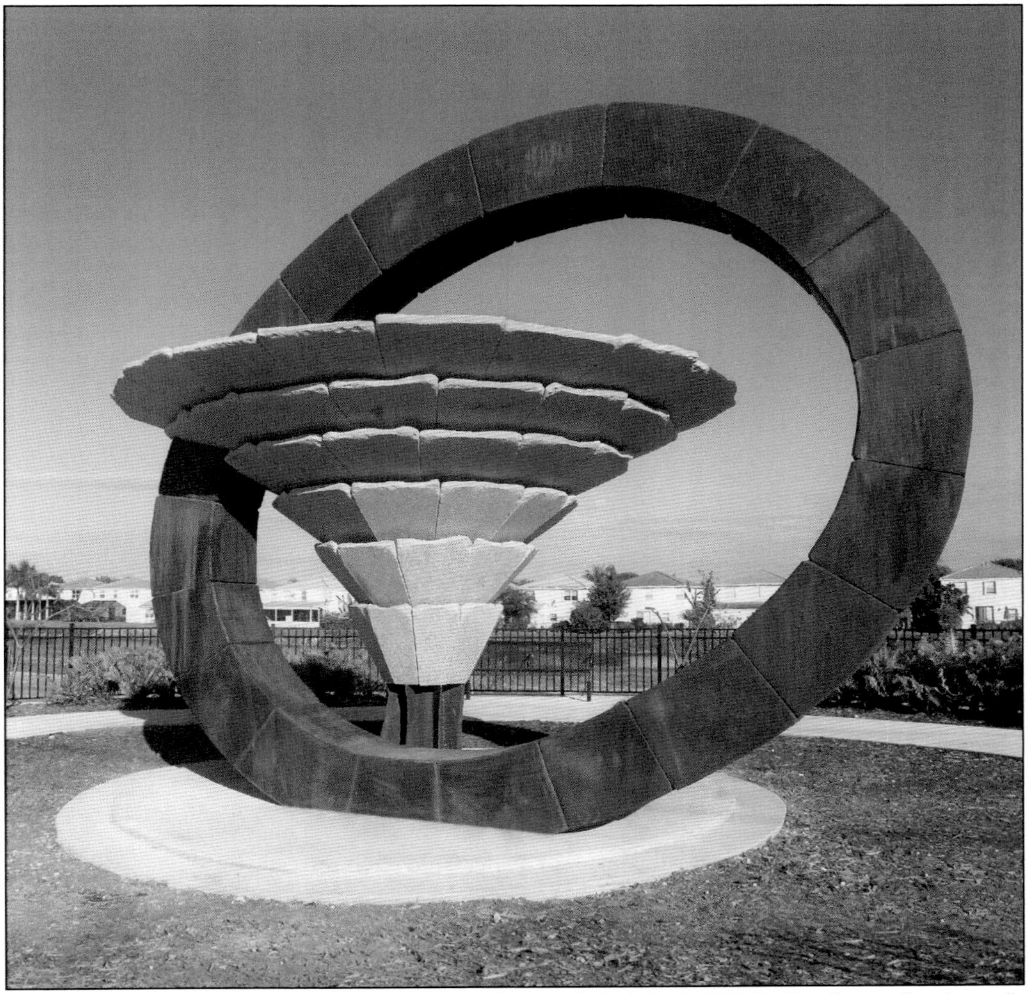

UNDER THE SHADOW OF A BIG TREE. Located at Tephford Park (10003 Southgate Boulevard), *Under the Shadow of a Big Tree* by Ilan Averbuch reaches out to create harmony with its immediate environment. Tephford Park is dedicated to Tamarac's fallen police officer, Brian Tephford, who was killed in the line of duty, and the sculpture represents the Israeli tradition of planting a tree after the death of an individual. At the heart of the sculptural environment is an elliptical form, made of modular units of weathering steel (Cor-ten), standing on its edge as if rolling or pulling away. Intersecting the large elliptical frame is a tree form made of flat granite stones, rising to approximately two-thirds the height of the ellipse. The tree has a wide canopy built like an inverted roof, growing out of a heavy-set and slightly leaning weathering-steel trunk. The elliptical ring is 14 feet high, 17 feet wide, and 1.5 feet deep. The tree is 10 feet high, 14 feet wide, and 14 feet deep. The sculpture frames the canal, the park, and surrounding buildings. (Courtesy of the City of Tamarac.)

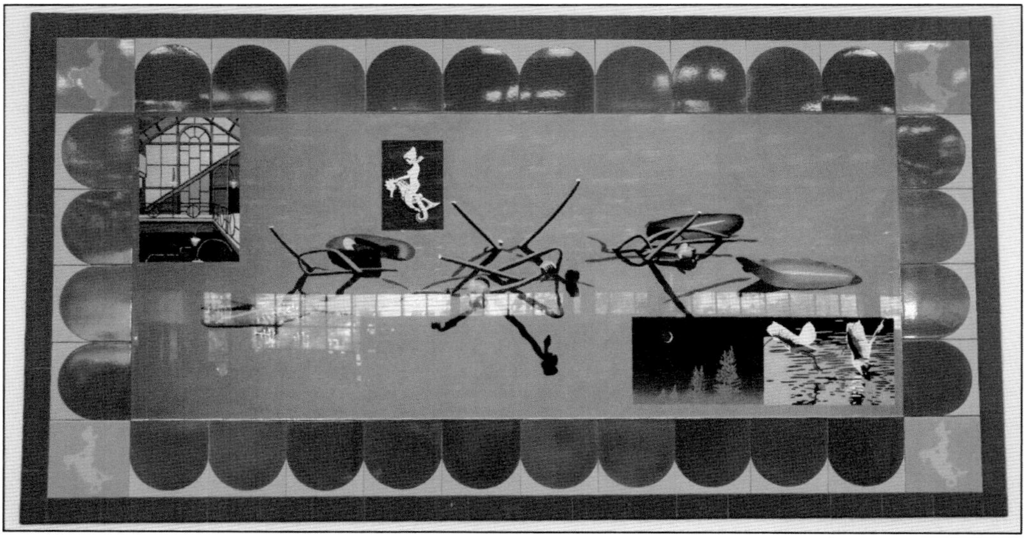

Moment in Tamarac: From Whence We Come. This mural by Raymond Olivero is located at Tamarac Community Library. It shows scenes from the city's past such as the park adjacent to the city's first housing development, the sea horse and mermaid at the entryway of an early Tamarac residential community, and the white bird on the city's second seal. The archway motif is meant to echo a locally popular architectural detail seen throughout Tamarac, including city hall. (Courtesy of the Tamarac Historical Society.)

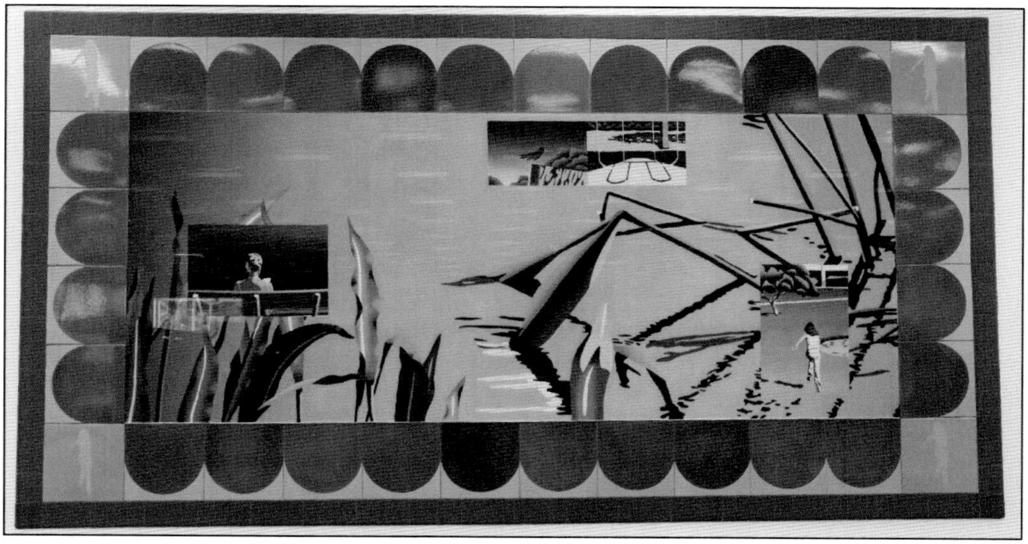

Moment in Tamarac: To Whence We Go. This mural by Raymond Olivero is located at Tamarac Community Library. It features scenes that symbolize the future of Tamarac such as city hall, the new moon, and a child running. (Courtesy of the Tamarac Historical Society.)

Nine

City Pioneers

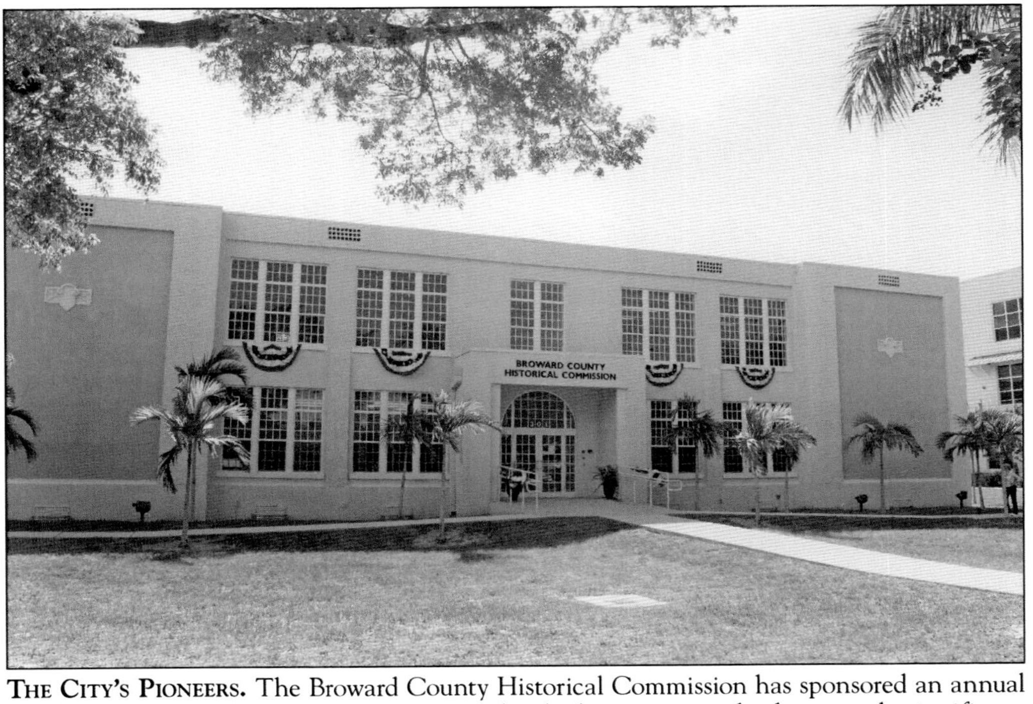

The City's Pioneers. The Broward County Historical Commission has sponsored an annual event since 1973. This event recognizes individuals or groups who have made significant contributions to preservation and education, while celebrating the county's rich history and the experiences that give each Broward city its unique character. The legacy of the county's early pioneers can serve as an inspiration to successive generations. (Courtesy of the Broward County Historical Commission.)

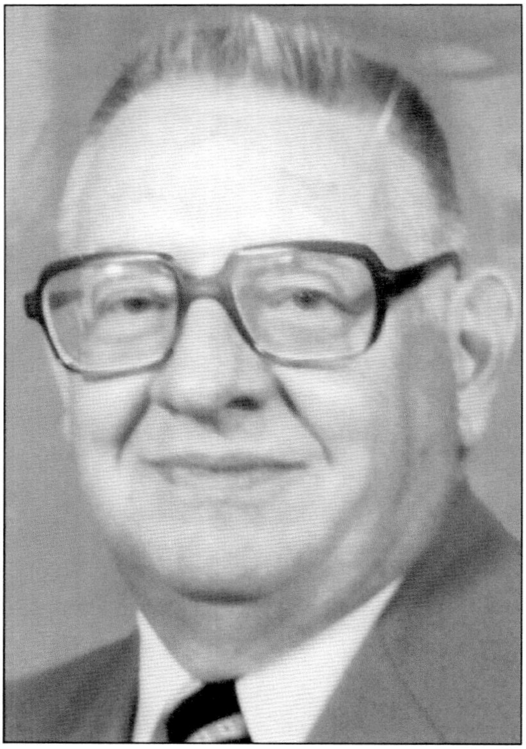

Walter W. Falck, 1998. Five years after moving to Florida, Walter Falck became a member of the Tamarac City Council in 1975 and was named mayor on March 12, 1976. Falck led the city through some of its worst growing pains, as the population grew from about 5,000 to more than 32,000 before he lost his 1984 reelection campaign. After leaving the mayor's office, he was appointed executive director of the Broward League of Cities, where he served for 15 years. He was also a member of the National Defense Executive Reserve until December 31, 1997. The Walter W. Falck Citizenship Award was established in his honor, to be presented to three public high school seniors in Broward County who exhibited outstanding citizenship. Mayor Falck was named Broward County Senior Citizen of the Year in 1987 and was inducted into the senior hall of fame in 1988. (Courtesy of the City of Tamarac.)

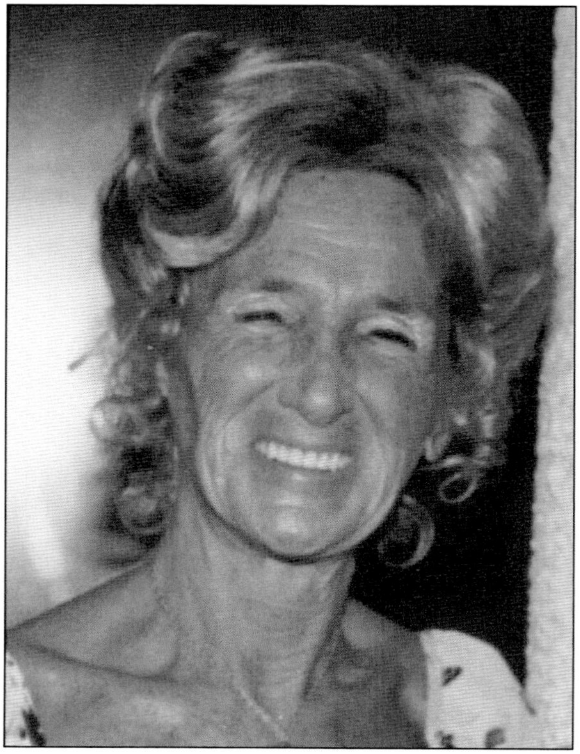

Helen Sobel, 2000. Helen Sobel moved to Tamarac from Brooklyn in 1970. The city had 5,000 residents at the time, and she "loved the rural life." Helen became active in city hall. Recognizing the need to help senior citizens who could not drive to doctor's appointments or the market, she started a volunteer group of about 50 drivers with their own cars. Eventually, this developed into Tamarac Social Services. Helen was a tireless volunteer for almost 30 years, supervising the city's social services department as volunteer director of the board. Her job was to find help for the sick, needy, and disabled of all ages. In addition, she delivered food and other necessities to shut-ins and helped establish the library system for Broward County. In 1993, the Tamarac chapter of the American Association of Retired Persons honored Helen Sobel as its "Woman of the Year." (Courtesy of the City of Tamarac.)

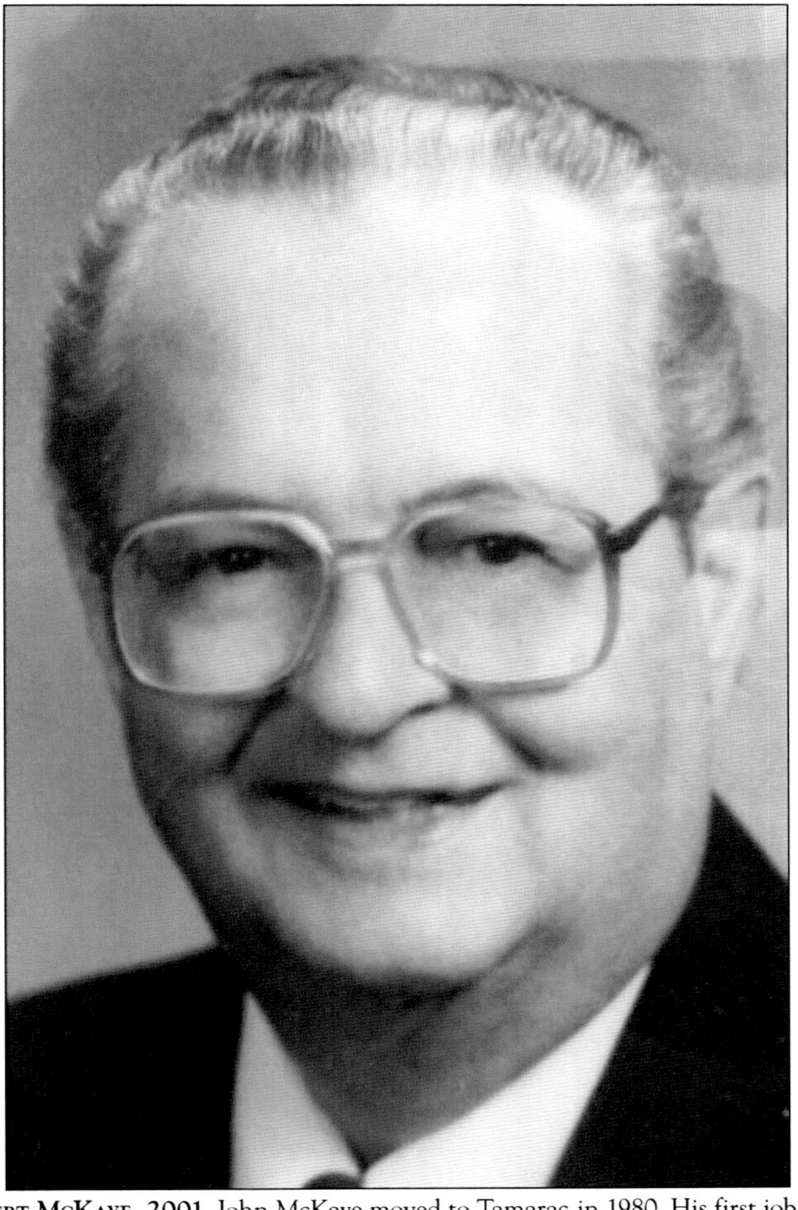

JOHN ELBERT MCKAYE, 2001. John McKaye moved to Tamarac in 1980. His first job in Florida was manager and instructor of food services at Miami Dade Community College North Campus. When the commute became too much, he switched positions to director of food for six retirement homes and later started a travel agency with his brother. McKaye became involved in civic affairs and served two terms as president of the homeowners' association for the Boulevards of Tamarac Lakes. An associate of Walter Flack, he became a city commissioner and later a Broward County commissioner. He ran for office and served a full term from 1996 to 1999. He subsequently sat on the Executive Airport Advisory Board. McKaye always marveled about how well the neighborhoods were maintained in the city. His mother, Miriam Lee Hale, purchased the first home built in Tamarac Lakes North in 1965. She collected every copy of *Tamarac Topics*, which led to her son's interest in the city's history. (Courtesy of the City of Tamarac.)

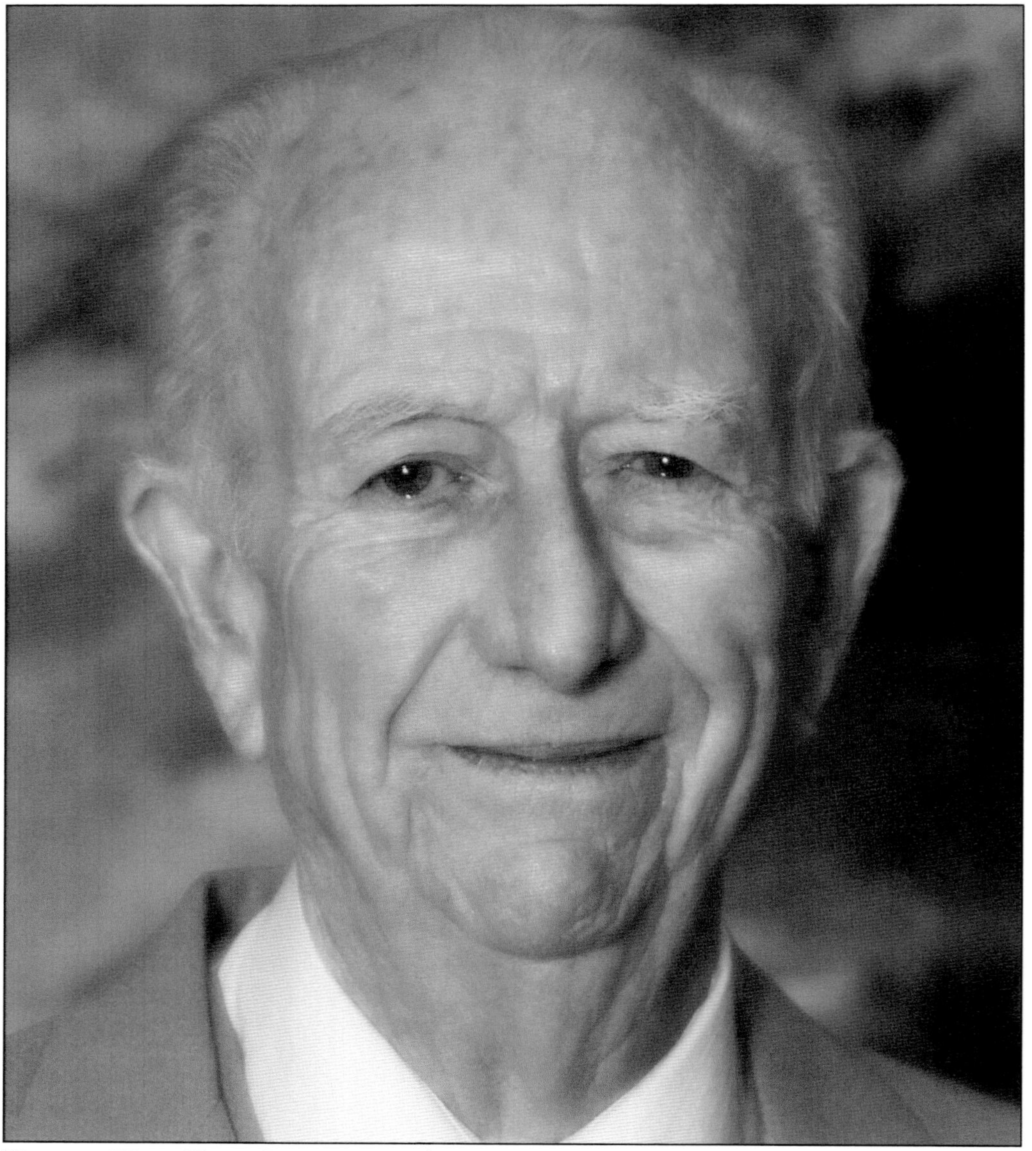

HERBERT WADE HAYES JR., 2002. Herbert Hayes Jr. came to Broward County in 1975 with a bachelor's degree from the University of Dayton (1943) and received two more bachelor's degrees from Fort Lauderdale College. Having settled in the Westwood Community, he served his community for more than 25 years as president of the Tamarac Presidents Council as well as a trustee. He served five years on the City of Tamarac Veterans Affairs Committee and was a City of Tamarac Investment Advisory Board member, a Broward County Sheriff's Office District VII Community Council member, junior vice commander of the Oakland Park Chapter of Ex-POWs, and a judge advocate of American Legion Post No. 265. Hayes also served as the City of Tamarac's liaison to the Tamarac Chamber of Commerce board of directors. (Courtesy of the Tamarac Chamber of Commerce.)

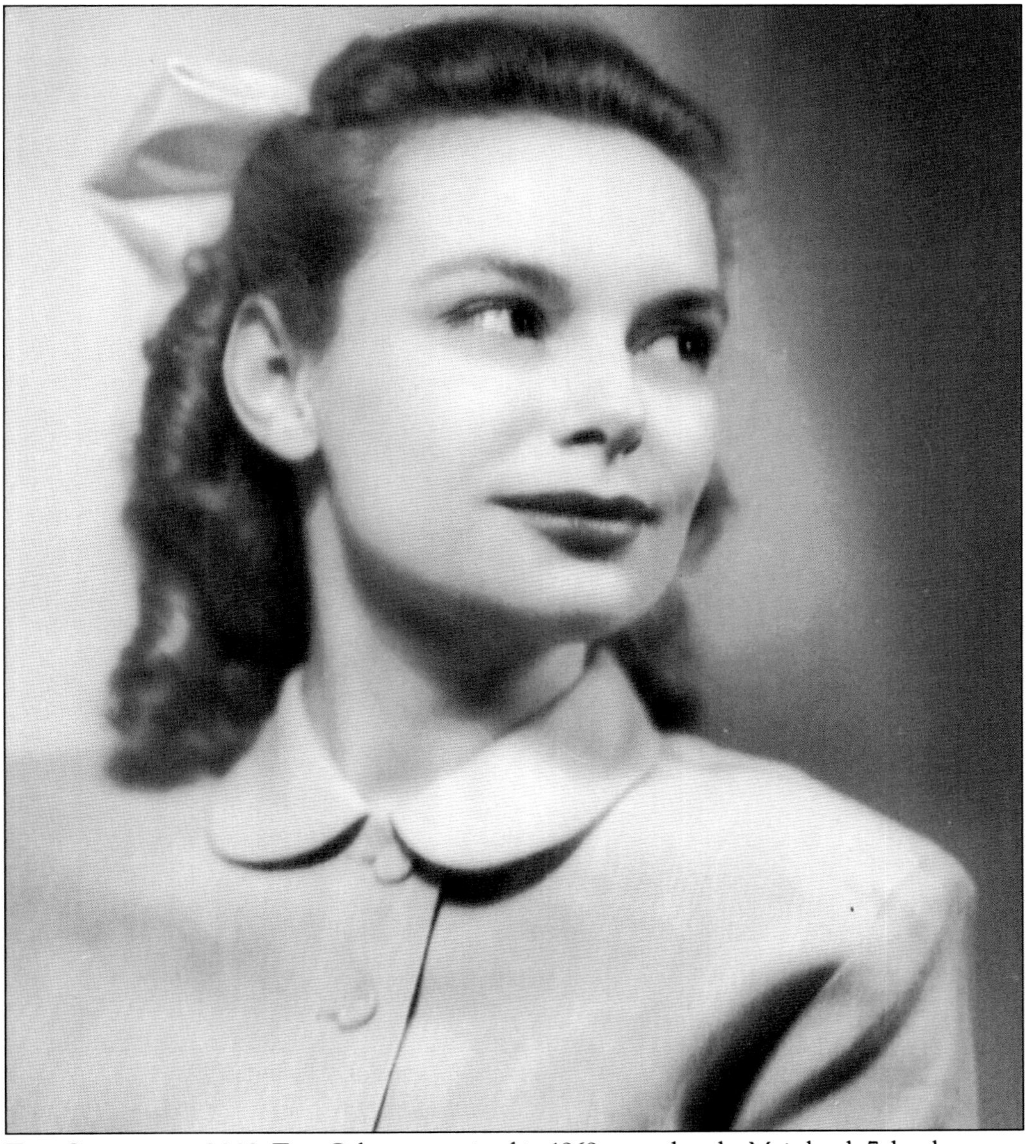

TINA CELANTANO, 2003. Tina Celentano arrived in 1969, moved to the Mainlands 7 development, and quickly became a community activist, prodding city officials until she got her way. She was the first editor of the Mainlands 7 Clubhouse newspaper, *Seven*, and regularly contributed to a column in *Tamarac Topics*. When Tina arrived in Tamarac, she and her closest neighbors did not even have phone service. Overwhelmed by the crush of new development in Broward County, the telephone company could not keep up with the demand. Tina fought for a pay phone at the Mainlands clubhouse. Afterwards, she reported that so many residents used the new pay phone that the coin box frequently overflowed. This first successful foray into community activism set the tone for her future endeavors. Often calling city hall with questions, she said, "I don't believe that you can't fight city hall, I believe that you don't have to, that most of the time people are willing to help you work it out." As a member of the City of Tamarac Social Services Advisory Board, she helped bring a stoplight to her neighborhood and lobbied the commission strenuously for the current city bus service. (Courtesy of the City of Tamarac.)

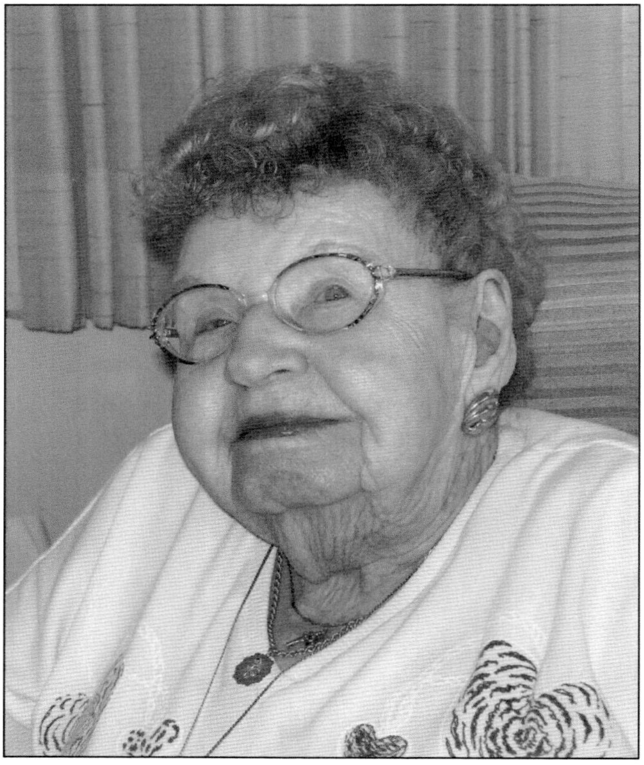

MARIAN FAY, 2006. The Fay family moved into Tamarac Lakes in 1964, the first development built by Ken Behring, later moving to the Mainlands 1 and 2. There was no Commercial Boulevard at the time; Marian used Oakland Park Boulevard and Prospect Road to travel north, south, east, and west. She remembered using a tunnel to get to University Drive. She was a founding member of the Mainlands 1 and 2 Women's Club, attended Faith United Church of Christ, was a member of the arts and crafts club, and communicated daily with several ladies who lived alone. In 2006, when she was named the city's pioneer, Marion Fay had lived in Tamarac for 42 years. Then aged 107, she was the longest-living resident of Tamarac. (Courtesy of Pamela Bushnell.)

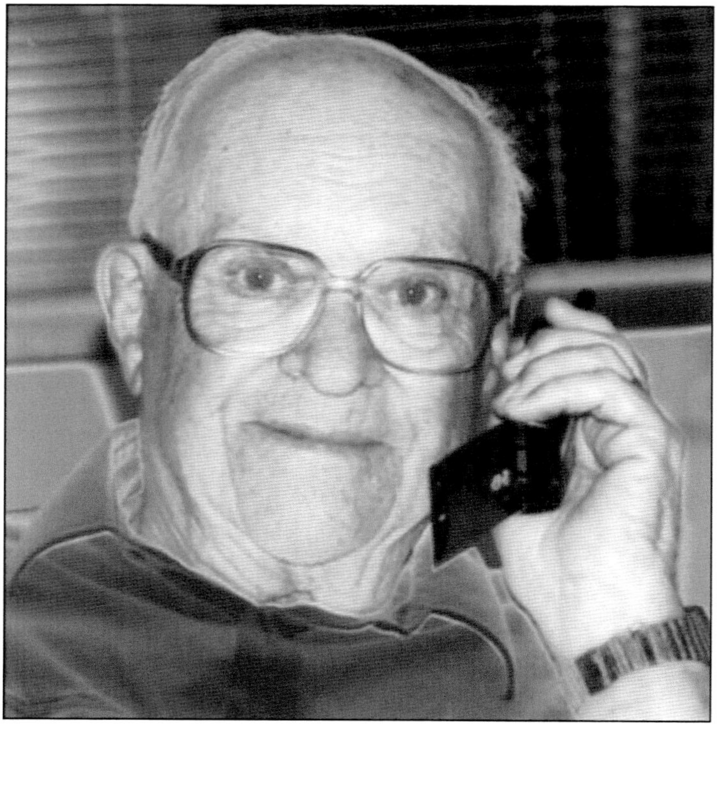

LEO KAPLAN, 2007. Leo Kaplan moved his family permanently in 1978, the year he retired. Initially living in Inverrary, Kaplan had a house built in the Woodlands. He had been active in his community and was on the board of directors for Woodlands Country Club. He spent his life working as an artist, specializing in assemblage art, or "art in a box." Acting as an unofficial historian, he collected newspaper articles for posterity and turned them over to city hall. (Courtesy of Karen Klein.)

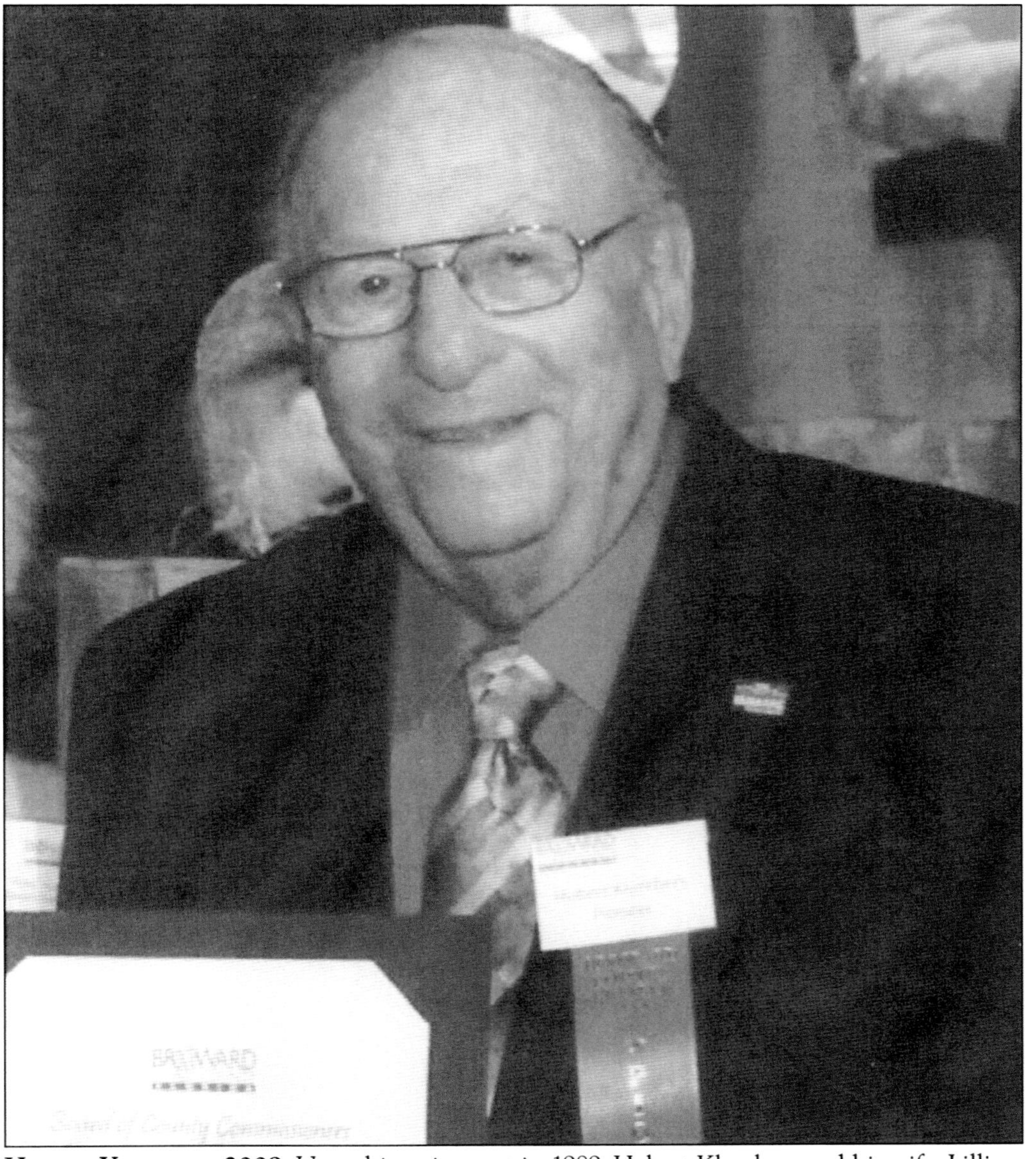

Hubert Klombers, 2009. Upon his retirement in 1989, Hubert Klombers and his wife, Lillian, settled into the Kings Point Devon community in Tamarac, Florida. Hubert enjoyed retirement but was restless. He became involved as a board member and president of his community's association and helped lead it through the transition from a developer-run association to a resident-run association. He also started the Serving Health Insurance Needs of Elders (SHINE) program in Broward County. He was a charter member of SHINE and worked tirelessly as a coordinator. The program helps keep seniors informed and gets them the help they need. Klombers served as a legislative aide for two Tamarac commissioners and as a member of the planning board, the insurance advisory committee, and the annexation committee. "Tamarac was my first 'small town' after living in the big city my whole life," explained Klombers. "Today, it is similar to when I first moved here in 1989, but with more people. I love the community. The people who work for the city are great; I am happy to be able to contribute to its success." (Courtesy of the City of Tamarac.)

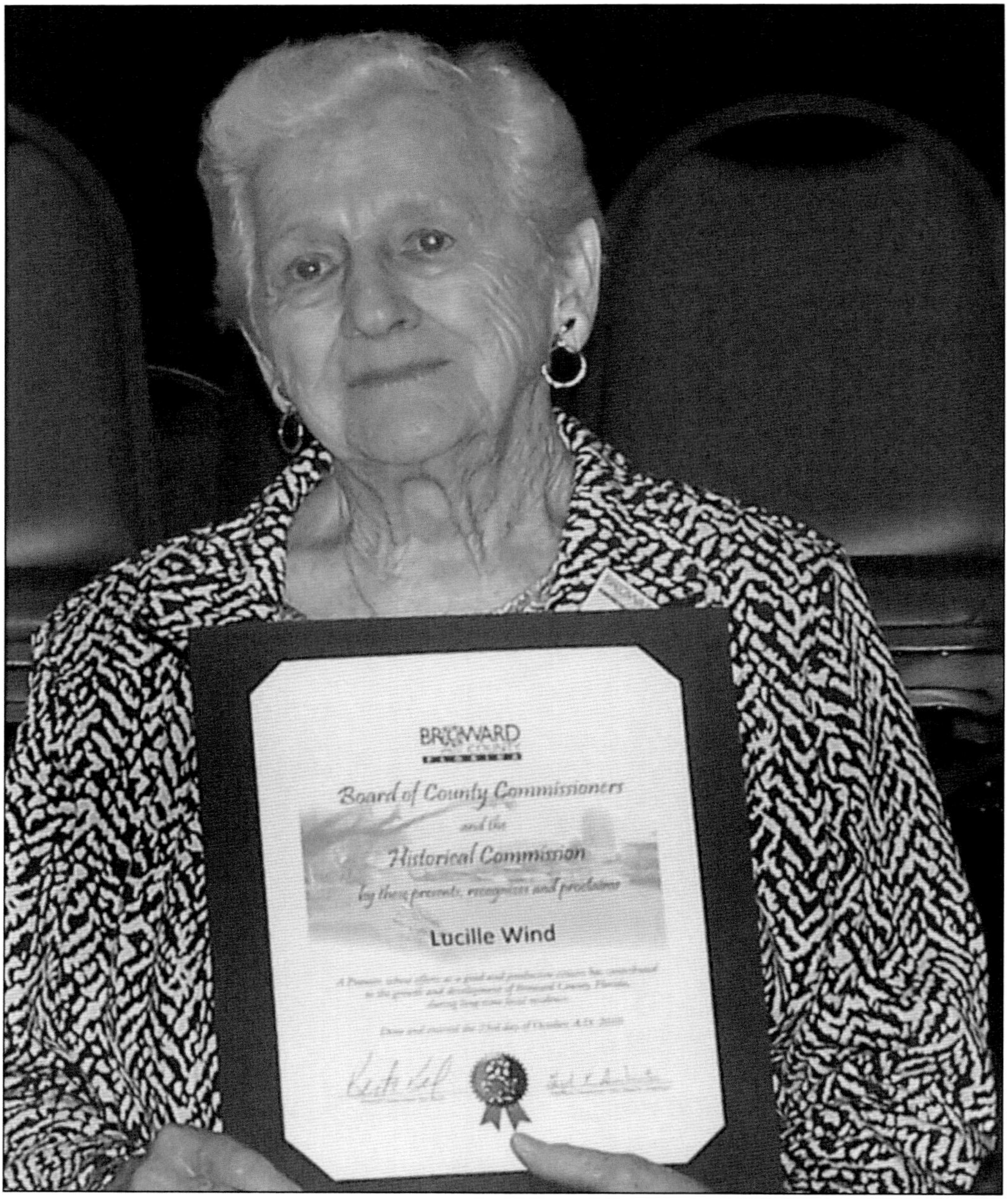

Lucille Wind, 2010. While vacationing in South Florida in 1964, the Winds were looking for property to purchase. A realtor showed them a new development, Tamarac Lakes in the newly incorporated City of Tamarac, and they met Ken Behring. The Winds fell in love with the property and signed a contract. Their home cost $8,990, and with the added features of air conditioning, a rear patio, and an expanded garage, it came to $10,030. They left a $200 deposit on a new way of life and maintenance-free living. On their return trip to Buffalo in a snowstorm, they decided that they were ready to move right away, though they previously told Behring they were not in a hurry. One phone call and six weeks later their home was ready. They closed on their home in March 1964 and moved by September. In 2010, Lucille Wind was Tamarac's only original resident still living. (Courtesy of the Tamarac Historical Society.)

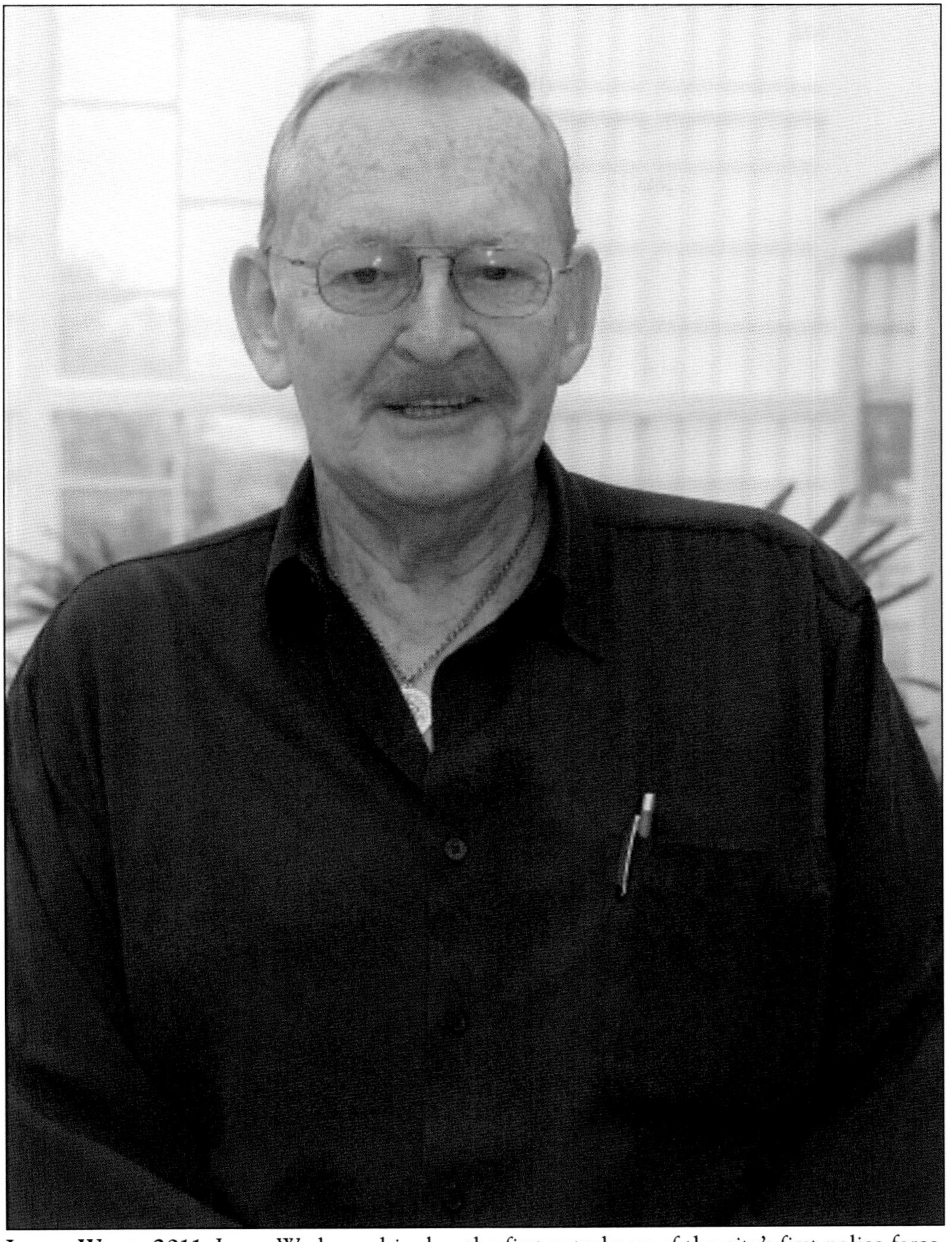

Larry Wark, 2011. Larry Wark was hired as the first patrolman of the city's first police force, with badge No. 1. "Back in my day with the Tamarac Police Force, most of the city was under construction," Wark said. "The majority of the police functions consisted of patrolling the city and keeping watch on the shadows of the many partially built homes. We occasionally wrote up traffic violations and on occasion deterred theft of construction materials." (Courtesy of the City of Tamarac.)

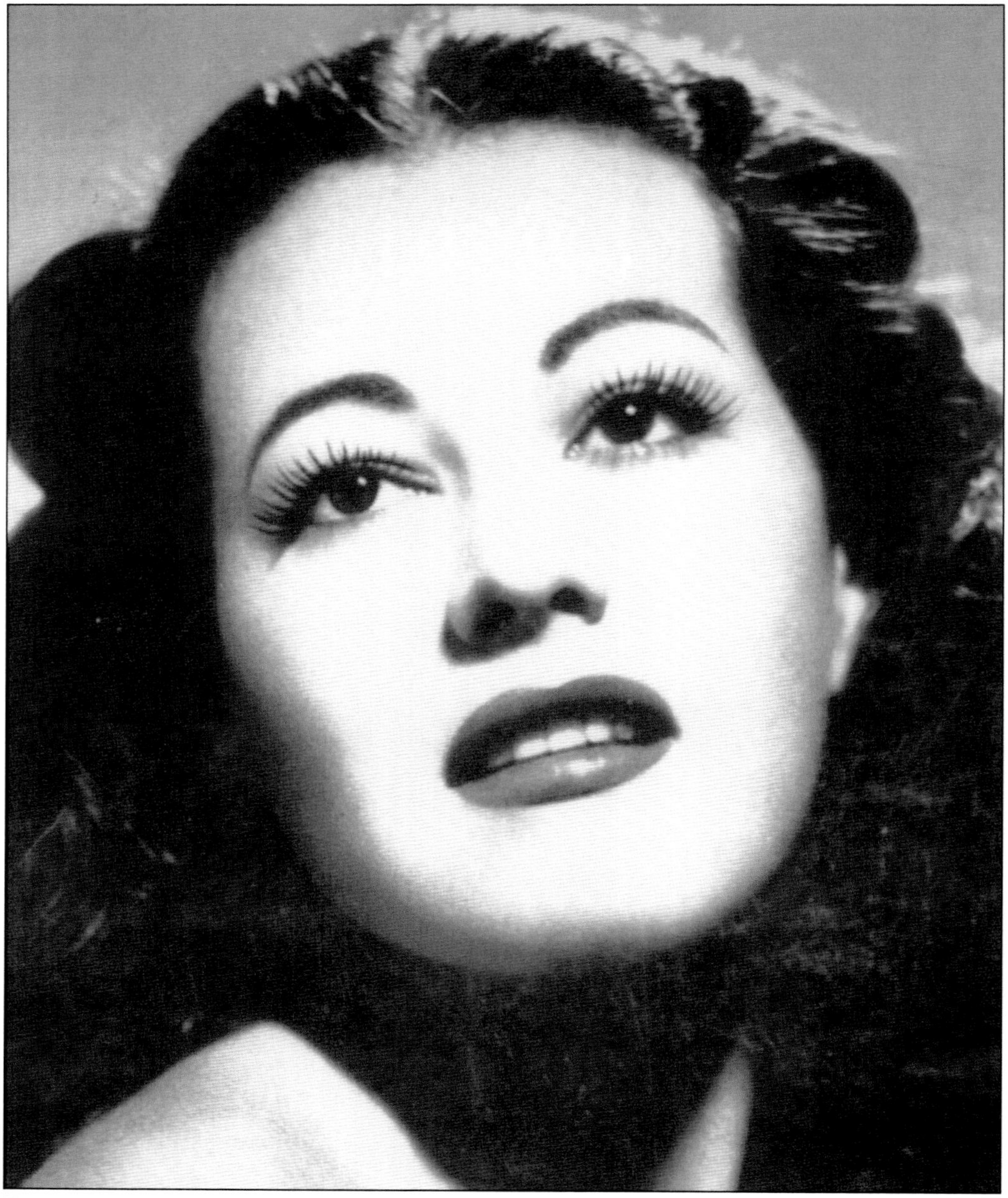

Dorothy Willis, 2012. Recommended by her high school teacher, she received a scholarship at the age of 17 to the Metropolitan Opera, where she performed solo at Carnegie Hall and Madison Square Garden. Later moving into acting, she appeared on Broadway in *High Button Shoes*, a Jerome Robbins musical. Dorothy married Chester Willis and had three children, and the family moved to New Jersey. Dorothy wrote and produced 21 shows and performed at local clubs. Moving to Tamarac in 1979, Dorothy wrote an autobiographical play about her aging mother and her live-in helper called *Fannie and Sadie*. Teaming up with Ann White, they created an alternative theater for local residents. Dorothy Willis is now the president of the Tamarac Theatre of the Performing Arts and has been entertaining local residents for 32 years. (Courtesy of the Collection of Dorothy Willis.)

Ten

City Historical Society

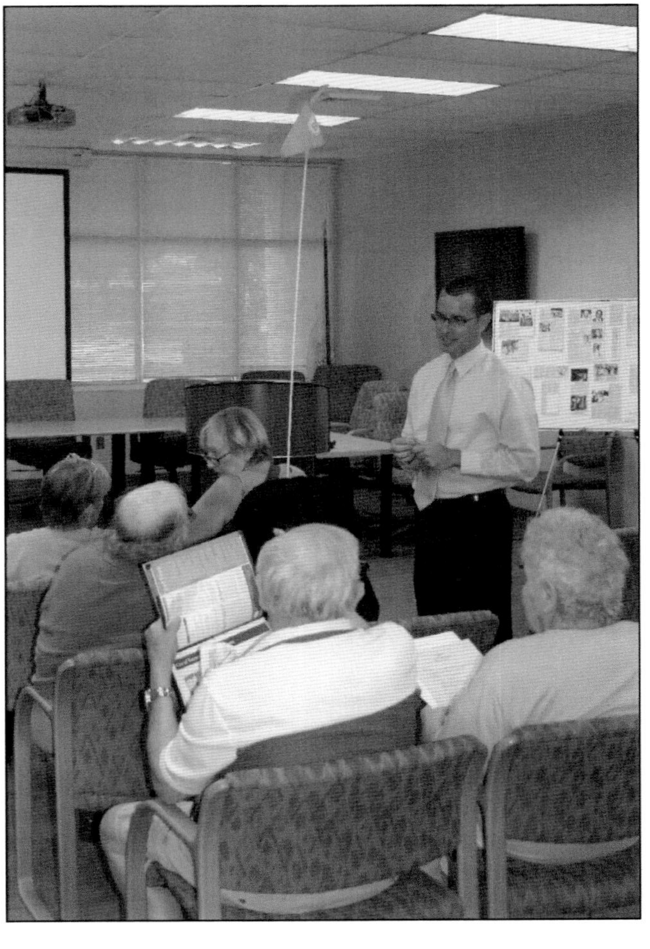

Tamarac Historical Society. The public information office would receive calls related to historical photographs of Tamarac. There was no central location for photographs or artifacts, and what was available was not in an easy-to-research repository. A plan was developed after having researched neighboring societies, and the idea gained the support of the city. On July 14, 2009, Chad Quinn, the founder of the Tamarac Historical Society (seen here), held its first organizational meeting and presented a collection of historical documents and photographs that had been stored in the city clerk's office. The meeting brought together many active residents in the community interested in the history of the city. (Courtesy of the City of Tamarac.)

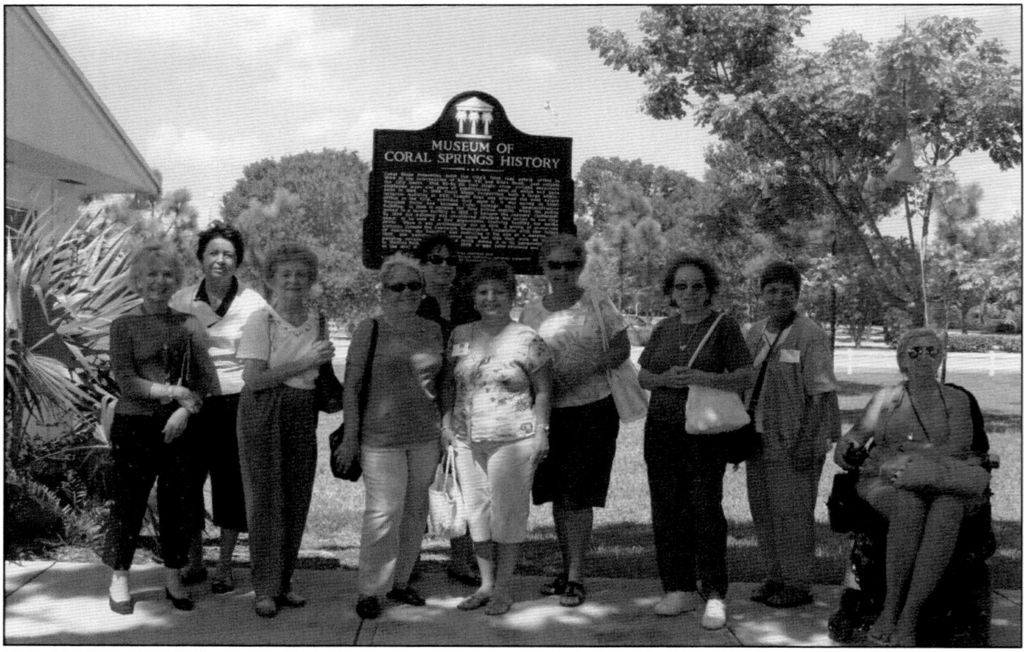

CORAL SPRINGS HISTORICAL SOCIETY. The Tamarac Historical Society traveled to the Museum of Coral Springs History where they met with Wendy Wangberg (far left), historian for the city of Coral Springs. The newly formed grouped listened attentively as she "talked and walked" history. The Tamarac Historical Society is grateful to Wendy for all her help. (Courtesy of the City of Tamarac.)

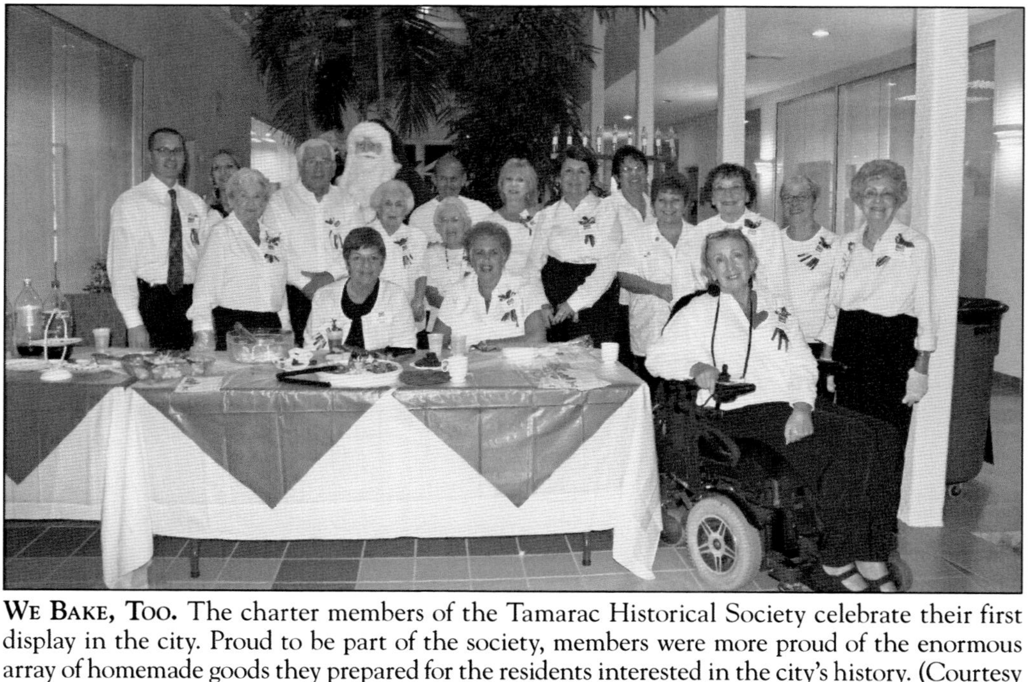

WE BAKE, TOO. The charter members of the Tamarac Historical Society celebrate their first display in the city. Proud to be part of the society, members were more proud of the enormous array of homemade goods they prepared for the residents interested in the city's history. (Courtesy of the City of Tamarac.)

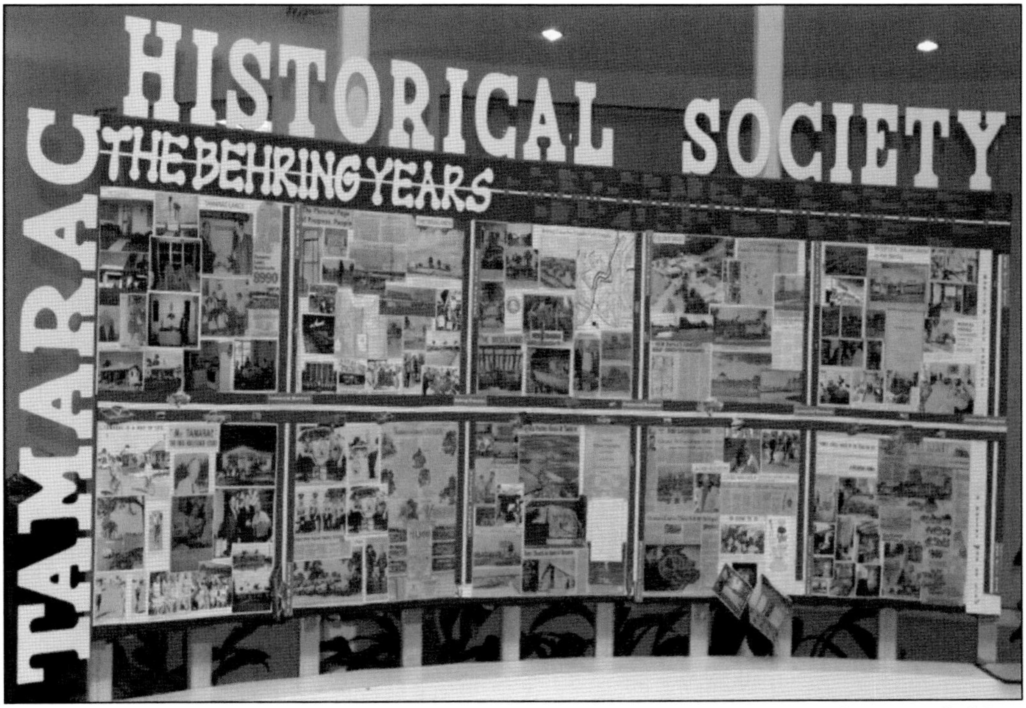

The Behring Years Display. On December 9, 2009, the Tamarac Historical Society held its first reception, which was named "The Behring Years." The historical society unveiled a pictorial display showing the growth and development of the city during the years of Kenneth Behring, city developer and founder. (Courtesy of the City of Tamarac.)

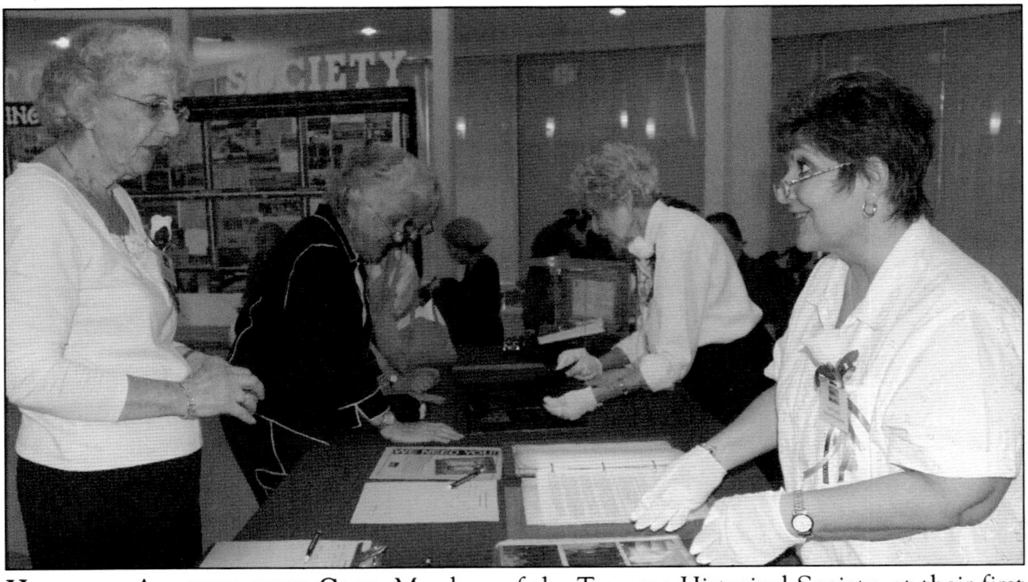

Handling Archives with Care. Members of the Tamarac Historical Society, at their first reception, wore white cotton gloves. The gloves are used to prolong and protect archived materials, as well as to protect the users' hands. Many of the collected scrapbooks shown at the reception are close to five decades old. (Courtesy of the City of Tamarac.)

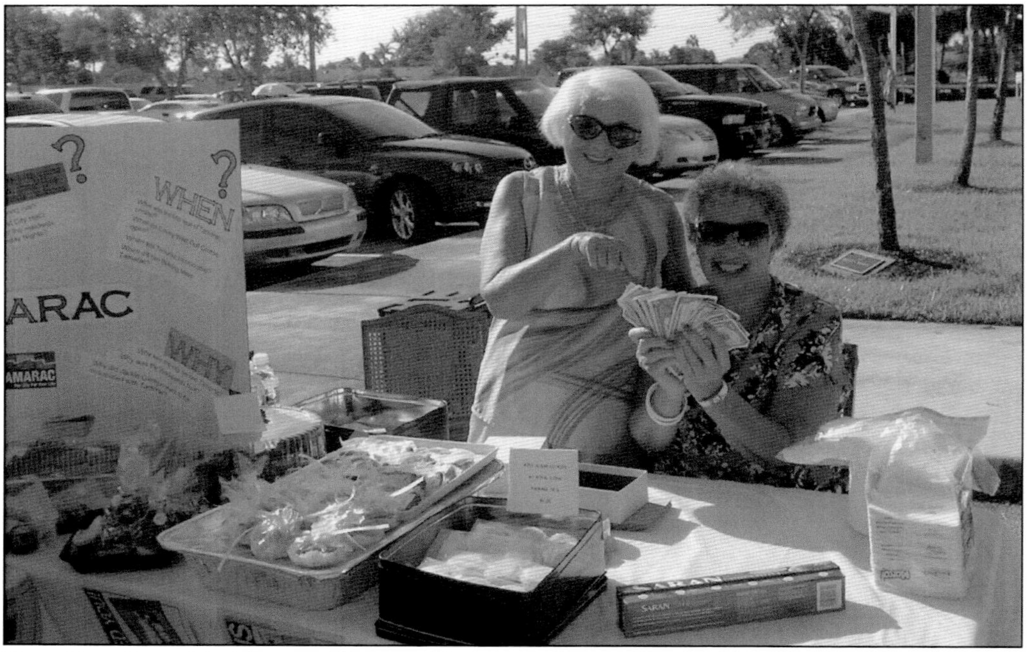

First Bake Sale. The Tamarac Historical Society has been a fixture at every community garage sale since 2009. As a sole means of revenue, members have been baking homemade goodies to sell. Pictured here is their very first bake sale. Since then, the group is ever-present in the same spot, wearing bright green shirts with the logo, to the delight of shoppers. (Courtesy of the City of Tamarac.)

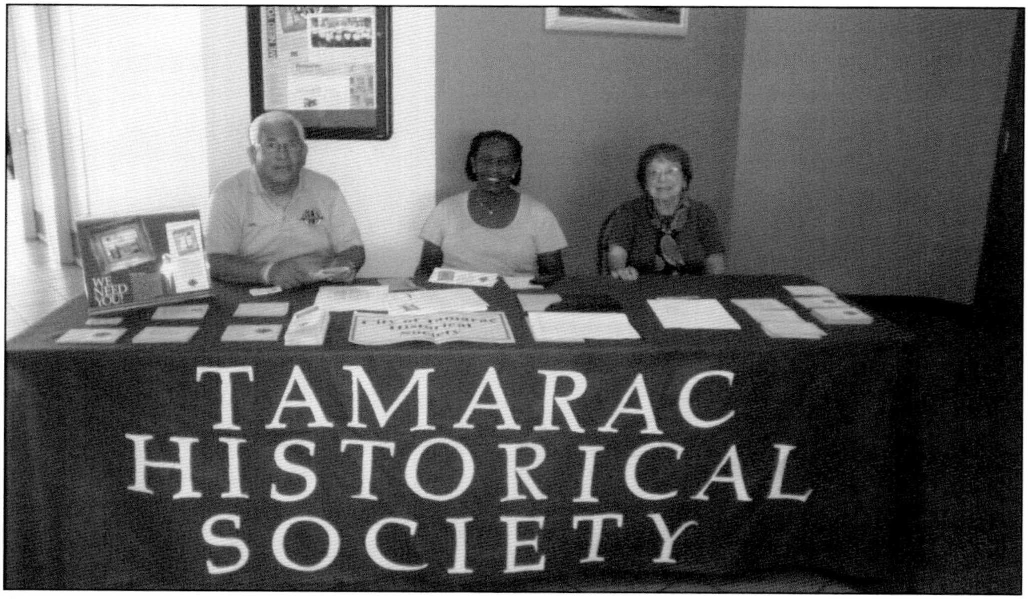

Community Center Informational Table. Members of the Tamarac Historical Society staff the informational table at the Tamarac Community Center at 8601 West Commercial Boulevard. Twice a month, the organization passes out information about the city through brochures and "Did You Know" cards. It also utilizes this opportunity to present fundraising events. (Courtesy of the Tamarac Historical Society.)

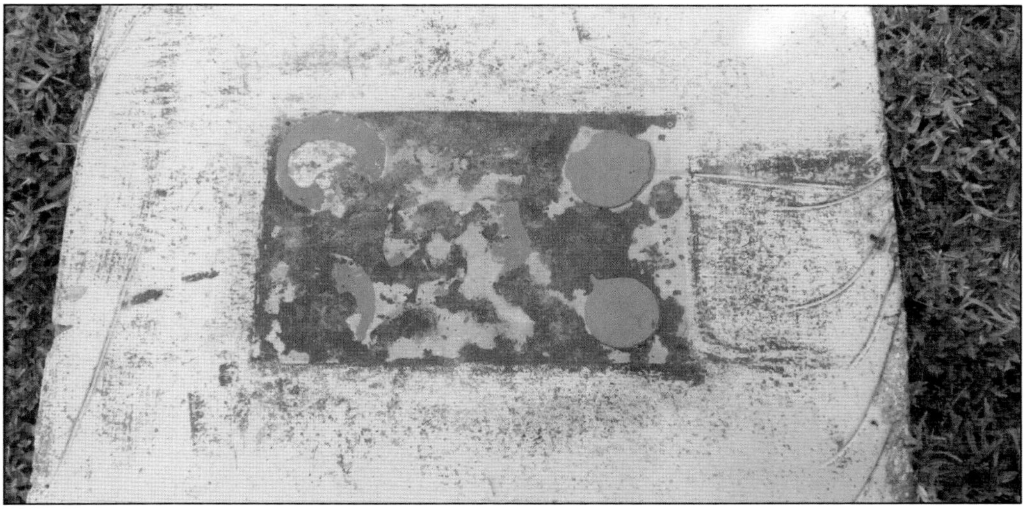

Lost Time Capsules. As the Tamarac Historical Society researched the history of the city, it found a few references to time capsules but no records of their locations. They remained on the society's "To Find" list for some time. (Courtesy of the City of Tamarac.)

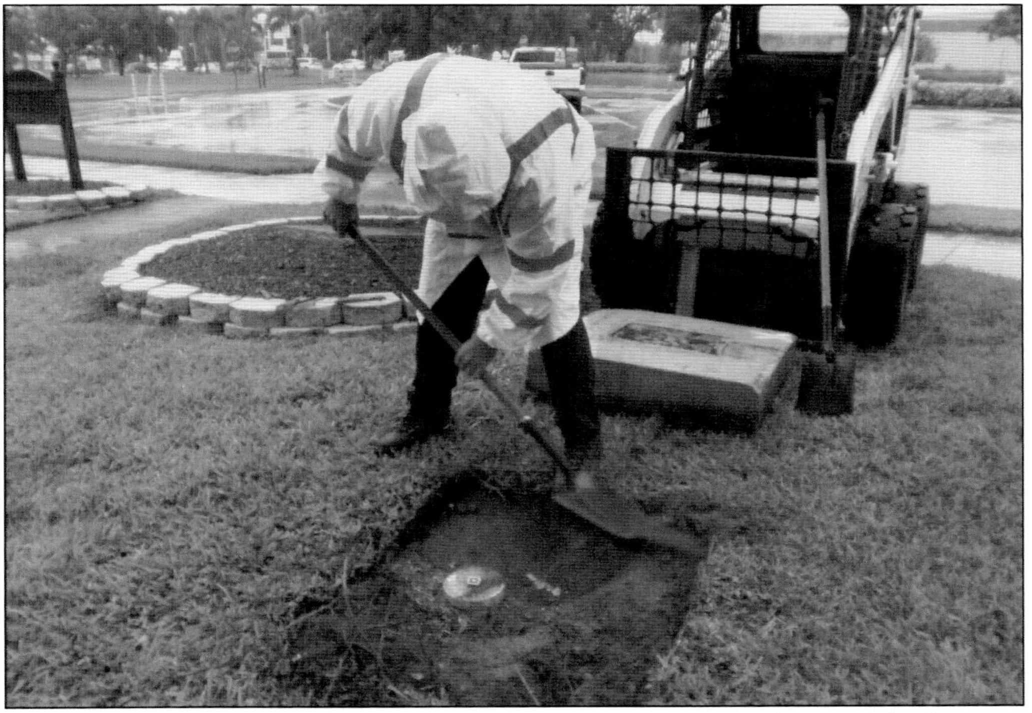

Time to Dig. At a Memorial Day celebration, someone almost tripped over a slab of cement. "Let's get this identified before someone gets hurt," was the parks director's message to the public works department. Upon digging up the slab, what was found was, perhaps, a time capsule. The next instruction was, "Return the slab to the ground, while I call the historical society." One can imagine how the news was received. A week later, representatives of the historical society and the parks department, along with public works employees Mike Morrison and John Ruiz, started digging in the pouring rain. (Courtesy of the City of Tamarac.)

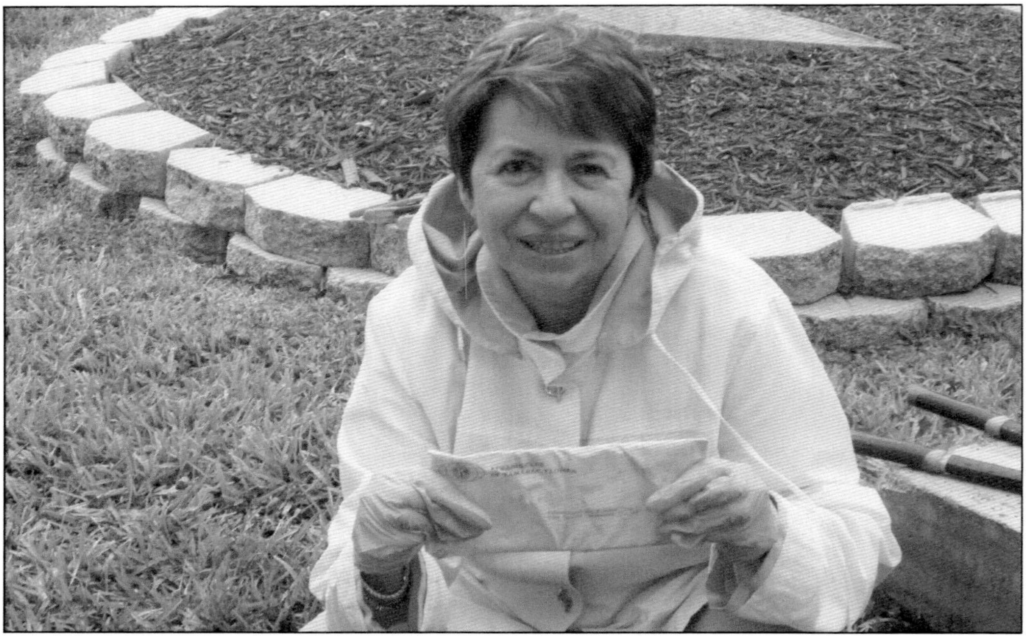

A Date Confirmed. The first item found in the time capsule was an envelope from the Kiwanis Club dated 1987. The Tamarac Historical Society took possession of the items that were wet, musty, and very dirty. Not satisfied, they began their hunt for more details. They discovered that the time capsule was buried September 17, 1987, at a ceremony to commemorate the anniversary of the signing of the US Constitution, indicating it should have been opened in 100 years. The items will be resealed in the 50th-anniversary time capsule. (Courtesy of the City of Tamarac.)

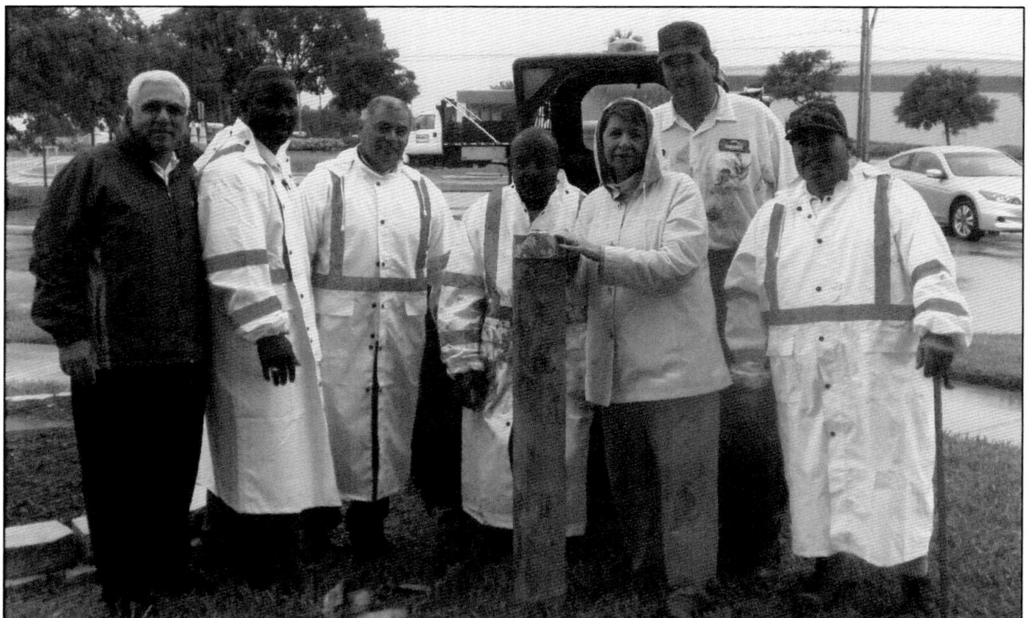

Capsule Contents. Two hours, one backhoe, and five public works employees later, the time capsule, a four-foot-long PVC pipe with a lid, was unearthed. (Courtesy of the City of Tamarac.)

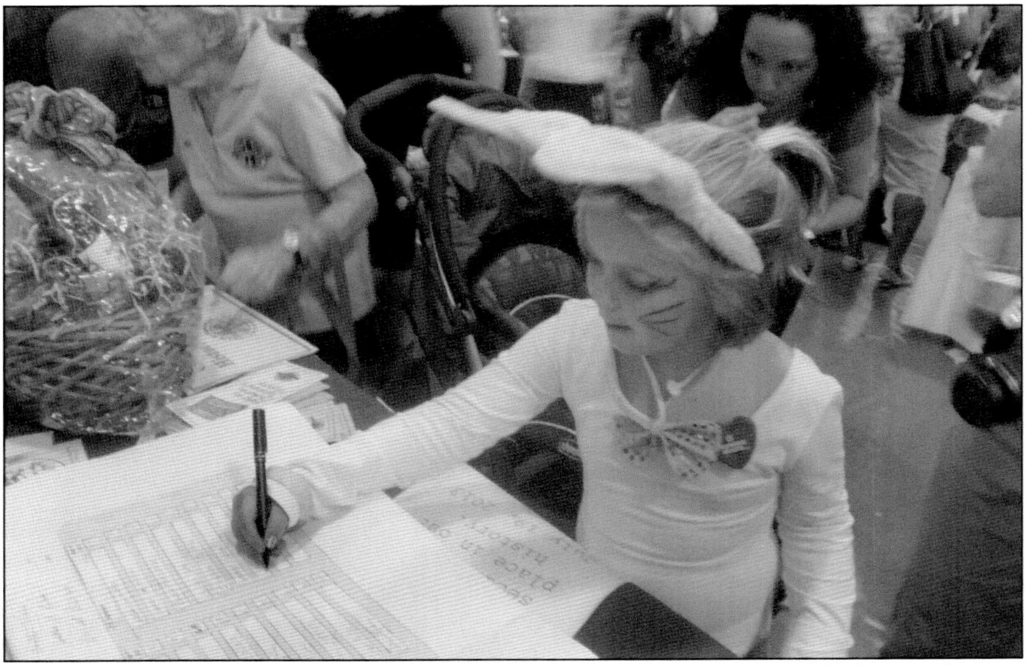

PART OF HISTORY. In preparation for the 50th anniversary of the city of Tamarac, the historical society decided to create a time capsule to be housed at the community center (aboveground and indoors). The public art committee designed an enclosure to preserve the capsule, a constant reminder of the capsule's existence, and the plan for it to be opened in 25 years. To commemorate this event, scrolls were signed by residents (including children) to be sealed in the time capsule. Signings were held at Fourth of July celebrations, Taste of Tamarac, and other events throughout the year. (Above, courtesy of the Tamarac Historical Society; below, courtesy of Sharon Aaron Baron.)

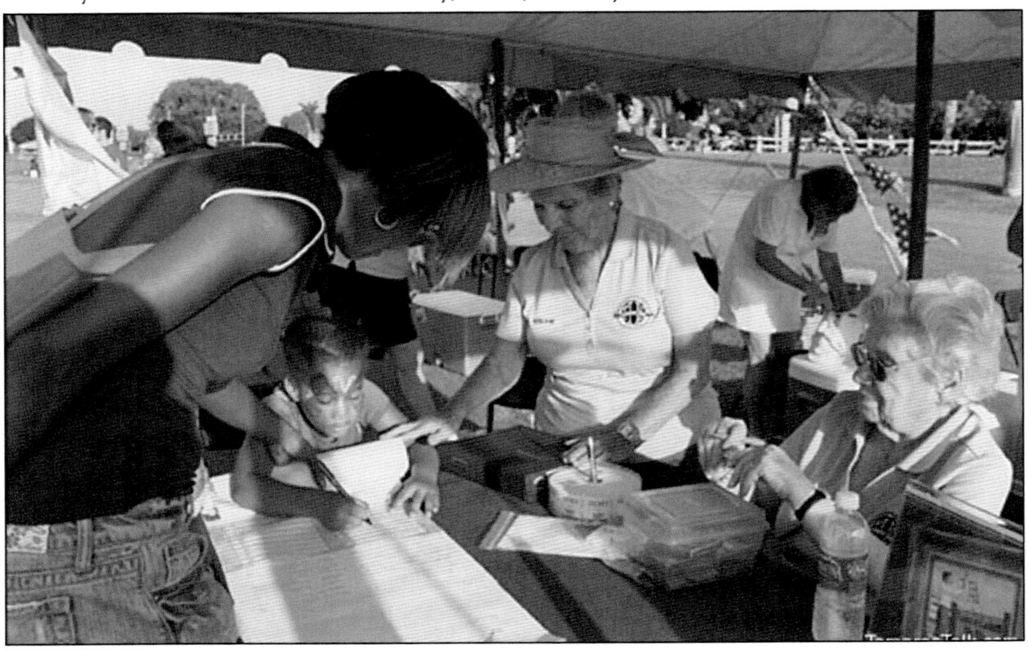

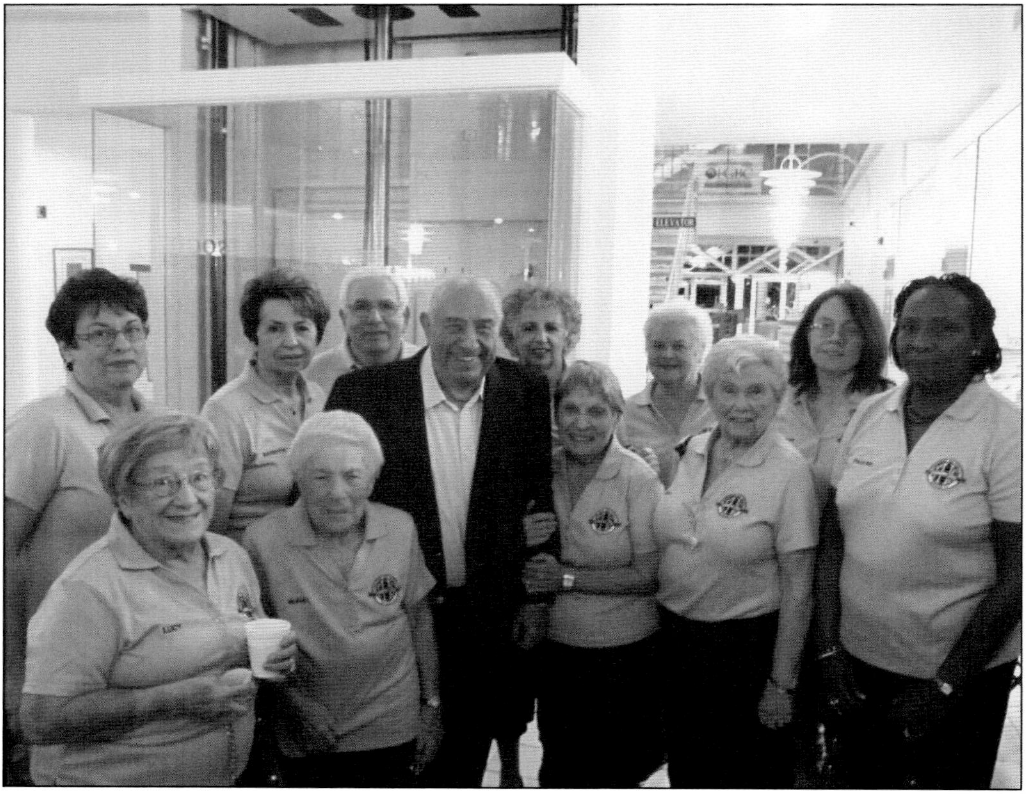

BEHRING AND THE TAMARAC HISTORICAL SOCIETY. Kenneth E. Behring is pictured with members of the Tamarac Historical Society. The society's mission is to research, collect, preserve, and exhibit the history of Tamarac with the goal of enlightening the community and passing on an enduring legacy for future generations. (Above, courtesy of Pam Davidson; below, courtesy of the Tamarac Historical Society.)

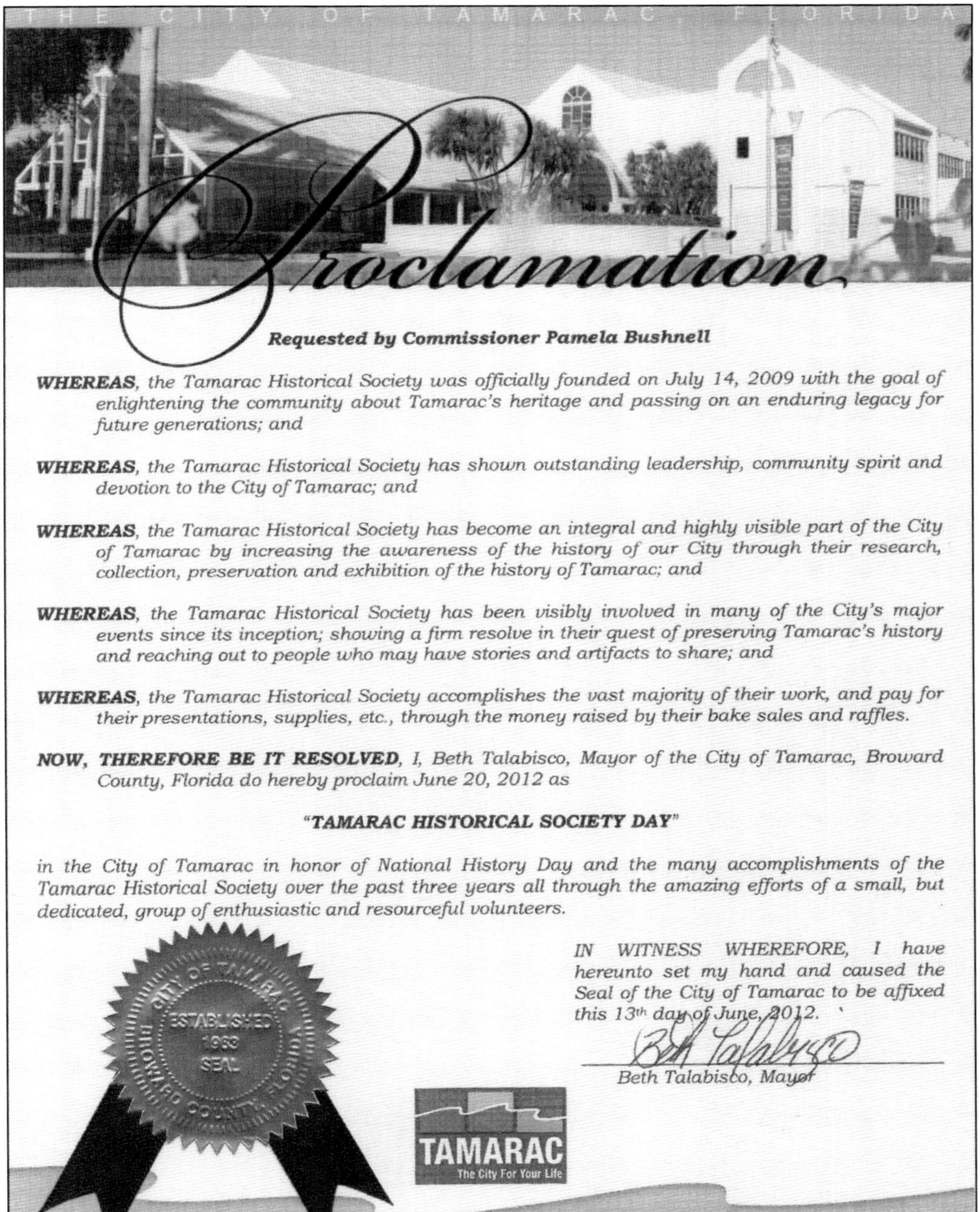

THE CITY OF TAMARAC, FLORIDA

Proclamation

Requested by Commissioner Pamela Bushnell

WHEREAS, *the Tamarac Historical Society was officially founded on July 14, 2009 with the goal of enlightening the community about Tamarac's heritage and passing on an enduring legacy for future generations; and*

WHEREAS, *the Tamarac Historical Society has shown outstanding leadership, community spirit and devotion to the City of Tamarac; and*

WHEREAS, *the Tamarac Historical Society has become an integral and highly visible part of the City of Tamarac by increasing the awareness of the history of our City through their research, collection, preservation and exhibition of the history of Tamarac; and*

WHEREAS, *the Tamarac Historical Society has been visibly involved in many of the City's major events since its inception; showing a firm resolve in their quest of preserving Tamarac's history and reaching out to people who may have stories and artifacts to share; and*

WHEREAS, *the Tamarac Historical Society accomplishes the vast majority of their work, and pay for their presentations, supplies, etc., through the money raised by their bake sales and raffles.*

NOW, THEREFORE BE IT RESOLVED, *I, Beth Talabisco, Mayor of the City of Tamarac, Broward County, Florida do hereby proclaim June 20, 2012 as*

"TAMARAC HISTORICAL SOCIETY DAY"

in the City of Tamarac in honor of National History Day and the many accomplishments of the Tamarac Historical Society over the past three years all through the amazing efforts of a small, but dedicated, group of enthusiastic and resourceful volunteers.

IN WITNESS WHEREFORE, I have hereunto set my hand and caused the Seal of the City of Tamarac to be affixed this 13th day of June, 2012.

Beth Talabisco, Mayor

THS Proclamation. The historical society was given a proclamation by Mayor Beth Talabisco naming June 20, 2012, Tamarac Historical Society Day. Requested by Commissioner Pamela Bushnell, the proclamation honored the society for its outstanding leadership, community spirit, devotion to the city, and many accomplishments over the past three years. (Courtesy of the City of Tamarac.)